CW00540034

Now my eyes have seen you

Titles in this series:

NEW STUDIES IN BIBLICAL THEOLOGY 12

Series editor: D. A. Carson

Now my eyes have seen you

IMAGES OF CREATION AND EVIL IN THE BOOK OF JOB

Robert S. Fyall

APOLLOS

INTERVARSITY PRESS
DOWNERS GROVE, ILLINOIS 60515

APOLLOS (an imprint of Inter-Varsity Press),
38 De Montfort Street, Leicester LE1 7GP, England
Email: ivp@uccf.org.uk
Website: www.ivpbooks.com

INTERVARSITY PRESS
PO Box 1400, Downers Grove, Illinois 60515, USA
World Wide Web: www.ivpress.com
Email: mail@ivpress.com

First published 2002

British Library Cataloguing in Publication Data
A catalogue record for this book is available from the British Library.

UK ISBN 0–85111–498–9

Library of Congress Cataloging-in-Publication Data
This data has been requested.

US ISBN 0–8308–2612–2

Set in Monotype Times New Roman
Typeset in Great Britain by Servis Filmsetting Ltd
Printed in Great Britain by Creative Print and Design (Wales), Ebbw Vale

Contents

To Thelma,
with love and gratitude

Series preface

New Studies in Biblical Theology is a series of monographs that address key issues in the discipline of biblical theology. Contributions to the series focus on one or more of three areas: 1. the nature and status of biblical theology, including its relations with other disciplines (e.g. historical theology, exegesis, systematic theology, historical criticism, narrative theology); 2. the articulation and exposition of the structure of thought of a particular biblical writer or corpus; and 3. the delineation of a biblical theme across all or part of the biblical corpora.

Above all, these monographs are creative attempts to help thinking Christians understand their Bibles better. The series aims simultaneously to instruct and to edify, to interact with the current literature, and to point the way ahead. In God's universe, mind and heart should not be divorced: in this series we will try not to separate what God has joined together. While the notes interact with the best of the scholarly literature, the text is uncluttered with untransliterated Greek and Hebrew, and tries to avoid too much technical jargon. The volumes are written within the framework of confessional evangelicalism, but there is always an attempt at thoughtful engagement with the sweep of the relevant literature.

For many readers, Job has been a closed book, or, at most, a book with which they have only a superficial acquaintance. They know it is about suffering, and not just any suffering but unjust suffering. They may even recall that such suffering is Job's lot, that God has permitted Satan to have a relatively free hand with the unfortunate man, and that Job begins by taking it very well, but over the course of several cycles of debates between Job and his 'miserable comforters' he becomes more and more convinced of his own righteousness and of the unfairness of what he is experiencing. Eventually, in several highly symbol-laden chapters, God scolds Job but does not give him a direct answer to his most burning questions. Then the book closes with a happy ending. This, more or less, is what casual readers know of the book of Job.

What are we to make of this? In fact, we do not begin to gain a real grasp of the message of the book of Job and of its contribution to the canon, apart from a more detailed grasp of its imagery and drama. Here Dr Fyall is a sure-footed guide: not only does he lecture in Old Testament, but he preaches regularly in a church that draws several hundred university students – something that does not usually happen unless the preacher has something to say from the Bible, and says it well. In this book many more can listen in with pleasure and profit.

D. A. Carson
Trinity Evangelical Divinity School

Author's preface

How long does it take to write a book? This work is a substantial rewriting of my doctoral thesis presented to the University of Edinburgh in 1991. Its roots, however, go further back to my undergraduate studies and beyond that to my late teens when I read the book of Job (in the AV) at a time when I was also devouring other works such as John Milton's *Paradise Lost*, the plays of Shakespeare and Homer's *Iliad*. In the study of Job my great loves of theology, of Bible exposition and literature came together especially powerfully and significantly.

Job studies have not stood still in the ten years since the thesis was presented, and this book differs in many ways from the original study. However, the basic argument at the heart of it is still the same: that the key to Job is its depiction of God dealing with and overcoming evil, represented by Behemoth and Leviathan. Over the last decade I have taught the book at St John's College, Durham and I am grateful to the many students who have sharpened my insights and raised new ideas and suggested new angles on the text. Many of them have urged me to see this into print, and encouraged me to return to this project three years ago when the serious writing began. I am also grateful to the 1992 executive of Durham Christian Union who asked me to give a series of talks on Job. These talks, somewhat expanded, were published by Christian Focus Publications in 1995 under the title *How does God treat his friends?* Marianne Young, former Course Administrator at St John's College, has transferred the whole thing on to computer disk and has my most grateful thanks.

To my former teacher and supervisor of the thesis, Professor John Gibson, who was also my mentor in matters Ugaritic, I give my grateful thanks. Also, thanks are due to Professor Emeritus Robert Davidson, the external examiner of the thesis and Dr Peter Hayman, the internal examiner. Both have my gratitude for their courtesy and shrewd comments.

It is a great joy to have this book published as part of the New

Studies in Biblical Theology. No-one could have been more helpful, encouraging and supportive than Professor D. A. Carson. His own immense knowledge and love of Scripture, and his concern for accuracy as well as the broad sweep of the argument, have constantly urged me on with this project. I also thank Inter-Varsity Press, and particularly Dr Philip Duce, for their courteous help. My hope and prayer is that this book will send people back with renewed interest to the book of Job and indeed to the Bible as a whole.

My family, as always, have provided the context of loving support in which the book was written. My children, Carmen and Drummond, now in their late teens, still show a somewhat bemused interest in 'Dad's books', and ensure that scholarship and living are held together. My wife Thelma has supported, encouraged and prayed this project to completion and I dedicate this book to her with love and gratitude.

Robert S. Fyall

Abbreviations

AB	Anchor Bible
AN Bib	*Analecta Biblica*
AnOr	*Analecta Orientalia*
AOAT	*Alter Orient und Alter Testament* (Neukirchen-Vluyn: Kevelaar)
AOS	American Oriental Society
AV	Authorized (King James') Version
BA	*Biblical Archaeologist*
BDB	F. Brown, S. R. Driver and C. A. Briggs, *Hebrew and English Lexicon of the Old Testament* (Oxford, 1906)
BHS	*Biblica Hebraica Stuttgartensia*, K. Elliger and W. Rudolph (eds.) (Stuttgart, 1968–1977)
Bib	*Biblica*
BibOr	*Biblica et Orientalia*
BTB	*Biblical Theology Bulletin*
BZAW	*Beiheft zur Zeitschrift für die alttestamentliche Wissenschaft* (Berlin)
CBQ	*Catholic Biblical Quarterly* (Washington)
Conc	*Concilium*
CML	*Canaanite Myths and Legends*, J. C. L. Gibson (ed.), (2nd edn. Edinburgh: T. & T. Clark, 1978; previous edn. G. R. Driver (ed.), 1956)
CTA	*Corpus des tablettes en cuneiforms alphabetiques*, A. Herdner (Paris: Imprimiere Nationale, 1963)
EBC	Expositor's Bible Commentary
Eng.	English (where numbering different from Hebrew)
EQ	*Evangelical Quarterly*
GKC	*Gesenius' Hebrew Grammar*, with E. Kautzch and A. E. Cowley (2nd edn., Oxford: Clarendon Press, 1910)

HTR	*Harvard Theological Reviews*
HUCA	*Hebrew Union College Annual*
ICC	International Critical Commentary
IEJ	*Israel Exploration Journal*
JAOS	*Journal of the American Oriental Society*
JBL	*Journal of Biblical Literature*
JJS	*Journal of Jewish Studies*
JNES	*Journal of Near Eastern Studies*
JPOS	*Journal of the Palestine Oriental Society*
JQR	*Jewish Quarterly Review*
JSOT	*Journal for the Study of the Old Testament*
JSOT Sup	Journal for the Study of the Old Testament Supplement Series
JSS	*Journal of Semitic Studies*
JTS	*Journal of Theological Studies*
KTU	*Keilaphabetische Texte aus Ugarit*, M. Dietrich, O. Loretz, J. Sanmartin (*AOAT* 24, Neukirchen-Vluyn: Kevelaar, 1976)
LXX	Septuagint
MT	Masoretic Text
NEB	New English Bible
NICOT	New International Commentary on the Old Testament
NIV	New International Version (1983, 1978, 1984)
Or	*Orientalia*
OTL	Old Testament Library
OTS	*Oudtestamentische Studies*
PEQ	*Palestine Exploration Quarterly*
RB	*Revue Biblique*
RSV	Revised Standard Version
SBL	Society of Biblical Literature
SBLDS	*Society of Biblical Literature Dissertation Series*
SBLMS	*Society of Biblical Literature Monograph Series*
SBT	*Studies in Biblical Theology*
SJT	*Scottish Journal of Theology*
SOTS	Society of Old Testament Studies Supplement Series
TynB	*Tyndale Bulletin*
Theol	*Theology*
TOTC	Tyndale Old Testament Commentaries
UF	*Ugarit Forschungen*

Ugaritica V	*Les Noveaux des Texte mythologigues et liturgigues de Ras Shamra/Ugaritica 5*, C. Virolleaud (Paris, 1968), 545–606
VT	*Vetus Testamentum*
VTS	*Vetus Testamentum* Supplements
WBC	Word Biblical Commentary
WTJ	*Westminster Theological Journal*
ZAW	*Zeitschrift für die alttestamentliche Wissenschaft*

Chapter One

Speaking what is right

A book of sermons by a distinguished biblical scholar and preacher bears the title *Trembling at the Threshold of a Biblical Text*.[1] This is a salutary caution to anyone who tries to expound the 'living oracles of God'. Few texts are more daunting and yet more fascinating than the book of Job; few have been the subject of such diverse interpretation, and the flood of commentaries and studies continues unabated. Bearing in mind the condemnation of the friends as 'not speaking what was right', it is important to approach this great book with humility, realizing that we do not know the answer to many of the problems. Indeed, the mystery of God's ways and the appalling evil and suffering in the world are at the heart of the book's massive contribution to the canon.

In this introductory chapter I shall outline the scope of this study; explain my approach; set out the case for the unity of Job; discuss some of the varied readings of the book and reflect on its genre and language.

The scope of this study

It is my aim to give a holistic reading of Job particularly in terms of its depiction of creation and evil. Naturally all the commentaries mention these, but there is a need for a synthesis and fresh treatment of the material and an attempt to assess their importance in the context of the study of the book as a whole. Commentaries diverge sharply in their treatment of these issues and these divergences colour their overall picture of the theology of Job.[2] I want to make three observations at this point that I hope will be useful.

The first relates to the importance of the divine speeches (chs.

---

[1] Crenshaw 1994.
[2] Generally speaking, older commentators such as Driver-Gray (1977) and Dhorme (1967) (supported by the later commentaries of Andersen and Gordis) argue for a naturalistic interpretation of Behemoth and Leviathan. Dahood and his followers, notably Pope and Michel, are convinced of a supernatural interpretation but barely glance at the theological implications of their views.

38 – 41). Here, surely, is the heart of the theology of Job, and it is my conviction that these chapters must control the interpretation of this book. Thus, two chapters (3 and 4) bear particularly on the first divine speech and four chapters (5 – 8) deal with the second divine speech.

Secondly, issues of creation and evil are of enormous importance for Old Testament theology as a whole. Thus, constant comparisons are drawn with a wide range of biblical material.

Thirdly, this study takes seriously the integrity of the whole of Job. Later in this chapter the case for the unity of Job is argued. Particularly important is the connection of the prose and the poetry and thus Job 1 and 2 are frequently referred to and 42:7–17 is analysed in detail.

The approach taken

This is not a full commentary on Job, nevertheless many passages are given very close attention. The argument of this study, that Behemoth is the figure of Death and that Leviathan is a guise of Satan, grows from a translation and exegesis of the relevant passages; likewise the central theme of the divine council includes a translation and commentary on Job 19:22–27. Many other passages, notably chapters 3, 9, 26, 28 and 38 – 39 are given close attention. In particular, I attempt to make sense of the Masoretic text of Job as it stands and to avoid speculative emendations. Close exegesis is the foundation of the study.

However, it is important not simply to explain individual words and phrases, but to be aware of nuance and literary genre and to give full weight to the magnificence of the poetry.[3] Thus, much of this study will focus on the imagery of the book.

I will also give a fair amount of attention to the extensive use of Canaanite and other mythical allusions. The use of these is discussed later in this chapter as well as in an appendix on 'Job and Canaanite myth'.

Is it a unitary work?

The author of Job is totally unknown and no sources have been found. He is mentioned in Ezekiel 14:20 along with Noah and Daniel,

---

[3] Clines (1989: xii) finely comments: 'The craftsmanship in the finest details, the rain of metaphor, the never-failing imagination of the poet, is surpassed only by the variety and delicacy of the theological ideas.'

which means that this story was known by the early sixth century BC. Many parallels have been adduced with other Ancient Near Eastern texts. These include stories such as the Egyptian 'Protests of the Eloquent Peasant'; laments such as the Sumerian 'A Man and his God'; and disputations such as 'The Babylonian Theodicy'. None of these, however, is particularly close to Job except for rather general similarities of subjects and format.

It is commonly argued that the book is the result of a long process of editorial activity by many people. This is not in itself a view which denies divine inspiration, but it does not seem to make particularly good sense in relation to the canonical book. If the book is the result of a centuries-long redactional process, then we have to try to recover each stage and the slant given to it by different authors; but if the book is the product of one controlling mind, then our task is to try to discover the overall meaning. More especially the question of the relationship of the prologue (chs. 1 – 2) and the epilogue (42:10–17) to the poetic dialogue must be explored.

There are a number of good reasons for seeing these as the product of one mind. The first is *structural*. Neither the prose nor the poetry can stand on its own. The prologue and epilogue do not constitute a story but only its opening and closing pages. Nor does the poem in all its magnificence stand plausibly on its own. Such volcanic emotions and implied traumas must have some adequate cause.[4]

There are a number of vital structural connections. The first is the establishment of the two levels on which this story is to operate. There is the sequence of events on earth and there is the reality of the orchestration of these events in the heavenly court. This establishes considerable dramatic irony in that the reader knows, but Job and his friends do not know, what has been happening in the divine council. We shall see that Job, from time to time, glimpses this reality. This ignorance, it will be argued, is no small part of the reason why the friends fail to 'speak what is right about God'. They have a flat, mechanical interpretation of the earthly events: Job is suffering badly, thus Job must be a particularly bad sinner.

A second structural connection is evident in 42:7–17. Verse 11 speaks of 'all the trouble the Lord had brought upon him' which clearly refers to the events of chapters 1 and 2. Yet the failure of the friends to speak what is right must refer to the poetic dialogue as they

---

[4] Those who wish to dissect the book are, of course, aware of this issue. Fohrer (1968: 325) identified five stages from a pre-Israelite legend to a final post-exilic redaction which blended prologue and dialogue.

say nothing in the prologue. Moreover, chapters 1 and 2 and 42:7–17 do not constitute a full story. Something like the present chapters 3 – 42:6 are necessary to complete the picture and to create the magnificent book as we have it.

A second connection of the prose and poetry is *thematic*. Some commentators argue that the Job of the prologue is a rural figure with flocks and herds grazing over wide spaces (1:14–17), while the Job of the speeches is a city dweller (29:7–11; 31:8–11). But this is to import a rigid distinction between city and country which is anachronistic and only truly emerges historically after the Industrial Revolution. Indeed, one of the features of Job is the creative way in which the author ransacks the whole of human activity for background and illustration.

Moreover, far from there being a contradiction between the patient Job of the prologue and the angry and strident Job of the speeches, both are necessary for a full understanding of Job's character. Without the prologue, the reader would have no reason to dispute the friends' increasingly virulent denunciation of Job. Without the speeches, the reader would be tempted to agree with Satan: 'Does Job fear God for nothing?' (1:9).

Thirdly, there is a strong *theological* link between the prose and the poetry. This bears most directly on the subject of this present study. We have already noticed the structural importance of the divine council. Arguably, the divine council (as ch. 2 will demonstrate) is theologically the controlling theme of the book. However, it is the role of Satan which binds the next chapters to the prologue. It will be argued in detail that Satan is unmasked in chapter 41 as Leviathan. A major part of this argument will be that such an identification is prepared for by numerous hints throughout the intervening chapters beginning in chapter 3. In other words, Satan is not simply a minor figure who has a walk-on part in chapters 1 and 2 and then disappears from the action. Rather the battle with evil is a major motif in the book as a whole. Once again the prologue is essential to establish two major truths. The first is that Yahweh is totally supreme; he alone has the power of life and death (2:6: 'you must spare his life'). The second is that Satan has enormous power and uses it to afflict Job grievously. This is the basis for the immensely powerful exploration of God's ways and the mysteries of creation and providence which are at the heart of Job.

Varied readings of Job

Unsurprisingly, Job has attracted a plethora of different readings and this continues. Here only a few comments can be made as an introduction to the main body of the study.[5] Early studies tended to emphasize the Job of the prose tale and dwell on the long-suffering Job rather than the passionate and angry Job of the speeches. Some scholars, including Dell (1991: 6), trace this emphasis on the patience of Job to James 5:11, but rather ignore 5:11c – 'and have seen what the Lord finally brought about'. Certainly the image of Job as the ideal and patient sufferer exercised a powerful grip on the imagination of all who wrote on the book.

By the twentieth century interest shifted to the poetic dialogue, and Job the passionate and unorthodox rebel became the focus of attention. Often this was linked with a tendency to dissect the book and see the prose and poetry as coming from different hands at different times. G. von Rad discussed Job and other wisdom literature and saw it, along with Ecclesiastes, as 'wisdom in revolt'.[6] This kind of interest is also reflected in H. G. Wells' novel, *The Undying Fire*, in which the owner of a country estate is visited by friends who come to console him over the death of his son in the First World War. Wells' framework is the dialogue of Job and his friends. This literary interest in the book of Job is evident earlier in Goethe's use of it in his prologue to *Faust* and in Blake's 'Drawings for the Book of Job'.

More recently, many comparisons have been drawn with Ancient Near Eastern myths, especially the chaos battle-theme. I will be discussing much of this in the following pages and assessing the value of such analogies. The commentary which makes most use of these analogies is that of Pope (1973), followed by the still incomplete philological commentary of Michel (1987). Both of these draw extensively on the work of Mitchell Dahood.

With the growth of interest in 'reader-response' criticism and deconstruction, the text of Job has been examined again in many studies. We may note the work of Athalya Brenner, now well known for her feminist readings of Old Testament texts. She argues that the book of Job is a sustained exercise in irony which in fact deconstructs wisdom literature's basic premise that virtue is rewarded.[7]

---

[5] A useful overview of the main lines of interpretation can be found in Dell (1991: 6–44). For an updated version of this work, see Dell 2001: esp. 361–364.

[6] von Rad 1972.

[7] Brenner 1989: 37–52. See the comments by Carson 1990: 156–157.

At first sight, Job appears to be a promising text for a 'reader-response' critic. It has no clear historical referents; it has no obvious relationship to Israel's legal and sacrificial system, and its depth and complexity are reflected in the widely varying interpretations already referred to. This non-realist view is the premise of much of the recent work of D. J. A. Clines on the book, especially in his paper 'Why is there a book of Job, and what does it do to you if you read it?'[8] Clines argues that the book is effectively a dream-like fantasy of what would happen to the author were he to lose his vast wealth. However, the author also imagines the overcoming of his death-wish and writes about the restoration of what he had both feared and wished to lose. He further states that the book exhibits inner conflict: affirming that piety does not lead to prosperity and then showing how the pious Job becomes more wealthy than ever. He then goes on to maintain that the book persuades readers that Job had the right to be rewarded, that his wealth was unproblematic, that there is a real objective cause to his suffering and that Job, far from being 'everyman', is a totally untypical human being. Clines wants to hold on to the book as great and powerful literature but to avoid readings which will be conditioned by dogma and will thus limit it.

Now if Clines is correct in his reading, many of the studies of Job (including this one) can safely be set aside. Deconstructionist readings, while they may throw some interesting sidelights on texts, are incompatible with hearing the voice of God in Scripture. Three considerations lead to a rejection of Clines' view of Job.

The first is a literary consideration. Deconstructionist readings claim that they are more sophisticated as readings because they distinguish between what a text apparently says and what it actually says. It is true that Job is a book of immense depth and power, with multiple layers of meaning. However, what Clines perceives as elements which undermine the text are imported by him into the text rather than arising from a reading of the text itself. Thus, the idea that great wealth somehow insulates Job from his calamities ignores the fact that loss of wealth is not raised as an issue in the dialogue. Also, the argument that the epilogue undermines the prologue ignores the fact that renewed prosperity is a gift of grace, not a reward for good conduct, and the reality that Job still needs to live the life of faith. (See further discussion in ch. 9).

The second consideration is theological. God is not carrying out

---

[8] In Beuken 1994: 1–20.

an experiment to see if Job's piety survives the loss of his prosperity. Clines relates this to God's lack of knowledge of what will happen and his inner need to know the truth about humankind. But our author is demonstrating exactly the opposite. He insists that suffering and calamity are under God's sovereignty. This is not a simplistic proposition and the suffering is real. The book abounds with hard questions and much mystery remains. Yet there is never a question that Job will turn away from God. His protests are not those of the atheist but of the baffled believer.

The third is canonical. As will be argued more fully in the final chapter, the book of Job is not freestanding and many of its themes are taken up elsewhere in the biblical canon as well as other complementary ideas introduced. In particular, the cosmic struggle between God and Satan is a major part of the whole biblical narrative, so we cannot simply take it as a narrative device, but must see the story of Job as an important experiment of the whole biblical revelation.

Thus we must reject deconstructionist readings and keep on wrestling to find a fuller understanding of this great book.

The literary genre of Job

No consensus has been reached on the overall genre of the book, and the fact that it contains both narrative and poetic dialogue should make us cautious in deciding too quickly how to classify the work. Dell (1991) has a useful chapter identifying various pitfalls such as assuming that the genre as a whole can be determined by finding a predominant minor genre, of too hastily and vaguely classifying it as 'wisdom' literature and of placing overmuch weight on recurring words and themes. She opts for parody as an overall genre and demonstrates many interesting links particularly with the Psalter. There is some truth in this approach, but it tends ultimately to isolate Job from much of the canon and to set it up in opposition to other biblical passages.

It is important to explore the idea of genre a little further as we establish some basic approaches to the book. Four observations might help.

First, it is to a large extent *sui generis*. This is not a counsel of despair, rather an acknowledgment that we cannot force the book into a straightjacket. The nature of the book is such that no one form can cover the variety of situations, emotions, questions, protests and characters that it introduces.

Secondly, the key, nevertheless, is in the skilful blending of the prose narrative and the poetic dialogue. This blending reflects the canon itself in miniature, with the narrative of God and his dealings with the universe and humankind and the commentary on that in prophetic, wisdom, epistolary and other texts. The story in Job is much more than a 'framework'; it is the essential seed plot from which the theology grows.

Thirdly, the prose has often been compared to the patriarchal narratives and to the book of Ruth. This is not unhelpful in itself, but does not take into account the interlocking of prose and poetry. While it may not be totally accurate to describe the book as drama, nevertheless the speeches are earthed in the narrative. This is not a debate or seminar on the problem of evil, it is an intensely rendered experience happening in the life of a named individual.

And fourthly, the poetry itself is rich and diverse. Dell is right in using parody as one of the prevailing forms (e.g. Ps. 8 parodied in 7:17–20; the traditional language of hymns of praise used in such evocations of God's power in creation in chapters 9 and 26). The lament genre is powerfully represented in speeches such as those found in chapters 13 – 15 and 19.

The present study attempts to take seriously the literary and artistic integrity of Job as well as its theological profundity. It is an examination of creation and evil as they are presented in the book and it particularly explores imagery, for there we find one of the most significant clues to the meaning of Job. It is to the relationship of imagery, myth and theology that we now turn.

The poet's use of imagery

In recent decades increasing attention has been given to the importance of metaphor in theology and it will be necessary to outline what I consider to be the gains and pitfalls of such an approach. We begin by noting that imagery and its effective employment by great poets is intended to engage the imagination as well as the minds of audience and readers. Robert Alter argues:

> It is probably more than a coincidence that the very pinnacle of ancient Hebrew poetry was reached in Job, the biblical text that is most daring and innovative in its imagination of God, man and creation; for here as elsewhere in the Hebrew Bible the literary medium is not merely a means of 'conveying' doctrinal

positions but an adventurous occasion for deepening doctrine through the play of literary resources, or perhaps even, at least at times, leaping beyond doctrine.[9]

I have some reservations with this statement, but it makes the important point that the imagery is of the essence of what is being said and is not merely colourful decoration. There has been a growing interest in the literary study of the Bible in recent years, much of it stimulated by the important work of Alter himself. Thus there is little excuse for ignoring the power and eloquence of this book. Since much of this study relates to the poetry of Job, we must examine carefully its powerful imagery and respond to that with our senses as well as our minds.

However, we must also avoid what I believe to be a misuse of the concept of metaphor. One of the significant books on metaphor and theology in recent years is by Sallie McFague.[10] Much of what she says is interesting and pointed, and she quite rightly asserts that religious language is profoundly metaphorical. She then, in my view, makes two wrong moves.

The first is to assert that the image of God as Father has become an idol. Christian tradition has narrowed and straightjacketed our images of God and there is a need to widen and democratize them. Doubtless the idea of God as Father has often been misused to oppress and exclude, but that is the fault of the user not the concept. To assert that one metaphor is incomplete in itself is quite right, it is illegitimate to set metaphors against each other and use the ones we like to discredit others.

The second illegitimate move is to set up a false dichotomy between a radical approach to Scripture which recognizes metaphor and an approach which absolutizes Scripture and fails to recognize metaphor. There may be such naïve approaches to Scripture, but it is difficult to find responsible conservative exegesis that approaches Scripture in such a flat and unnuanced way. Taking Scripture seriously means taking form as well as content into account when listening to a text.

This need for a balance of form and content has a direct bearing on the present study of Job. The basic premise of the interpretation offered here is that the divine speeches are the key to understanding

---

[9] Alter 1987: 15.
[10] McFague 1983.

the book as a whole. These speeches (chs. 38 – 41) are the peak of the poetry of the book. We must therefore read them as poetry, unpacking the imagery, trying to discern the flow of thought and resisting the temptation to come out with a series of propositions: 'What the book of Job really says is . . .' We must respond with all our hearts and our imaginations.

Moreover, this balance bears on another major issue in the interpretation of Job. It is frequently argued that God fails to address the issues of the book. In one sense that is true. We are given no easy answers to the mystery of suffering, nor are we told why the calamities came in the first place. Yet at a more profound level Yahweh does respond to the cries of Job. Many images and metaphors that have been used earlier, not least in Job's first agonized cries in chapter 3, are taken up in chapters 38 – 41. Failure to see this, in my view, has often led to inadequate readings of the divine speeches.

Myth and theology

Much of the imagery, especially relating to death and evil, appears to come from the milieu of Canaanite and other mythology. The links with Canaanite myth are discussed in an appendix (pp. 191–194), but something must be said here.

C. S. Lewis made some shrewd comments on the nature of myth and these are relevant to our study. His arguments are subtle and scattered throughout many of his writings;[11] but in essence he argues that pagan myths are 'good dreams' sent by God in preparation for the gospel. He further maintains that when we awake from the dream into the daylight of the 'Great Fact' we need to receive this with the same imaginative embrace that we accord to the dream myth.

My argument is that the author of Job and other Old Testament writers respond imaginatively to these ancient stories and use elements from them. They employ these partial insights and integrate them with the revelation given about the true nature of God and his relationship with his creation. These images and the myths to which they refer are a fundamental component of the book's theology. We cannot simply demythologize otherwise we will merely end up with a series of duller and less pointed images.

A further word needs to be said about the relationship between

---

[11] See e.g. 'Myth become Fact' in Lewis 1979. Lewis also wrote myth, notably in the Narnia stories, as did his friends J. R. R. Tolkien and Charles Williams.

imagery, myth and theology, for the above must not be taken to mean that these terms are being used interchangeably. Imagery, particularly in its most common manifestations of metaphor and simile, sees each object or person as having a significance beyond itself as an image of something or someone else. The poet rejuvenates language by creating new images or by using hackneyed images in new contexts. Poetry, in its compression and allusiveness, is thus a powerful way of embodying the richness and complexity of the world. Imagery and myth are not identical (e.g., images of trees, clouds and lakes in Job are not mythological). However, as demonstrated in the analysis of chapter 38, natural images often have mythological nuances. Similarly, to say that Leviathan has characteristics of the crocodile and the whale is not to say that it is such a creature, but rather to suggest that evil is rooted in the natural world.

The next step is to try to arrive at a working definition of myth. One point must be made immediately. Even if it could be demonstrated that the allusions to Canaanite myth were simply poetic rhetoric (whatever that means), we would still be left with questions about how and why they are used. The purpose of metaphor is to clarify and give a richer understanding. Moreover, since imagery works at a very deep level, the characteristic imagery of an author is a guide to his worldview and the characteristic cast of his mind.

By 'myth' I do not mean a story of 'make-believe', rather an attempt to embody in narrative the great truth of good and evil, of origin and consummation, of truth and error. When we use terms such as 'light' and 'darkness' about spiritual as well as physical realities, we are underlining the link between the natural and supernatural worlds. Myth takes this a step further and embodies these concepts in divine figures who battle for mastery. Baal and Yam, Osiris and Seth, Marduk and Tiamat are examples.

Thus the author of Job uses these stories as a potent vehicle for conveying the reality of the great cosmic battle between Yahweh and his adversary, the battle adumbrated in Genesis 3:15. That reality is expressed also in prose in chapters 1 and 2 with the picture of the heavenly court.

This means that some understanding of how Canaanite myth is used in Job is necessary for an appreciation of much of the imagery. The principles governing the use of these texts as well as some illustrative examples are laid out in the appendix on Job and Canaanite myth. However, I would like to make three observations about the author's use of the material.

The first observation is to do with the nature of revelation and inspiration. If the biblical use of Canaanite and other motifs were simply evidence of a common mythology, then it would be difficult to maintain a doctrine of special revelation. What we do have, here and elsewhere in the Bible, is creative use of such motifs to present a distinctive message. The inspired word comes in a variety of genres, through different personalities, and bears the stamp of the creativity of the different human authors.

Secondly, the author of Job is interacting with the worldview of Israel's neighbours. He is establishing the incomparability of Yahweh as against the gods of the nations. By using and engaging with their stories, he is showing an understanding of their worldview.

Thirdly, it is important to realize what the allusions to Canaanite myth do and do not do. The Canaanite evidence, as will be demonstrated, gives very strong support to a supernatural interpretation of Behemoth and Leviathan. What it does not and cannot do is to prove that interpretation to be the right one. Indeed the argument of this book does not depend on Canaanite parallels; these are, however, important supporting evidence.

The shape of this study

So far I have argued that the book of Job is a literary and theological unity and that a study of its imagery is necessary in any responsible interpretation of the book as a whole. The title *Now my eyes have seen you*, taken from Job 42:5, encapsulates neatly the basic thrust of this study. What is it that Job has seen, and how is this anticipated in the unfolding drama?

Chapter 2 discusses the basic legal metaphor which underlies and gives coherence to the book of Job. Beginning with an outline of the flow of Job, it traces this theme throughout the book and in particular discusses the 'Redeemer' passage in 19:21–27. The heavenly court is an expression of the doctrine of providence and thus chapter 3 discusses creation theology in Job and defends the unity and integrity of chapters 26 – 31 more especially as a setting for the wisdom poem in chapter 28.

The sub-title of the study is *Images of creation and evil in the book of Job*, and chapter 4 examines the raging sea, the most basic Old Testament image of the forces of evil. That study lays a foundation for chapters 5 – 8 where the implications of all these other images are focused in Behemoth and Leviathan.

In chapters 5 and 6 I will examine Behemoth and explain how this figure has been anticipated right from chapter 3. Then in chapters 7 and 8 I undertake a similar exercise for Leviathan. An important feature of these chapters is a translation and exegesis of the relevant passages.

Chapter 9 concentrates on Job 42 and argues that the interpretation advanced for the rest of the book makes this chapter no anti-climax but a powerful climax of the theology of Job and the unity of its prose and poetry. Some comments are also made on the canonical place of the book.

The book of Job is far more than any possible interpretation of it and it continues to defy easy classification. Yet it is important that we make the effort to listen to it, to be moved by it and see its progress from shrieking protest to repentance and vision.

Chapter Two

An advocate in heaven?

What is the book of Job about? We must face this question before proceeding to more detailed exploration of parts of the text. In the previous chapter we examined different readings of the text and in particular explored the relationship of theology, myth and imagery and established the importance of imagery for a theological understanding of Job. But what does the book 'mean'? By this I am referring not simply to the plot but to the intention of the author and how the text as we have it embodies that intention. Since the text is part of Scripture, we must also have regard to the *sensus plenior*, with the inevitable implications that has for the canonical status of the book of Job.[1]

This chapter will explore the legal imagery of the book of Job, which is not so much a separate area as the framework in which all the other images operate. Habel puts it thus: 'This metaphor is a major literary device which integrates narrative procession and theological motif.'[2] An exploration of this metaphor will therefore provide a basis for the examination of the images of creation and supernatural evil which are at the heart of the book of Job and which bear on God's providence and how this is experienced. In particular the theme of the heavenly court or divine council will be explored. The heavenly court will be seen to dominate the various parts of the book and particular attention will be given to the three 'witness' passages (9:33–35; 16:18–22; 19:20–27) where the legal metaphor is at its most obvious and striking.

First, however, it will be helpful to outline briefly the flow of the drama of Job. The book opens (chs. 1 and 2) with a patriarchal[3] figure

---

[1] For a full exploration of the 'meaning of meaning' see Vanhoozer 1998. See esp. 'On the definition of meaning as author's intention: a brief excursus' (253–255); and 263–265 on the *sensus plenior*.

[2] Habel 1985: 54.

[3] This says nothing about the time of writing; rather that the language and setting (including the absence of any reference to Israel's cultic system) recalls the days of the patriarchs.

named Job who is a wealthy landowner in 'the land of Uz'.[4] As well as being wealthy, he is notably pious and a man of integrity. Yet in the prologue to the book, in a series of hammer blows he is deprived in quick succession of his possessions, his family, his health and almost his sanity. As if this were not bad enough, we learn that these events on earth are orchestrated in the heavenly court and in that court there is an adversary who is anxious to destroy Job. Three friends of Job, Eliphaz, Bildad and Zophar, come to commiserate with him, but before a word is spoken, the group sit in silence for seven days and nights.

Job breaks the silence with an immensely powerful soliloquy (ch. 3) which expresses a bleak nihilism about his situation and prospects and sees no help or solace in God. This is the first of thirty-nine chapters of poetry and it sets the scene for the speech-cycles where Job and his friends engage in increasingly heated and bitter debate.

The next section is chapters 4 – 31 which can be subdivided further into three speech-cycles. Eliphaz opens the first (chs. 4 – 5) with a defence of traditional wisdom teaching as well as a claim to revelation through a vision (4:12–17). Job's first reply (chs. 6 – 7) is a complaint that both God and his friends have rejected him. Bildad now intervenes, and in a characteristically brusque speech (ch. 8) asserts that God is just and the obvious implication must be that Job is unjust. Job's second reply (chs. 9 – 10) centres on the mystery of God's sovereignty and justice. Zophar's first intervention (ch. 11), in tones of strident dogmatism, speaks of the transcendence of God. Job's third reply (chs. 12 – 14) dwells on the frailty and transience of humans and the apparent arbitrariness of God.

In the second speech-cycle an increasingly vitriolic tone marks the friends' speeches and an increasingly anguished and desperate tone marks those of Job. Eliphaz now questions Job's wisdom and innocence (ch. 15), and Job's fourth reply (chs. 16 – 17) focuses on the enmity and hostility of God. Bildad intervenes (ch. 18) with a grisly tirade on the fate of the wicked (i.e. Job). This evokes a passionate fifth reply from Job (ch. 19) with a challenge to God to clear his name followed by the famous passage on vindication (vv. 25–27) which we will consider later in this chapter. Zophar is not impressed and (ch. 20) assures Job that retribution will come. This cycle ends with Job's sixth reply (ch. 21) that fate does not always correspond to virtue.

[4] Uz appears in Gen. 36:28 among the descendants of Esau and in Lam. 4:21 in parallel with Edom.

The third cycle (chs. 22 – 31) does not neatly follow the pattern of the previous two. Only Eliphaz speaks at any length (ch. 22), attacking Job directly for his sins. Job's reply (chs. 23 – 24) wrestles with the problem of God's justice. Bildad (ch. 25) replies only briefly with a sour tirade on God's power, and Zophar does not speak at all.[5] In Job's eighth reply (chs. 26 – 27) he speaks of the mysteries of God's power and providence. The wisdom poem (ch. 28) eloquently lingers on the divine wisdom at the heart of creation. The final long section of Job's speech (chs. 29 – 31) is an eloquent apologia for his way of life and a defence of his integrity.

At this point, when we might expect the intervention of God, we have instead the introduction of a totally new character, Elihu, whose words form the substance of chapters 32 – 37. He says much that is good, but he is brash and angry and his words often sound too much like a Ph.D. thesis on suffering. In chapters 32 – 33 he condemns the friends and also Job for a lack of true understanding of God's justice. In chapter 34 he defends God's government of the universe, but, like the friends, fails to suffer along with Job, and in chapter 35 he dismisses the idea that God will appear to Job. (How wrong he is to be proved!) Finally, in chapters 36 – 37 he turns to God in creation and providence, evoking the splendours of creation in an eloquent passage (37:5–24). These chapters are integral to the book: they build up suspense, they allow theology a fair run for its money and they outline the main issues of the book as the drama approaches its climax.[6]

Now God himself speaks in four majestic chapters (38 – 41) which form the peak of the book and the heart of its theology. In the first speech (chs. 38 – 39) God speaks of the marvels of inanimate and animate creation. In the second speech (chs. 40 – 41) he presents Job with the two great powers, Behemoth and Leviathan, and asks if he can subdue them. Since discussion of these chapters form the bulk of this book, I shall make only two observations here. The first is that it is Yahweh, the Lord of the Covenant, who answers Job from the storm. This is the *gô'ēl* for whom Job had longed. The second is that Yahweh does not charge Job with sins he has not committed, but he does charge him with ignorance. This leads to Job's repentance and a restored relationship with God (42:1–6).

[5] I give reasons in ch. 3 (pp. 66–68) for seeing Job 26 – 31 as a coherent and carefully planned whole, thus rendering unnecessary the attempts of some commentators to reassign and rearrange these chapters.

[6] See Habel 1985: 36–37 for a further defence of the integrity of the Elihu chapters.

The book ends with a prose epilogue (42:7–17) where Job intercedes for his friends and is restored to even greater prosperity than he had enjoyed earlier. The final word is of Job dying in peace surrounded by a loving family.

To return now to the heavenly court or council, even the brief summary of the flow of the book has indicated something of its importance. It is the mainspring of the narrative of chapters 1 and 2; it is reflected in the debate-like format of the poetry; it is evidenced in the extensive use of legal language and most of all in the fact that Yahweh himself appears in his court in chapter 38. Job had wished to bring God to trial (*lārîḇ*, 9:3) and Yahweh himself accepts the legal framework and refers to Job as one who has a case (*rōḇ*) with the Almighty (40:2), and it is he who finally pronounces the verdict (42:7).

The prose tale

In order to understand the place of the heavenly court in the theology and drama of Job, six matters are of great importance. It is to these we now turn.

The nature of the heavenly court

The first is the nature of the court itself. Here, the Old Testament uses the concept of a meeting place of the gods. Sometimes, as in Canaanite mythology, this is a mountain.[7] Psalm 82:1 speaks of God standing up in the council of the gods. In 1 Kings 22:8–28 Micaiah ben Imlah tells of a vision of the heavenly court where a lying spirit is sent to speak through the mouths of false prophets. The later chapters of Daniel speak of heavenly beings involved in the destinies of nations (10:13–14); in the business of revelation (9:22–23) and in the answer to prayer (9:23). Psalm 103:20 speaks of angels as 'You mighty ones who do his bidding, who obey his word.' The 'sons of God' of this prologue are, therefore, no mere decoration echoing a primitive mythology but the realization that there are powers in the universe other than God and that they exercise great influence on the course of events.

The characters

Secondly, it is helpful at this stage to introduce the characters. Three main figures stand out: God, Job and Satan. Some commentators

---

[7] There are a number of books which explore this idea in some detail. Perhaps the most useful and accessible is Clifford 1972.

have gone very close to casting God as the villain of the piece.[8] This, among other things, is a misunderstanding of the nature of what is happening. In dramatic terms we can refer to this as a 'wager' and this certainly captures the suspense of the situation and the huge issues at stake. What would be illegitimate is to press this notion further and present God as a cosmic dramatist interested only in a suspenseful story and so indifferent to the lives even of his servants that he plays with them to win a bet.

In theological terms, this story is a fascinating glimpse into God's providence. The court simultaneously distances and involves God in Job's circumstances. Clines argues that here God is not omnipotent or omniscient: 'But not even Yahweh knows what has not yet happened; his knowledge does not encompass all possible hypothetical situations.'[9] He maintains that if Yahweh knows that Job will not waver, he can dismiss Satan's questions out of hand. Two things can be said. First, the issue is not what Yahweh knows, but what Job does not know and what he must therefore learn by the only way he can (i.e. by bitter experience that his faith is indeed equal to what lies ahead of him). More exactly, through his experience he is to learn that God is to be trusted fully, although for most of the book the evidence points in the opposite direction. Second, it is around Yahweh's *power* not his knowledge that the problem centres. Can the Lord provide? The whole story has striking parallels with the binding of Isaac in Genesis 22. This is no 'legal fiction'; God's justice is on the line and everything depends on the final verdict. God must act to vindicate not only Job but himself.

The character of Job is introduced as both a godly and a wealthy man, and the prose tale's description of him provides the essential foundation not only for his protestations of innocence and integrity in a general sense, but for his legal standing (the emphasis of chs. 29 – 31 in particular). The words used of Job underline his standing in the eyes of God and the heavenly court. He is 'blameless' (*tām*), a word used of clean animals offered for sacrifice (e.g. Lev. 22:18–20), a word with ominous nuances in light of what follows. The word is also used of the Torah (Ps. 19:8) and of Noah in Genesis 6:9. Job is also 'upright' (*yāšār*), a word used of God himself (Deut. 32:4). It is also used of the reforming kings Hezekiah and Josiah (2 Kgs. 18:3 and 22:2). The word implies integrity and faithfulness to God and his

[8] See esp. Clines 1989: 41–42 and more recently Whybray 1998, who writes: 'It cannot be said that Yahweh comes well out of the encounter' (p. 29).
[9] Clines 1989: 29.

Word. Positively 'he feared God' and is thus the kind of man whom Proverbs 1:7 identifies as associated with wisdom. Negatively, he 'shunned evil'. If Michel is right in his suggestion that *rā'* is personal and mythological (i.e. the evil one),[10] we have an anticipation of trouble to come.

Thus the writer presents Job as a righteous man free from specific sins which merit heaven's condemnation, and God appears to have blessed him in accordance with his uprightness. In an interesting article, Alan Cooper argues that the connection between prosperity and piety is not made by God nor by the narrator but by Satan.[11] It is Job's piety not his prosperity that God emphasizes, and thus prosperity is not to be an issue in the heavenly court, nor indeed does God mention the matter in chapters 38 – 41.

This brings us to the role of Satan[12] in the heavenly court. We will look at his exact relationship to the heavenly court, and go on to question whether he has a continuing role in the book.

Commentators make much of the definite article, '*the* satan', and argue that he is not to be identified with 'the great dragon . . . that ancient serpent called the devil or Satan, who leads the whole world astray' (Rev. 12:9). But that is unconvincing; 'the devil' in the New Testament, as in the passage quoted, is a very real personality.

Satan 'also'[13] came with the sons of God. He is the only identified person among them and thus is somewhat distanced from the others. This accords with and foreshadows many of the fundamental themes of the book: the existence and mystery of evil which is both part of creation and yet a threat to it; and a providence which cares but is surrounded by much mystery. There may be a deliberate contrast implied between Job the intercessor (v. 5) and Satan the accuser.

It is important to try to decide exactly against whom Satan is adversary: is it God or Job? At first sight, Satan's spite appears to be directed wholly at Job and his family. However, the narrator subtly suggests that God is in fact the main target. The indirect 'Does Job fear God for nothing?' (v. 9) and the way God is made the subject of the verbs in verse 10, 'Have *you* not put . . . *You* have blessed . . .',

---

[10] Michel 1987: 29, n. 5.

[11] Cooper 1990: 69–79.

[12] For an assessment of the role of Satan in the Old Testament see Day 1988. This is a well documented and fascinating book but tends to restrict itself to the word 'Satan' and thus misses many passages (including Job 41) where Satan appears in other guises.

[13] BDB (p. 169) says that 'Independence and emphasis is sometimes given by *gam* to a new idea.'

show that Satan is more concerned with the Giver than the gifts and with God than Job.

The question of whether he has a continuing role in the book is related to how we understand the abundant references to spiritual powers in succeeding chapters. He certainly is not called 'Satan' again, but scarcely has he disappeared when Leviathan makes an appearance in 3:8, and I shall argue that Eliphaz's vision in 4:12–21 is not in fact God but the enemy masquerading as him. The portrait of Satan is to find its culmination in the figures of Behemoth and Leviathan.

Moreover, if the heavenly court is not only the narrative device for setting the plot in motion but the controlling reality behind the whole book, then we must presume that Satan's activities continue.

The use of dramatic irony

The third important matter is the clever use of dramatic irony throughout chapters 1 and 2. Job, unlike the reader, has no knowledge of what is happening in the heavenly court. This has two effects. The first is to make an important theological point. Job is to become massively aware of hostile presences in the universe whose power seems overwhelming and who all but destroy his faith. Thus in Job's experience there is a perceived dualism, in that God seems unwilling to help him or even to communicate with him. Yet we know that in the last analysis there is no actual dualism because Satan cannot step outside the bounds God has laid down. Only at the end does Job realize this: 'I know you can do all things; no plan of yours can be thwarted' (42:2). Yet this irony has established the narrative thrust of the book: the man of faith has to live with crushing questions.

Secondly, it rules out some discussions of irony recently advanced by deconstructionists. For example, in an essay already more fully discussed in chapter 1, Clines postulates that the author is essentially creating a dream and the various actors in the drama are aspects of the dreamer.[14] Job is not typical of the human condition; there is no injustice in what he suffers and no deserving in his later prosperity. Thus the alert reader must deconstruct the book and will see that Job 'is labouring under a vast illusion'. However, irony is not something that the reader brings to the text and imposes on it, rather it is of the essence of the story and its underlying theology. We are allowed to 'listen in on God's council', to use Eliphaz's sneering words to Job in 15:7, and thus glimpse the nature of reality.

[14] Clines 1994.

The literary nature of the scene

This fourth issue establishes the importance of dialogue in the narrative sequence. As Habel points out, this is another close link between the prologue and the main body of the book which itself consists of extended dialogue.[15] The effect of the dialogue is to give the reader an insight into the motives of the characters, and to build up a world in which the activities and judgments of the heavenly court are no mere abstractions.

The final verdict

The prose tale twice anticipates the final verdict. The first occurrence is in 1:22: 'In all this Job did not sin by charging God with wrongdoing.' This is not a crude anticipation of the 'happy ending' because Job is to charge God vehemently and the first-time reader must wonder if Job is indeed going to curse God. The second instance is in 2:10: 'In all this Job did not sin in what he said.' This anticipates God's verdict in 42:7 that Job has 'spoken what is right'. Right speaking is of fundamental importance and God's condemnation of the friends shows that it is no minor matter.

Interpretation

Finally, the heavenly court is so firmly established in the reader's mind that its presence is a major factor in interpreting what happens in the rest of the book. Failure to recognize the importance of the heavenly court is a large part in the friends' misunderstanding of what is happening, just as awareness of it (without, of course, precise knowledge of what happens there) is an important factor in Job's eventual vindication.

In the rest of this chapter I will explore further how the heavenly court crucially impinges on earthly events, giving particular attention to the 'witness' passages. However, it is vital that we don't see these passages as isolated units but as points where the underlying preoccupation with the heavenly court surfaces in a particularly striking way. The first 'witness' passage (9:32–35) comes in the first speech-cycle and the other two 'witness' passages (16:18–21 and 19:23–27) feature in the second speech-cycle. This does not mean, as we shall see, that the heavenly court ceases to be important thereafter.

---

[15] Habel 1985: 81.

Job 9:32–35

Chapter 3 has established the atmosphere of lament and mystery, yet has placed these firmly within the providence of God. The cry of verse 23 is that of someone convinced of God's sovereignty and prepared to argue with him and challenge him to vindicate his justice.

> 'Why is life given to a man
>   whose way is hidden,
>   whom God has hedged in?'

He will not hide behind the easy platitudes of the friends; he will bring his case to court. Eliphaz, by contrast, speaks as if he were delivering a set-piece wisdom oration (much as Queen Victoria is said to have accused Gladstone of addressing her as if she were a public meeting). Indeed, Eliphaz denies Job access to the heavenly court: 'To which of the holy ones will you turn?' (5:1). He concludes his speech by declaring that an earthly court (i.e. traditional wisdom) has already declared on the matter: 'We have examined this, and it is true. So hear it and apply it to yourself' (5:27).

Job's speech in chapters 6 and 7 continues the preoccupation with God's providence and perceived hostility, and in a bitter parody of Psalm 8 challenges God to confront him directly (7:17–21). Bildad in chapter 8 appeals to mechanical laws of retribution and essentially presents a deist view of creation in which there is no place for Job's agonized questions.

All this is the background for the magnificent chapter 9 where, with great eloquence, Job unfolds the mysteries of creation and providence. Thus God and Job are seen in a much wider context than simply Job's own sufferings. The chapter subtly interweaves the language of the lament psalms with the rhetoric of the law court. Yet the key to unlock the dark prison lies tantalizingly close to Job's hand, indeed his fingers brush against it in verse 24: 'If it is not he, then who is it?' In this context it prepares the way for a mediator in the heavenly court and leaves open the possibility that the apparent hostility of God may have a more complete solution.[16]

This is the background to Job's pleas for an arbiter (v. 33); a figure

---

[16] If Michel (1987: 221, n. 134) is right in following Dahood and taking *rāšāʿ* (v. 24a) as 'the Wicked One', this would give an additional reference to Satan in his role of prosecutor. Against this view is the fact that 'wicked' is parallel to 'judges'.

who can be understood only in the context of the heavenly court. A textual point here is of some importance. The MT reads *lō'yēš* ('there is not'). Some manuscripts, however, prefer *lû'yēš* ('would that there were'). In any case, the question of the need for an advocate is being raised and, by raising it, Job is both emphasizing the apparent impossibility of speaking in the heavenly court and the deep desire that this should happen.

In this passage the identity of the putative advocate is not specified,[17] but he is described as one who could 'lay his hand upon us both'. Already in the prose tale God has forbidden Satan to lay his hand on Job (1:12), and Satan in turn challenges God to put out his hand and touch Job (2:5). In 2:10 Job speaks of receiving good and evil from the hand of the Lord.

It is fascinating to see how Job treats the prospect of such a lawsuit with apparent alacrity. The unusualness of this is well expressed by Clines: 'A psalmist prays to be delivered from such a threat (Ps. 143:2); Isaiah uses its imminence as a threat (Isa. 3:13–14); and Qoheleth uses it as an ultimate sanction against excessive self-indulgence (Eccl. 11:19).'[18] Job is also scared to death by the prospect (cp. 13:14–15), but like Abraham in Genesis 18 he overcomes his fears and pushes God in argument.

A further phrase which calls for comment is 9:35b. The line could be translated literally 'for I am not so with me', which is very unclear. Michel argues, not with entire conviction, that *kēn* means 'just', and translates 'for not honest am I before him'.[19] More helpfully, Habel argues that 'it is not so' is an inclusio, balancing 'it is so' of verse 2.[20] This is a useful reminder of the coherence of the chapter. Following Habel's suggestion a little further, it is interesting to note the context of the words 'I know that is so' (v. 2). They are a reply to the accusations of Bildad (8:20–22) which uses language that echoes the prologue. God, he asserts, will not reject the blameless, a clear reference to and implied criticism of the Job of the prose tale. The verb *mā'as* is often used in covenanted contexts of a judicial decision of God.[21]

In this first 'witness' passage we can discern three elements. The

---

[17] He is called a *môkiaḥ* (the Hiphil participle of *yākaḥ*). Job uses the verb in 13:10 of God rebuking those who presume to present his case for him, and Elihu uses it in 32:12 of how no-one has refuted what Job has said.

[18] Clines 1989: 242.

[19] Michel 1987: 234.

[20] Habel 1985: 183.

[21] E.g. Jer. 2:37; Amos 5:21.

first is the realization that there is a heavenly court and thus the possibility, however remote, that there is an advocate whose identity is as yet unknown. The second is that the blend of psalm-like and legal language has a particular potency. The language of the worshipper and of the litigant create a powerful sense both of the majesty of God and of the justice of Job's case. Thirdly, and this complements the first point, in the developing drama of the book, once the question of a mediator has been raised, it cannot simply be left. It is here a forlorn wish, and after the next passages he slips back into near despair. But each time the impossible hope becomes stronger.

Job 16:18–22

Again a few comments on the intervening chapters will help to put the passage in context. In chapter 11 Zophar responds to both the litigious and hymnic aspects of Job's speech, but in a rather rationalistic and mechanical fashion. He uses the litigious language to accuse Job of being a sinner who not only has no case to put but has been treated leniently (11:5–6). His hymnic language (11:7–9) has no sense of the awesomeness of the mysteries of which he speaks; like Bildad, who uses similar language in chapter 25, he is much more concerned to put Job in his place. That place is spoken of as a prison in verse 10 and, as we shall see in the discussion of death, that prison is probably Sheol.

Job's reply in chapters 12 – 14 is full of images of death and creation. There is a greater sense of calm and control here; the tone is melancholic rather than angry. Yet at its heart there is still the cry for a legal contest. He again denies he is guilty (13:19) and challenges God to produce a record of his sins.

Eliphaz's response in chapter 15 is a fascinating point in the development of the imagery. He raises the issue of the heavenly council only to dismiss it: 'Do you listen in on God's council?' (v. 8). Moreover, the passage is full of images of darkness, distress and the death of the wicked and somewhat anticipates Bildad's grim evocation of 'the king of Terrors'.

This leads directly to the next 'witness' passage in 16:18–22. Job's speech is a direct rebuttal of the taunts of Eliphaz in 15:25–26 and an allegation that it is God's violence to him and not his to God which is the issue. The violence of God is expressed in images foreshadowing Leviathan and will be of great significance in interpreting chapter 41.

Chapter 16 is one of the low points of the book; Job is in the blackest despair as he is attacked mercilessly by this savage adversary he believes to be God. It is important, however, to observe the legal nature of this chapter. There is a clear contrast between the 'witness' of verse 8 and that of verse 19. In verse 8 it is Job's own gaunt and emaciated appearance that rises up as a visible witness against him. In verse 19 the witness is Job's defender.

The language of verses 18–22 recalls the covenant settings of such passages as Deuteronomy 31:28: 'call heaven and earth to witness against them'. Similarly, in Genesis 4:10 Abel's blood cries for vengeance, and in Ezekiel 24:7–8 God is moved to vengeance by the blood of those massacred by the King of Babylon. Perhaps most strikingly, in view of the heavenly court context of Revelation 4 – 5, is Revelation 6:10 where the souls of the martyrs call out: 'How long, Sovereign Lord, holy and true, until you judge the inhabitants of the earth and avenge our blood?' The NIV rather loosely translates verse 18b as 'may my cry never be laid to rest!' However, this paraphrase may in fact bring out the shade of meaning of *māqôm* ('place') as 'burial place' and have the connotation of Sheol. Thus Job's plea would include all three parts of creation: heaven, earth and under the earth – and give it the tremendous solemnity of a universal assize.

Who then is the 'witness', and could he be God himself? Clines takes an individual line and argues that verse 20a should read:

> 'It is my cry that is my spokesman;
> Sleeplessly I wait for God's reply.'[22]

This is partially supported by the NIV: 'My intercessor is my friend'; although it identifies the intercessor as the witness of verse 19. The RSV's 'my friends scorn me' (this follows MT: see also NIV footnote) would also make excellent sense as Job is emphasizing his utter aloneness, hence he calls on heaven, earth and the netherworld as witnesses, since he has no human witness to stand by him or speak for him.

Clines argues that 'the truth of his innocence has been placed on record in the heavenly court'.[23] That is, of course, the point of the

---

[22] Clines 1989: 384ff. He takes *rēʿāy* to mean 'longing', from *rʿh* (BDB, root III) and reads singular *mᵉlîṣay* ('my spokesman'). He connects *dlp* with Akkadian *dalapu* ('to be sleepless') and argues that the cry for justice will be his witness in heaven whether anyone is listening or not.
[23] Clines 1989: 390.

prologue where God has attested Job's innocence. But that also places a question mark against Clines' view. Job's cry in itself is not enough; Satan will contest its validity and thus Job's cry needs an advocate. It has no existence in itself, and indeed is the expression of Job's need for vindication, not that vindication.

Textual considerations also point in the same direction. The connection between verses 18 and 19 does not suggest that 'cry' is to be equated with witness. A wish that his cry may find no resting place does not fit easily with an affirmation that it is now in heaven. The MT of verse 20a has plurals and these refer most naturally to his friends who are being of no help, as Job has said so scathingly in verses 3–5. It is to God that his tears ascend. There is no *waw* in verse 20b, so it is not easily understood as circumstantial (cp. NIV's 'as my eyes pour out tears to God') but rather as a statement paralleling verse 20a. The syntax suggests that Job wants his cry to ascend to heaven, for God even now is there as his witness. The friends scorn him (and God seems unreachable), but he cries tearfully to God that he might argue for him in heaven.[24]

This brings us neatly back to the question of the identity of the witness and how he can be God even if the flow of the passage and the syntax point that way. He is called *'ēd* and thus must be connected with the use of the word in verse 8. There the witness is his bodily appearance which gives the lie to his protestation of innocence. This is compounded by God's deadly enmity in verses 9–14. Hartley makes a most penetrating comment:

> Here Job comes close to reconstructing the scene of the heavenly council in the Prologue, but he turns it inside out. He identifies God as his enemy rather than his advocate. At this crucial point he is tested to the ultimate. From his perspective he is led to wonder if the God in whom he trusted is not in reality his satan.[25]

Hartley's suggestion of the confusion of God and Satan goes a long way towards answering the charge that the witness could not be God himself. In the chapters on Leviathan I shall develop this theme (i.e. the confusion of God and his adversary which appears often as two

---

[24] Verse 21 begins with a *waw* followed by an imperfect of purpose which suggests that this clause is not a new beginning.

[25] Hartley 1988: 302.

gods arguing against each other). In such a contest his own cry would scarcely be a convincing advocate.

Two notable advances have been made in this passage. The first is the placing of Job's cry in covenant-like language and this can be finally satisfied only by an appearance of the covenant Lord himself. Secondly, the fierce conviction that there is a witness in heaven is far stronger than the desperate hope of chapter 9.

Job 19:20–27

Job's immediate words are not encouraging; his mind is obsessed with death, an obsession which Bildad is to fuel with grisly relish in chapter 18. Chapter 19 shows Job at his most harassed and persecuted. What if now he dies unvindicated? In 19:7–12 he describes God's attacks on him in a series of vignettes: a lone victim of a mugging ignored by passers by; a traveller faced with a landslide in a darkening landscape; a disgraced and ostracized ruler; an uprooted tree; and, worst of all, his pathetic little tent attacked by God's vast armies. In verses 13–19 his former well-ordered family and societal life has collapsed around him and he is an object of contempt and ridicule. It is just at this point that the great *gô'ēl* passage comes. Because of its crucial importance I shall begin with a translation and base my exegesis on it.

Translation

[20]My bones are showing through my skin and my flesh and I have escaped by the skin of my teeth.[a]

[21]Have pity on me, have pity on me, you friends of mine, for the hand of God has struck me.

[22]Why do you pursue me as God does? When will you ever be satisfied with my flesh?[b]

[23]O that my words were written! O that they were inscribed on a stele![c]

[24]O that with an iron stylus and with lead[d] they were engraved on a rock for ever.

[25]Yet[e] I know that my Vindicator lives and that in the end he will stand upon the dust.[f]

[26]And that after they have struck off my skin – this shall be – though my flesh has gone[g] – I shall see God.

[27]I shall see him for myself; my own eyes will see him and not a stranger. My heart faints within me.

Notes on the translation

[a]This verse has been the subject of numerous emendations but these are not especially relevant to the present study. Clines provides a comprehensive list of suggestions and emendations (pp. 430–432).

[b]The translation here tries to bring out the continuous force of the imperfect.

[c]I have translated *sēper* as 'stele' to try to capture the idea of a permanent record in stone which would be a continuous testimony to Job's innocence.

[d]Taking *bᵉ* with both nouns.

[e]I have translated *waw* as 'yet' to suggest the contrast between dead stone and lead and the living vindicator.

[f]'Dust' has ambiguities.

[g]Taking *mîn* in essentially a temporal sense (cp. 38:21: *mîn yāmêḵa*: lit. 'from your days', i.e. 'since you were born').

The passage falls naturally into three parts: Job's present situation (20:22); his desire for a permanent record of his words (20:23–24); and the *gô'ēl* (20:25–27).

Verses 20–22 form a pause for assessment and have many echoes of the prose tale, but the reference to skin recalls 2:4–6 where Satan taunts God that Job's skin and flesh have not been harmed. This verse shows that in fact this has now happened; Satan has done his work thoroughly. Ironically, what Job complains about here is in fact a result of what has happened in the heavenly court, and thus unknowingly gives further weight to his protestations of innocence. This is reinforced by the reference to the 'hand of God' (v. 21) because it is the interplay of the hand of God and the hand of Satan that is presented with such subtlety in the prologue.

An additional element introduced in verse 21 is Job's twofold cry for pity. This must be an element of God's condemnation of the friends in 42:7; in their desire to prosecute Job they had so mistaken the nature of the Judge as to speak with the voice of his adversary.

The real adversary, as Job perceives it, is God. 'Hand of God' is metonymy for the power of God, and is often used, especially in relation to the exodus, of God's power on behalf of his people. But here it has a negative sense that is developed in an image of savagery in verse 22b about eating flesh. The hidden nuance of 'slander' and the use of the Syriac term for the devil are pointers to the reality of the activity of the Satan figure behind the words of the friends.

These two verses give us a concise summation of Job's current and continuing agonies that demand redress. The rest of the passage shows the response to this situation in two ways: desire for a permanent written record (vv. 23–24) and desire for a living vindicator (vv. 25–27).

Verses 23–24 express the hope that the legal case would be recorded in a permanent medium.[26] It may be that Job is deliberately contrasting this with other previously used metaphors of the brevity and fleeting quality of his life (e.g. the cloud of 7:9; the tree of 14:10; the lake of 14:11). Job wants something that will not only vindicate him and his integrity but that in after ages will be a memorial to his fight for justice. He has lost his family, his place in society and his reputation, and he fears that death will come and cover him in oblivion. 'Rock' is also, of course, used metaphorically for God, especially as the defender of his people (e.g. Deut. 32:4; Is. 32:2). Thus Job wishes his words to be inscribed in a medium that has the solidity of God himself.

Yet this is cold comfort. Just as Shakespeare in his sonnets longs wistfully 'that in black ink my love may still shine bright' and yet longs for the living lover (Sonnet no. 65), so here Job, not content with memorials in stone, longs for a living *gô'ēl*. In examining this passage (vv. 25–27) I shall begin with what is tolerably certain before considering the identity of the *gô'ēl* and the time of Job's vindication. The *waw* in verse 25 I have taken as one of contrast with both the preceding sections, not only the persecution (vv. 20–22) but also the desire for a permanent record (vv. 23–24). The AV and the RSV translate it as 'for', suggesting logical sequence rather than contrast. The NIV leaves it untranslated.

The 'I' is emphatic; the friends may not believe in Job's vindication but, in spite of all, he is capable of a leap of faith. Moreover, *yāḏa'* ('to know') is often used in forensic contexts (e.g. 9:28: 'I know you will not hold me innocent'; also in 10:14 of God's purpose to mark him down as a sinner). Also worth noting is the use of *yāḏa'* in covenant contexts (e.g. Amos 3:2: 'You only have I chosen of all the families of the earth'). It is a rich word with implications of relationship.

An unmistakable emphasis is on 'seeing God'; mentioned three times in verses 26–27. The language here, as so often in Job, is reminiscent of the Psalter. A striking parallel is Psalm 17:15:

'And I – in righteousness I shall see your face;
    when I awake, I shall be satisfied with seeing your likeness.'

[26] The technical details are surveyed in Gehman 1944: 304–307.

The context is a plea for vindication from deadly enemies: 'May my vindication come from you' (v. 2). Similarly Psalm 24:6 speaks of seeking the face of the God of Jacob; those who do so have received vindication from God the Saviour (v. 5). Psalm 27:4 speaks of gazing 'upon the beauty of the LORD and [seeking] him in his temple'. There the psalmist is claiming refuge from enemies who 'advance against me to devour my flesh' (v. 2). These and other passages in the Psalter place the seeing of God in the context of legal vindication and the protection of God, the *gô'ēl* of his people.

Plainly, the 'seeing' must also be linked with Job's words in 42:5:

> 'My ears had heard of you
> but now my eyes have seen you.'

To anticipate briefly, I shall argue in the final chapter of this book that the 'seeing' is in no small measure the discerning of the difference between God and his colossal adversary. All Job's flashes of insight (e.g. 9:24) and this present glimpse of the reality of the heavenly court are to be vindicated fully by a vision that simultaneously rewards and humbles him.

Now we need to examine who or what the *gô'ēl* is. Throughout the Old Testament it is a legal and relational term referring to Yahweh as champion and kinsman of Israel, and the term applied to humans sees them operating essentially as Yahweh's representatives. It is, in fact, easy to trace many of the nuances of *gô'ēl* in this passage. There is the *gô'ēl haddām* whose duty was to avenge a relative by tracking down and executing the killer (e.g. Num. 35:19). This is reflected in the images of violence against Job in the earlier part of the chapter and also recalls 'O earth, do not cover my blood' (16:18). The book of Ruth shows that marriage could be part of the duties of the *gô'ēl*, and this goes beyond legal stipulations to the theme of relationship that is at the heart of covenant. Interestingly, in Ruth 4:5, Boaz, using the verb *qwm* (as here), speaks of the *gô'ēl* as the one 'to maintain the name of the dead with his property'. This suggests the continuation of the work of the *gô'ēl* beyond this life. Thus the *gô'ēl* is to be to Job as Yahweh himself; to be everything the friends have failed to be.

The title *ḥāy* ('lives') is also significant. Hartley says 'this adjective "living" stands in bold relief against Job's fear of dying'.[27] Once again there are comparisons with the Psalter. Psalm 42:2 speaks of the

[27] Hartley 1988: 293.

psalmist's soul thirsting for the living God and the context is of opposition both human and supernatural. Indeed Psalm 43, usually seen
as a companion piece if not originally part of the same psalm, calls
on God to defend and vindicate the psalmist's cause (v. 1).

It is plain that the words most naturally suggest that Job's vindicator can be none other than God himself. Nevertheless, the bulk of
scholarly opinion is against this interpretation. Habel argues that:

> A major argument against viewing God as the *gô'ēl* is that it
> would mean a complete reversal in the pattern of Job's thought
> to date, a pattern which also persists after this famous cry of
> hope. Job has portrayed God consistently as his attacker not
> his defender, his enemy not his friend, his adversary at law not
> his advocate, his hunter not his healer, his spy not his saviour,
> an intimidating terror not an impartial judge.[28]

I would like to make three observations here. The first is that Habel
does not give sufficient weight to Job's passionate desire to meet with
God and his refusal to give up the struggle to see him. In particular,
Habel fails to see the development in the three 'witness' passages. Job
is serious about God and, like Jacob in Genesis 32, will not let him go
without receiving a blessing. His hot and bitter words about God are
those of an anguished lover desperate to hear from the beloved that
he is not hostile. Thus his cry here could be a voicing of his deepest
convictions with an implied appeal to God that it might be so.

Secondly, this view gives insufficient weight to the canonical status
of Job. The book is not freestanding and ideas and words which carry
massive theological weight in other contexts cannot simply be evac-
uated of that here. I have already cited some of the Old Testament
evidence for the status of the *gô'ēl* as well as passages in the Psalter
about seeing God. Habel comments: 'the allusions to God as *gô'ēl* in
the Psalter are not pertinent; the context here is forensic, not cultic,
and the need is for deliverance from God, not by God'.[29] Too sharp
a distinction is drawn here between forensic and cultic. Job frequently
combines the language of worship and the law court and thus
removes his situation from a merely forensic transaction. In any case,
seeing God implies Job's vindication, otherwise he could not stand in
the heavenly court.

Taking the canonical aspect a bit further, it is appropriate to ask

[28] Habel 1985: 306.
[29] Habel 1985: 305–306.

how viewing the *gô'ēl* as God fits into the complete canon. Once again much scholarship denies that there is any foreshadowing of Christ here. J. A. Wharton argues: 'It is important for Christians to recognise that when we identify the "Redeemer" of Job 19:25 with the Risen Christ of the Gospels, it is our faith we are expressing, not the faith of Job.'[30] In a sense Wharton is right, for Job did not see Christ risen or otherwise, yet this is a clear example of Hebrews 11:13: 'They did not receive the things promised; they only saw them and welcomed them from a distance.' Wharton further argues that to interpret the ultimate meaning of this passage Christologically would be to admit that Job is in fact a sinner after all in need of a Redeemer. But that is unconvincing. No-one argues that Job is sinless; after all he offers sacrifices. What is being challenged is the rigid deterministic view that suffering is a sign of God's punishment for specific sins. As Andersen says: 'It is possible for sinful men to be genuinely good.'[31] It seems if we take the concept of canon seriously, we cannot but think of the advocacy of Christ here and see this as one of the Old Testament intimations of the light that was to come into the world.

Thirdly, Habel does not sufficiently consider the full implications of verses 25b and 26 with their many hints of a judgment beyond this life. Indeed, he does not deny the possibility of 'surviving death in some sense'; but, in common with many other commentators, rules out the serious possibility of such an interpretation.

This brings us to a consideration of verses 25b–26. The *gô'ēl* must be someone whose voice carries weight in the heavenly court, a figure such as Michael, who in Daniel 12:6 'stands up' to protect the people of Israel. Job glimpses the paradox that in spite of God's apparent hostility it is to God he must appeal.

The interpretation of these verses is very closely related to an examination of the Old Testament view of death and the life beyond. The theme of death in Job will be our subject in chapters 3 and 4, but some comments are necessary as we try to understand this passage. Again the weight of scholarly opinion denies that here we have a glimpse of resurrection. For example, Whybray argues, 'In view of Job's admission elsewhere in the book that no one can return from the realm of death and that God himself has no power over the underworld it is out of the question that he should here express such a hope.'[32]

---

[30] Wharton 1999: 89.
[31] Andersen 1976: 79.
[32] Whybray 1998: 96.

This view does not take sufficient account of the diverse literary genres of Scripture. It is indeed true that Job expresses pessimism and hopelessness about the world beyond the grave (see e.g. 3:11–19; 7:9–10; 10:20–22), but these are dramatic not theological statements and express what Job is feeling at that moment. Similarly, when the writer of Ecclesiastes says, 'All go to the same place; all come from dust, and to dust all return' (3:20), he is reflecting the perspective of life 'under the sun' and not giving a definitive statement about the destiny of the departed.

However, this passage, with its formidable theological freight and its clear links with the heavenly court scene of the prologue and with 'seeing God' in the epilogue, has a visionary even revelatory character. To put it another way: Job's glimpse here of the realities of the divine council that set the plot in motion and his vindication by God at the end show that this is supremely a passage in which he has spoken what is right.

In 19:25 we read: 'In the end he will stand upon the dust' (my translation). 'In the end' could simply be rendered 'in days to come' and have as its primary reference legal vindication during Job's early life.[33] The trouble is that such vindication would not in itself restore Job's relationship with God. J. A. Motyer has a useful comment on rightly handling the Old Testament material on life after death:

> There are, in fact, three dangers in dealing with death and Sheol in the Old Testament: one is painting the dark scenes too dark; the second is failure to take the light scenes at their face value; and the third is to omit to bring the sentiments of Old Testament saints into comparison with those of the New Testament, for, in both Testaments, death is a dread enemy (1 Cor. 15:26; cf. Isa. 25:7–8; Job 18:14).[34]

The second of Motyer's comments is particularly pertinent. These considerations do not minimize the translation difficulties but emphasize the two clear elements: there is a *gō'ēl* and Job will see him.

A few other textual points need comment. Firstly, 'He will stand

---

[33] The numerous writings of M. Dahood have identified many places in the Psalter and elsewhere that can be taken as referring to a life beyond death. Dahood, usually on the basis of Ugaritic, argues for this view which causes him to rewrite many traditional renderings of the Psalter. For a convenient overview of this evidence see Tromp 1969.

[34] Motyer 1996.

'al 'apār' (lit. 'upon the dust'). The word has nuances of 'underworld', as will be shown in the next chapters, and can be seen as Yahweh trampling on death on Job's behalf. Just as he 'tramples on the back of Yam' (9:8; see treatment of this in ch. 3), so here he will defeat the deadly powers which hold Job in a vice-like grip.

Verse 26a is very difficult to understand. The reference to skin and flesh presumably harks back to verse 20 which, as already demonstrated, is probably a deliberate echo of the prologue. Literally the text reads 'And after my skin they have stripped off – this.'[35] I have taken the phrase to mean that Job expects the experience which follows to take place after his skin has wasted away in death. The AV understands the unidentified 'they' as the worms who devour the corpse: 'and though after my skin worms destroy this body'. 'This' can be paraphrased as 'this shall be' and referring to the next clause about seeing God. It seems probable that Job is referring to 18:13:

> 'It eats away part of his skin;
>   death's firstborn devours his limbs.'

Thus Job is claiming that far from being 'marched off to the king of terrors', he will see light in the divine presence.

The phrase *mibbᵉšarî* can be understood in quite different ways: 'from within my flesh' or 'from without my flesh'. The translation offered here takes *min* in a temporal sense and sees it as an after-death experience.[36] The phrase remains odd.

'Seeing God' has already been the subject of comment, but it is worth pausing for a moment on the additional phrase in verse 27: 'and not a stranger' (my translation). The verbal form of the word occurs in verse 13: 'He [i.e. God] has alienated my brothers from me; my acquaintances are completely estranged from me.' Basically it is the opposite of *gô'ēl*, and at the heart of Job's cry is not only the wish for legal vindication, but also for the renewal of a relationship. The book, in fact, is not ultimately about the problem of evil and suffering in isolation but about a true relationship with God.

This is probably underlined by the final phrase of verse 27: 'My heart faints [longs, yearns] within me!' In an old but still useful commentary on Job, A. B. Davidson writes: 'This thought was so intense

---

[35] For a concise survey of possible interpretations and emendations see Habel 1985: 293.

[36] This does not imply a disembodied experience. Rather it implies that *this* body has gone.

that it almost recognised itself. Job's assurance of seeing God was so vivid that it virtually became a vision of God and he faints in the ecstasy of his faith.'[37] This shows powerfully the profundity of Job's experience here which virtually becomes an adumbration of God revealing himself. In the prologue Satan had said that it was one thing to honour God if he lost everything he had, but that it would be a different matter if his skin and flesh were harmed (2:4–5). Job has indeed been 'stripped' – his body has been attacked viciously so that he feels flayed and destroyed. Yet, in spite of it all, he can still want to see God and indeed, by the power of that wish, can partially see, and by partially seeing receives an intimation of the final vision. Thus the basic reality of the heavenly court is for Job more than a plea for legal vindication; it is at heart a longing for an unclouded relationship with God.

This lengthy consideration of the 'witness' passages began with a concern to see these not as isolated parts of the book but to demonstrate how they focus the centrality of the divine council in the overall interpretation of the book. To complete the task it will be necessary to examine briefly how that continues in the latter part of the book.

Two chapters conclude this second speech cycle. In chapter 20 in his second, and last, contribution, Zophar pronounces legal condemnation on the wicked, by whom he clearly means Job:

> 'Such is the fate God allots the wicked,
>   the heritage appointed for them by God' (20:29)

It is interesting to note how Zophar views happiness in largely material terms. Moreover, he denies all possibility of a favourable verdict in the heavenly court; far from there being a vision of God, 'The eye that saw him will not see him again' (20:9). This is countered by Job in a speech which amounts to a legal justification of himself and constitutes a reply to the accusations of the friends (ch. 21). This speech is in fact a legal complaint (v. 4) and rounds off this speech-cycle.

The third speech-cycle (chs. 22 – 31)

In Eliphaz's final speech (ch. 22) he effectively argues that Job must submit to God and by repenting regain his former favour. With

---

[37] Davidson 1884.

unconscious irony he anticipates, Caiaphas-like, that the innocent will achieve favour for the guilty. Verses 27–30 are to be fulfilled in 42:7–10. Job's reply in chapters 23 – 24 reaffirms his desire 'to state my case before him' (23:4). In a brief final tirade (ch. 25), Bildad denies any possibility of a person being righteous before God.

The long final speech of Job (chs. 26 – 31) is discussed later (see pp. 67–68), but it is important to notice at this point that its closing section (chs. 29 – 31) is a final declaration of innocence and an appeal to the Almighty to hear him (31:35).

The Elihu speeches (chs. 32 – 37)

We cannot examine Elihu's long contribution in detail here, but three comments will help to highlight how his remarks bear on the legal metaphor of the book. The first is that he is concerned to defend the justice of God but in a way that veers dangerously close to the callousness of the friends. He does indeed speak of a mediator in 33:23 but fails himself to show empathy with Job.

Secondly, in chapter 35 Elihu denies that Job is innocent. The trouble is that he fails to detect any compassion in God: 'If you sin, how does that affect him?' (35:6). His God is the God of deism who does not respond to repentance and faith (vv. 12–14). Verse 14, 'you do not see him', totally ignores the magnificent leap of faith of 19:25–27.

Thirdly, in chapters 36 and 37 Elihu's platitudes are overtaken by a splendid evocation of the glories of creation and of God in awesome majesty coming from Mount Zaphon,[38] the place where the divine council will deliver the long-awaited judgment.

God and Job (38:1 – 42:6)

When God appears he makes it very plain that he has not come as plaintiff but as judge; he will ask the questions. At this stage there is only one point we need to make: whatever the detailed meaning of these chapters, they spectacularly respond to the *gô'ēl* passage: 'now my eyes have seen you' (42:5). This leads Job to repentance, not for the many sins alleged by the friends, but for ignorance and presumptuousness. Andersen helpfully draws attention to Job's likeness to

---

[38] Probably *ṣāpôn* here does not simply mean 'north' but contains a hidden reference to the cosmic mountain. See the further discussion in ch. 7.

Abraham here.[39] The passage to which he refers, Genesis 18, is one in which Abraham 'sees' God.

The epilogue (42:7–16)

This will be fully discussed in the final chapter (see pp. 178–185), but here it suffices to say that God publicly vindicates his servant in two ways. First, Job virtually acts as *gô'ēl* for his friends and prays for them as he had prayed earlier for his family (1:5). Secondly, his prosperity is restored, indeed increased. Thus God publicly replies to Job's pleas and to his suffering, and the Judge of all the earth is seen to have done right.

General comments

Three comments will serve to bring together some of the significant threads of this consideration of the heavenly court. The first concerns the literary nature of the passages discussed. As already noted, they show a blend of legal and psalm-like language. The lamentation psalms are of especial relevance here as many of them call on God to vindicate the psalmist. Moreover, much of the language found, for example, in Psalms 42, 43 and 44 uses words of doubt, depression and despair, but these are balanced with leaps of faith that God will and must vindicate his people.

The lament psalms are also full of an intense longing for God and for the sanctuary (cp. again Psalm 42). Thus the hope expressed goes beyond mere legal vindication and is a desire for deep and unbroken fellowship with God.

Secondly, the theology of the divine council provides a context for an exploration of some of the other most significant passages and themes in Job. Death, supernatural evil and the fundamental mysteries of creation must be related to God's providence which is deeply related to the reality of the heavenly court. Job is not, as the friends allege, trapped in a flat mechanistic universe. Powers other than God are active and it is the relationship of these powers to God which will be explored in succeeding chapters. The unifying theme of the heavenly court which binds the book of Job together is the necessary context for our examination of other themes.

Thirdly, the theology of the divine council shows the centrality of

---

[39] Andersen 1976: 292.

Job in the canon. Although this will be explored in detail in the final chapter, a few words at this point will be useful. Here the book of Job joins hands with the rich devotion and agonized prayer of the Psalter, with the intercessions of Abraham and Jeremiah, with the covenantal theology of Deuteronomy. 'Rise up, O Judge of the earth' (Ps. 94:2) is a concise summation of much of what Job has to say.

Chapter Three

The tragic Creator

Part of the power and depth of the Job poet's treatment of evil and suffering arises from his linking these with the issues of creation and providence. Evil is a universal problem but it is a peculiarly difficult one for those who believe that a loving God not only once created but is continually involved in his creation. Thus any exploration of the book must engage with its picture of creation and providence. To do this, the imagery of nature must be explored.

The imagery of nature in Job is part of the Bible's presentation of creation which is at the heart of the biblical story. In Genesis 1 and 2 God creates and over and over again pronounces his creation to be 'good' or 'very good'. Yet into this good creation comes the serpent, and the subsequent 'fall' involves not only the sin and death of humans but a curse extending to the whole created order (Gen. 3:16–19). Thereafter creation is still good and beautiful (see such Psalms as 65 and 98) but is subject to frustration and longs for its transforming (Rom. 8:19–22). Job is not only experiencing suffering and disaster but sharing something of the anguish of creation itself. Thus it is no surprise to find that the book is alive with images of creation and in several places develops more fully a 'theology' of creation.

Imagery of nature occurs widely throughout the book. There is animal imagery: for example, lions (4:10ff.), eagles (9:26), a wild donkey (11:12), and various creatures in ch. 39. There is botanical imagery: grass (5:25), papyrus (8:11), and trees (14:7–9; 19:10). There is also cosmological imagery: clouds (7:9; 37:5–11), and stars (9 and 38). The panorama of heaven, earth and sea is evoked in vivid and colourful detail and linked with the main themes of the book: streams in the desert (6:15–16), with the faithfulness of the friends; and clouds (7:9), with the transience of human life.

A full examination of these (and there are numerous others) would take a whole book. What I shall do is select two key areas of imagery and three significant chapters. The two areas of imagery are the starry heavens and the life of trees; the three chapters are 28 and 38 – 39 which occur at crucial junctures in the book and provide a necessary foundation for the later discussion of supernatural evil.

'He also made the stars'

'Two things fill me with awe,' said Kant, in the conclusion to his *Critique of Pure Reason*, 'the starry heavens above me and the moral law within me.' At various crucial points, the Job poet introduces references to the starry heavens and wrestles with how creation and the 'moral law' can be reconciled. We have already noticed the 'mythological' connotations of the stars, especially the parallel in 38:7 where *kôkbê boqer* corresponds to *bᵉnê ᵉlōhîm*. Moreover, there is in these passages some splendid nature poetry or, more accurately, poetry about creation.

To place these passages in their widest context it will be useful to say something about the general Old Testament depiction of the stars. Apart from their use as simple markers of time in Nehemiah 4:21, where the builders on the wall of Jerusalem continued work 'until the stars came out', all other references belong to significant areas. Following the basic statement of Genesis 1:16, 'He also made the stars', a number of passages, mainly in the Psalter, refer to the stars as a sign of the power of God and a reminder to humankind of the duty of praise (Pss. 8:3; 147:4 and 148:3; also Jer. 31:35). Further passages speak of the descendants of Abraham (i.e. the creation of God's people)[1] and compare their number to that of the stars. The primary passages are Genesis 15:5; 22:17; 26:4; and there are also a number of passages which refer to these (Exod. 32:13; Deut. 1:10; 10:22; 28:62; 1 Chr. 27:23 and Neh. 9:23).

A further group of passages reflect the danger of worshipping the stars (Deut. 4:19 and 2 Kgs. 21:3). Related to these are a number of passages where the stars are associated with judgment: on a personal level in Ecclesiastes 12:2, on an international level in Ezekiel 32:7 and Joel 2:10 and 3:15. In Judges 5:20 'the stars fought from their courses . . . against Sisera'; in Obadiah 4 judgment is promised on Edom although he aspires to the stars; and in Nahum 3:16 the Ninevite merchants are said to be more in number than the stars of the sky. Also relevant here is the significant passage in Isaiah 14:12–13 of Helel ben Shachar exalting himself above the stars of El. Two other passages – Joseph's dream in Genesis 37:9 and Baalam's prophecy in Numbers

---

[1] For the choice of Abraham's descendants as a new creation see esp. Craigie 1969.

24:17 – associate the stars with vision and prophecy. Like the Old Testament as a whole, the star passages in Job are related to the great biblical doctrines of creation, election and judgment and it is to these we now turn.

Job 3:9

Here Job, cursing the day of his birth, exclaims: 'May its morning stars become dark.'

The full impact of Job's statement becomes apparent when it is compared with Genesis 1:16, 'He also made the stars.' Job is virtually assuming the prerogative of the Creator and doing so in order to 'uncreate'. That this power is far beyond him is to be demonstrated in the wisdom poem in chapter 28 as well as in Yahweh's questions in chapter 38. Habel expresses the underlying thrust of the verse thus: 'The stars are the lights which give the night its character from dusk to dawn. The execrations are intended to eliminate any celestial light or beings who give the night its identity.'[2] Job's misery here becomes a microcosm of human misery, for to put out the morning stars would not simply be to prevent the day of his own birth but the dawning of creation itself.[3] Thus, early in the poetic dialogue, Job's calamities have ceased to be simply his personal suffering and have become a profound questioning of the wisdom behind creation.

At the level of Job's own experience, stars (which would normally be images of hope and joy) become simply a suffocating reminder of his own desolation.[4] Moreover, since *nešep* denotes both the morning and the evening twilight, it is the whole day and, by implication, all days that Job wants to vanish into the abyss of darkness. The stars, which to Abraham were signs of hope both for his own future and that of his descendants, become for Job mere objects that mock his misery.

The friends

This negative view of the stars is best followed by an examination of the allusions in two of the friends' speeches.

[2] Habel 1985: 108.

[3] A striking parallel can be found in one of the poems of the Great War. Wilfred Owen in 'Futility' (1918) moves from sorrow about a young soldier's death in the trenches to a profound pessimism about the whole purpose of creation: 'O what made fatuous sunbeams toil / To break earth's sleep at all?'

[4] We may compare *Hamlet*, Act II, Scene 2, pp. 90ff.: '. . . this brave overhanging firmament, this majestical roof fretted with golden fire – why it appeareth no other to me than a foul and pestilent congregation of vapours.'

The first allusion is in 22:12:

> 'Is not God in the heights of heaven?
> And see how lofty are the highest stars.'

Eliphaz here slanders Job, accusing him of vicious and evil behaviour to his fellows, which he sees as proof of Job's belief that God does not see or care; a bizarre parody of Job's own agonizing fear. The phrase *rō'š kōkābîm* is rather strange; literally it means 'the head of the stars'.[5] Gordis usefully suggests that in *rō'š* there may be an allusion to the hosts of heaven.[6] If this is so, it is yet another example of how obtuse Eliphaz is and how limited his insight. He is not moved to awe and worship by the loftiness of the stars, nor does any hint of the heavenly court and its activities disturb his flat mechanical universe presided over by its deist God.

A similar atmosphere prevails in Bildad's sour tirade in chapter 25. There in verse 5 Bildad alleges that even the moon and stars are not pure in God's sight. Bildad produces no evidence for this statement, but probably the poet is making a significant point here. Job, in his agony, had wished for the stars to be blotted out. Bildad, without any such reason, damns as corrupt and evil the work the Creator had pronounced 'good', and sees in the heavens simply a reflection of his own sour spirit. Like Eliphaz, Bildad does not look up with a sense of awe and reverence.

Job 9:9 and 38:31–33

These passages are probably the most important of the star references and are interestingly paralleled in the doxology of Amos 5:8–9. There Yahweh is hailed as the maker of the Pleiades and Orion and as controller of light, darkness and the waters of the sea.

Driver, in a most interesting article, finds other constellations in verse 9. The usual translation, 'He flashes destruction on the stronghold and brings the fortified city to ruin', becomes 'who makes the Bull to rise hard on (the rising of) the She-goat, and causes the Bull to set hard on (the rising of) the Vintager.'[7] Driver then argues: 'In effect he bids the Israelites worship the true God who has made the starry firmament and fixed the alternation of day and night, who has

---

[5] BDB suggests 'heights' as the meaning, but shows some uncertainty and gives no other examples (147).

[6] Gordis 1965: 247.

[7] G. R. Driver 1956b: 8–10.

put earth and sea in their places, and who has determined the rotation of the seasons which control man's livelihood on earth, by the rising and setting of certain stars and constellations.' This is most relevant to Job 9:8 where the idea is in effect turned on its head. Job, as much as he is able, has done the righteous works which Amos's contemporaries have despised, and yet this God, the maker of Pleiades and Orion, is to him an elusive and vengeful deity.

There are two ways, however, in which Job shows himself different from the friends. He is aware, as the reference to Rahab (9:13) shows, of the supernatural agencies at work. Also he shows the very awe and wonder in the presence of the majesty of God which the friends state as a dogma but of which they have no imaginative consciousness.

Moreover verse 7, 'he seals off the light of the stars', is a significant advance on 3:9 where Job himself had wanted to assume the powers of the Creator to do that. Job's naming of the constellations is also of some importance, for this act is later to be seen as an essential part of the Creator's work and involvement in his creation.

It is important to notice some of the literary techniques of these passages. In 9:9, 'He makes the Bear' ('*ōśeh 'āš*) uses alliteration to underline both words and suggests the precision and detail of the Creator. The obscure phrase 'chambers of the south' (*ḥaḏrê ṯēmān*) has interesting nuances. Schiaparelli refers to Luther's translation: 'die Sterneggen Mittag' ('the stars towards the south'),[9] and Pope, comparing it with the word used of the south wind in Psalm 78:26 and Song of Songs 4:16, renders it 'chambers of the south wind'.[10] The word *ḥeḏer* in most of its appearances means 'private or innermost chamber'; so there is probably a nuance here of the innermost secret which God alone knows, thus pointing forwards to the wisdom poem in chapter 28.

The verbs in the star passage in chapter 38 are also of interest. Yahweh does not use the word 'create' about the stars, but initially uses verbs relating to binding and loosing. The verb *qāšar* (38:31a) is also used of Leviathan (40:29) and thus a link is suggested between control over creation and the containing of evil. *Pāṯaḥ* (38:31b) is also used of the daring venture of opening Leviathan's mouth. *Nāḥāh* (38:32b) is used of the pillar of cloud leading the Israelites (Exod. 13:21). *Yāṣā'*[11] is used in 28:11 of human ability to bring treasure

---

[8] This raises interesting questions about the relative dating of Job and Amos. It may be that both are drawing upon a common doxological tradition.

[9] Schiaparelli 1905: 53–73.

[10] Pope 1973: 71.

[11] In the Exodus passage the verb is used in the Hiphil form.

from the earth but inability to find wisdom any more than cause the rising and setting of the stars. All these are summed up in the crucial question in verse 33:

> 'Do you know the laws of the heavens?
> Can you set up God's dominion over the earth?'

The verb *yāḏaʿ* has the implication of fully comprehending with the knowledge of the Creator himself. Sin, in the sense of fixing boundaries, is also used of setting limits to the sea in verse 10 (also in Ps. 104:9 and Jer. 5:22). These verbs all have implications of creation as a continuing and active work and show something of the richness and variety of God's control of the universe.

Another point worth noting is that God not only mentions the same constellations as Job has in chapter 9 but he also adds further details. In effect he is saying that Job's knowledge was true as far as it went, but that further revelation was needed. Binding and loosing, whether in the natural and supernatural worlds, are the Creator's prerogatives and these are illustrated by control of times and seasons. Thus the binding of the Pleiades would prevent the coming of spring, for their rising heralded the time when it was safe to begin sailing again; the loosing of Orion would presage winter with the beginning of the rainy season.

Two general comments can now be made on the star passages. The first is that they are marked by poetic grandeur created partly by some of the literary devices mentioned. They encapsulate something of the awe and wonder of humans gazing up at the starry heavens, and evoke a sense of the vastness and mystery as well as the providential guiding of the universe.

Secondly, Yahweh's own speeches evoke the mysteries of the universe in images of haunting power. A similar sense of vastness is to be discerned in the speeches of Job; and indeed a notable advance from the irony of chapter 9 to the awe of chapter 26. This element of awe is missing in the speeches of the friends who use the starry heavens as a theological bludgeon, as indeed does Elihu in chapter 37. Thus, although Job has much to learn, part of his saying 'what is right' (42:7) about God is this imaginative response to the grandeur of the universe.

The tree of life

Another potent image from the realm of nature used to great effect by the Job poet is the tree, the symbol of life. Kirsten Nielsen, in an exploration of this image, writes: 'The use of the tree by the author of Job to describe the life-force is not an idea that came to him spontaneously but a centuries-old tradition of which evidence is to be found in several passages of the Old Testament.'[12] The most basic of these images is that of the tree of life in Genesis 2 and 3 with all its resonances of creation and fall. The righteous person is like a fruitful tree (Ps. 1:3 and Jer. 17:8) and wisdom is described as a tree of life (Prov. 3:18). The metaphor remains an evocative one, and in Revelation 22:2 the tree of life grows in the middle of the heavenly city.

The use of this image in some key passages in Job witnesses to the power of the symbol, and, as is characteristic of the book, gives to the traditional a new depth and resonance.

Job 14:7–9

This passage occurs in the long speech of Job (chs. 12 – 14) that begins the second round of the dialogue, much of which is a meditation on death. The immediate context is the frailty and transience of humans: 'of few days and full of trouble'. *Ādām* is given a prominent place as the first word in the chapter, and in a few evocative phrases the brevity and misery of human life are encapsulated.[13]

The image used here is very precise and echoes other parts of the book. Job is thinking not just of his own death but of that of all humankind. The young shoots are a poignant reminder of the death of his own family. The 'flowing' that causes the tree to revive in spring is in stark contrast to the vanishing streams in the desert (6:14–17) which are a symbol of Job's faithless friends and their inability to bring him renewed hope and vitality.

Moreover, the tree is a particularly potent symbol of creation. Creation is a continuing process and the reborn tree and its renewed budding is a sign of the continuing providence of God. The use of the word *'āpār* (v. 8) is probably significant. As will be demonstrated, this word is often used of Sheol and may have the implication that even from there life can spring.

The tree is further contrasted not only with human life and mortality but with the disappearance of waters and the crumbling of

---

[12] Nielsen 1989.

[13] *Kî* in v. 7 is interesting and may be used in a contrasting sense, i.e. the vitality of trees and the mortality of humans. The word *tiqwâ* is not common in Job and its other occurrences are in similar contexts with the theme of death prominent: 7:6 where grim and hopeless death follows arduous toil; 17:15 with its vain calling for hope in Sheol; and 19:10, the second of the tree passages.

mountains; this latter in verse 19 compared with God's destruction of human hopes. This is a fascinating reversal of the apparent attributes of trees and mountains. Trees look fragile and do in fact decay; mountains look indestructible. Yet it is the flimsy tree that survives and not the substantial mountain, because the tree has life in it.

Job 19:10

The image of a tree and hope come together again here in a more sombre way. Habel speaks of the image of God as the divine adversary who besieges Job and breaks the walls of his fortress. He then comments: 'With mortals God goes a step further; he "uproots" them and thereby destroys any new hope emerging from the dust.'[14] What must be noticed, however, is that the object of 'uproots' is not 'tree' but 'hope'. Tree remains a positive image. In fact, it is probable that 14:7–9 is being alluded to here.

Moreover, the essence of the metaphor which is life beyond physical decay is carried on in the famous passage, verses 20–27, with its leap of faith. Thus all these images of gloom and decay are faced and there is an attitude of defiance towards them.

Job 24:20

Job returns to the tree image and this time sees wickedness 'broken like a tree'. Habel attributes the speech to Zophar and argues: 'The reference to a broken "tree" seems to be an allusion to Job's powerful image of the tree as a supreme symbol of hope in the face of death and disaster.'[15] However, Job has not denied that the wicked are punished but rather affirmed that he is not one of them. Moreover, it is wickedness, not life, that is destroyed like a tree, thus the image is not so much a refutation or cynical echo of its earlier occurrences but a new use of it from a different angle.

In general, the tree image is a very effective one in the book's development. Like Job it is subject to the reality of death but it raises possibilities for a life beyond.

Both stars and trees illustrate how the poet uses images from the natural world to comment on the issues of the book. It is time now to turn to the poet's more detailed presentation of 'creation theology' in the key chapters 28 and 38 – 39.

[14] Habel 1985: 301.
[15] Habel 1985: 362.

'Where can Wisdom be found?' (ch. 28)

Chapter 28 is important for a number of reasons. First, in its own right, it is a magnificent poem. It strikes the reader as being out of place in terms of theme and tone. The speeches surrounding it are frenetic, unlike the calm, measured tone of this passage. Thematically it appears to anticipate Yahweh's speeches and thus be somewhat of a false dawn. The text as it stands treats the chapter as part of a speech by Job. Yet chapters 27 – 31 are inordinately long and the lack of speeches of reply by the friends and apparent glaring inconsistencies (notably between 27:1–13 and 27:13–23) suggest that some serious dislocation has taken place. Bildad's speech (ch. 25) is uncharacteristically brief and Zophar does not speak at all, unless he is given 27:13–23[16] or chapter 28 itself.[17]

To do justice to chapter 28 in its present position[18] we must examine the dynamic flow of the imagery and theology. Thus it will be necessary to say something about the underlying thrust and imagery of the surrounding chapters; then the structure will be examined and finally some theological comments made.

Context

The opening word *kî* ('surely, certainly'), whatever its precise meaning, certainly invites us to look for connections with the preceding chapter. A general point must be made first. The MT implies that the whole of chapters 26 – 31 is by Job. If this is the case, his speech is excessively long, whereas Bildad's speech (ch. 25) is a paltry six verses. Eliphaz fell silent as long ago as the end of chapter 22 and Zophar does not speak again at all. It may be that the dramatic point being made is that the characters have run out of things to say. Zophar sputters out in angry silence in chapter 20 and Job turns his words against him in 27:13–23. Similarly, Eliphaz gives a legalistic indictment of Job in chapter 22 (much of which Job answers in chs.

---

[16] Habel (1985: 385) draws attention to 20:29: 'Such is the fate God allots the wicked', which is echoed in 27:13; and argues that the latter part of ch. 27 is the continuation of that earlier speech. I suggest an alternative explanation of this later in the chapter.

[17] Clines (1989: lix) comes cautiously down on this side; Zophar has made similar points in 11:7–20.

[18] This is not to prejudge the issue. Whoever wrote the chapter, someone must have decided that the chapter fitted into its present context in the final form of the book. Given the consummate artistry of the canonical book there would have to be good reasons for so deciding.

29 – 31) in a manner akin to the final summing-up of a prosecuting counsel, whereas Bildad peters out in sour commonplaces. (We shall return to this in the discussion of Leviathan.) There can be little doubt that the poet did not intend simply to replicate the first two cycles of speeches, for that structure could become an ever-repeating cycle with no goal or denouement.

I want to argue that chapters 26 – 31, and not only chapter 28, have an essentially choric function[19] and bring together much of the theology and imagery of the earlier chapters and thus provide a secure base for Yahweh's speeches where all these matters are definitively addressed. Chapter 26, which will be discussed in detail in the Behemoth and Leviathan chapters, encapsulates much of the imagery of creation and evil. What is worth noticing here is that this chapter in a small compass anticipates the structure of Yahweh's speeches in chapters 38 – 41. Verses 1-4 are a challenge; Yahweh also begins with a challenge. Then verses 5-10 correspond to chapters 38 – 39 with their evocation of the mysteries of the universe, and verses 11-14 touch on the mystery of supernatural evil which is the thrust of chapters 40 – 41.

Chapter 27 turns to legal imagery and to the court scene with the adversary. The imagery and theme have thus moved from God's power to his justice, and Job's reference to the 'ways' of God (26:14 lit.) have reminded him forcibly of the mystery of divine providence and his inability to explain these ways. In verses 11–12, Job employs an *ad hominem* argument and goes on to use the words of Zophar not only against him, but against the other friends. The list of calamities here is now applied in human rather than cosmic terms: personal (starving children and destitute widow); deprivation of possessions (loss of wealth and house); and supernatural (terrors).

Chapter 28 shows that behind all the other questions is the basic one of the place of wisdom which lies behind creation itself, and thus this chapter is a metaphor of the entire book. The various images will be examined later, but it is worth noting that the picture of mining is a characteristically subtle blend of physical realism and theological nuances. Chapters 29 – 31 constitute a *māšāl* in the sense of a legal statement of Job's innocence.

Andersen comments: 'Chapters 29 – 31 grow out of 28:28; for Job is the wise man and we learn here in detail what it means to fear God

---

[19] In the sense that these chapters act essentially as a 'chorus' in a play, and comment on the flow of the book thus far.

and shun wrong.'[20] This shows a coherent and plausible connection on one level between chapters 28 and 29. There may also be another connection between these chapters. The images of ordered society in chapter 29 are a reflection of the order of the cosmos evoked in chapter 28 and indeed depend for their stability on that order. Thus the imagery is not only legal but very much concerned with creation and providence. The legal metaphor underlies the rich imagery of a full and peaceful life. The chapter is a picture of *šālôm*, which is far more than the absence of conflict but suggests being in tune with creation and drawing nourishment from the life flowing from God to the whole ordered cosmos.[21]

Chapter 30, by contrast, shows images of deprivation and terror and thus draws on the dark side of the mystery of God's ways in creation. The evocations of human life at its most exposed and perilous are reminiscent of chapter 24. Perhaps also the allusions to the wasteland anticipate the mysteries of these places outlined in chapters 38 and 39. The imagery of enemies recalls that of the lament psalms. The pictures of siege and attack in verses 12–15 recall similar images of violence in chapters 13, 16 and 19. In verse 15 the word 'terrors' recalls the 'king of terrors' (18:14) and carries implications of a life overshadowed by death. Most significantly, the word *'akzār* ('cruel, harsh'), here applied to God, is used of the 'rousing' of Leviathan in 41:2 and is one of the many confusions Job falls into about the roles of God and Satan. Moreover, chapter 30, like chapter 3, contains images of 'uncreation', such as light turning to darkness (v. 26), which are a protest and challenge.

Chapter 31 represents the culmination of the legal language in the cycles of speeches with Job's protestations of innocence and purity. This is made more effective rhetorically by being cast in the form of challenging questions that assume negative answers. The emphasis in this chapter is on inner attitudes rather than on outward actions and this again has a choric function. The philosophy of the friends has been based on the assumption that they could read Job's motives and,

---

[20] Andersen 1976: 231.

[21] A minor crux in v. 18 is worth a mention. Is *ḥôl* 'sand' or 'phoenix'? Rabbinic tradition as early as the Talmud favours the translation 'and like the phoenix'. This may receive some support from Ebla where the word *ḥl* occurs accompanying a Sumerian logogram indicating some kind of bird. This would certainly accord with the image of the roots in v. 19 echoing the tree image of 14:7. It would thus be another of these gleams of hope which occasionally flash through Job's dark night. Ambiguity remains, for 'multiply days' would fit 'sands', whereas, 'phoenix' would need something like 'renew'.

indeed, by implication also read the innermost secrets of the universe. Moreover, this passage recalls Job's earlier pleas for an advocate. However, the closing verses (38–40) are perhaps the most significant. In his references to the land and its produce, Job is returning to the theme of creation and the ordered cosmos which essentially guarantees his righteousness. He is in tune with nature and thus his case deserves an answer.

This pattern of imagery is characteristic of the book as a whole as we have seen. It suggests a discernible pattern in chapters 26 – 31 which makes a reordering and reassigning of these passages unnecessary. Chapter 28 is a pivot and a basis from which all these conflicting emotions can be assessed.

Structure

It is quite easy to discern a threefold structure in chapter 28: mining for precious metals, reflecting the search for wisdom (vv. 1–11); the inaccessibility of wisdom (vv. 12–22); wisdom and creation (vv. 23–28). I want to demonstrate how this threefold structure in many ways mirrors that of the whole book and casts its shadow backwards and forwards not only over chapters 26 – 31 but over the entire course of both story and dialogue. Habel points out that there are numerous allusions to other images in the book.[22]

The first section (vv. 1–11), with its use of mining as a metaphor, is introduced by the particle *kî* with connecting force, but what exactly is the connection being made? The word *māqôm* ('place') here has nuances of the underworld and reminds us of its significant use in 16:18, 'May my cry never be laid to rest.' More immediately the word is used in 27:21 and 23 with supernatural connotations. The *kî* thus shows that what follows is a new stage of the argument, yet one linked closely with what precedes it.

Indeed, verses 1–11, with their metaphor of mining, can be taken as an image of Job's suffering thus far. There are numerous echoes of the journey already taken: for example, the possible reference to Nergal (v. 4);[23] the probable reference to Leviathan (v. 8) and the nuances of

[22] Habel 1985: 393.

[23] See esp. Dick 1979: 216–221. He points out that the MT *mny-rgl* has caused problems and emends to *minnergal* ('stooped over by Nergal' – i.e. the Mesopotamian god of disease). He maintains: 'The subtlety of mentioning in a description of miners the god who rules over the subterranean worlds and who inflicts man with disease is fully equal to the ability of the author of Job XXVIII.' Later, I argue a similar case for the expression 'sons of Resheph' in 5:7 (see pp. 119–120). It is characteristic of the Job poet to use language which resonates with far more than its surface meaning.

the sources of the rivers (v. 11). These are potent reminders of the experiences of Job and the sufferings inextricable from a true search for wisdom. Moreover, in a manner characteristic of Job's earlier speeches,[24] there are hints of the ultimate solution. Verse 1, about the refining of gold, plainly echoes 23:10: 'when he has tested me, I shall come forth as gold'. Indeed, in that chapter the previous verses contain the search motif as here and thus form an anticipation of this speech. Similarly, the description of the darkness in the bowels of the earth may recall many of the passages about Sheol (e.g. 10:21; 24:27).

Habel points out the significance of probing and searching,[25] and this is underlined by the commodities mentioned in verses 5–6: *bread* (RSV), with its implications of the process of sowing and reaping and the sustaining of life, and *precious stones*, whose suggestions of costly effort remind us of the main issues of the book. Verses 7 and 8 will be examined for their possible mythological allusions in the Leviathan discussion. Verses 9–11 compare human and divine activities. In 9:5 it is God who overturns mountains. As already noted, in Canaanite legend both mountains and rivers are associated with El's dwelling place and council.

Thus I would suggest that verses 1–11 both mirror and are a metaphor of the earlier part of the book. Human wisdom and achievement are not denigrated, any more than Job's wealth and happiness were in the prologue. In essence the picture of mining becomes a metaphor for Job's search for the divine wisdom that lies behind creation.

The questions implied in verses 1–11 are now addressed in the second section (vv. 12–19) on the inaccessibility of wisdom. The key terms of 'wisdom' (*ḥokmâ*) and 'understanding' (*bînâ*) are taken up extensively by God in chapters 38 and 39. First, in verses 13–14 it is stated that wisdom is not located in the material or human universe, with the implication that it is beyond and antecedent to these. Moreover, wisdom cannot be bought and its worth far excels earth's most precious substances. Perhaps this may hint at something else. Job has been stripped of all these, but none of them has guaranteed wisdom and understanding, indeed they have prevented him acquiring these in the truest sense. Wisdom is not to be found by extensive search.

---

[24] This does not imply that the speech is necessarily spoken by Job. The narrator, providing a choric commentary, could equally do this. Yet it seems reasonable to see Job as speaker.

[25] Habel 1985: 396.

This section has surveyed human, animal and supernatural power and skill and shown they are inadequate in a true understanding of wisdom. This has also been the burden of the book as a whole as it has grappled not just with the problem of evil but more fundamentally with the issue of creation itself.

In the final section (vv. 23–28) it is interesting to note that wisdom is scarcely mentioned; rather it is God's power in creation that is celebrated.[26] This focus on creation is illustrated in verse 23: 'God understands the way to it and he knows its place' (RSV), implying that God's knowledge is based on his creation. The emphasis on 'seeing' is a vivid way of speaking of God making what is already present in his mind.

The actual details of creation in verses 25–26 are full of interest. In line with the theology of the chapter they represent a statement of order and thus point forward to Yahweh's speeches. Thus those very aspects of creation generally deemed most elusive and intangible – wind, rain, thunder and lightning – are seen to be governed by fixed patterns, 'the ordinances of heaven' of 38:33 (RSV). Probably mythological elements lurk in the references to God's control of the raging waters and the theophanic language of the thunderstorm. There is further the ambivalence of these forces, their beneficence and destructiveness, which is exactly the riddle about the ways of God that is at the heart of the book.

In this carefully crafted chapter it seems plain that verses 27 and 28 belong together. Verse 27 is a general statement about creation and verse 28 a specific one about the providence which guides the just. The full implications of verse 27 are still to be explored in chapters 38 and 39. Similarly, verse 28 is not a platitude but a vital reminder of the God-fearing character of Job emphasized in chapter 1 and vindicated in chapter 42. It is also a salutary reminder of human limitations and ignorance. The 'fear of the Lord' had not prevented Job's suffering and indeed it is largely in protest against this that he makes his final speech in chapters 29–31. Thus, further revelation from God himself is necessary.

[26] This point is given interesting treatment in Harris 1983: 419–427. Harris takes the four verbs in v. 27 which each have a third personal singular feminine pronominal suffix ($r\bar{a}'\bar{a}h$; $way^esapp^er\bar{a}h$; $h^ek\hat{i}n\bar{a}h$; $h^aq\bar{a}r\bar{a}h$) and suggests that the subject 'it' is not 'wisdom' but creation, i.e. the heavens and earth introduced in v. 24. He argues that it is grammatically acceptable that the content of the preceding sentence (vv. 23–26) could be referred to as 'it'. Moreover, the verbs of v. 27 are elsewhere used in creation contexts: $r\bar{a}'\bar{a}h$ in Genesis 1 is the most noteworthy.

Reflections

Some additional remarks need to be made on the function of the chapter in the developing theology of the book.

The main issue is whether chapter 28 anticipates Yahweh's speeches in such a way as to make them an anti-climax. This can be approached on two levels: literary and theological. On the literary level, the first general point is that it is unreasonable to expect a long work to have only one high point.[27] Rather we have intimations and motifs that provide a vantage point for the final stage of the journey.

Another obvious feature of the poem is its calm and measured tone in contrast to the frenetic energy of chapters 3 – 27. This gives weight to the suggestion that the chapter is choric commentary. Habel draws attention to some of the main features which support this view: 'It is not addressed to any of the participants of the dialogue in Job. There are no indictments, complaints, interactive comments or direct responses to previous assertions of other speakers.'[28] Yet he rightly points out that the language and themes of the chapter have deliberate echoes of earlier speeches and thus constitute a reflection on the debate.

The space for reflection is vital at this point as a signal that the petering out of the speeches is not evidence of a disturbed text and careless editing but a deliberately crafted interlude. The metaphors and themes are brilliantly employed to further the flow of the book.

The theme of wisdom and its intertwining with creation and providence is expressed here in a vivid metaphorical manner. The evocation of mining has connotations not only of suffering and solitude which mirror Job's plight but of the mysteries of the underworld which are a powerful reminder of the supernatural dimensions of these sufferings. Moreover, there is a profound admiration for human

[27] For example, *Macbeth* has at least three points of high tension: the murders of Duncan, Banquo and Lady Macduff's children. These do not simply repeat each other but are linked to Shakespeare's depiction of the deterioration in Macbeth's character and the increasing dominance of his mind by the witches. The parallel is closer than it might seem. Job may have originally been 'heard' rather than 'read'. Thus a play which exists in the first place to be seen and experienced as it is spoken and acted is a good comparison with an ancient text addressed to hearers.
Another example from a culture and literary form perhaps closer to that of the Job poet is *Beowulf*. Again it has three high points: the battles with Grendel, Grendel's mother and the dragon; each anticipates the other and the later reflect the earlier.
[28] Habel 1985: 392.

71

ingenuity which is in stark contrast to Bildad's sour dismissal of man as 'a maggot'; yet it also shows human limitations, for with our god-like powers we are unable to find wisdom. The metaphors of hidden treasures and precious stones and metals with their solidity reflect the reality of the experience. When these are combined with the more dynamic images of rain, wind and thunder, a most vivid and dramatic evocation of the mysteries of both the visible and invisible universe is created. Thus the imagery points back and co-ordinates the concerns of the earlier chapters of the book.

However, the imagery also points forward to Yahweh's speeches. The depths of the earth are also evoked there in 38:16–18 with the primeval ocean and the gates of death. The 'way' to light in 38:19 is reminiscent of the unknown way to wisdom (28:13); 'the ordinances of heaven' (38:33 RSV); of 'a decree for the rain' (28:26); 'a way for the thunderbolt' (38:25 RSV); of 'a path for the thunderstorm' (28:26). Moreover, the rhetorical questions of 28:12 and 20 anticipate those of Yahweh in chapters 38 – 41. None of this imagery has the effect of lessening the impact of the divine speeches. Rather it prepares the hearers for the speeches and increases their power by showing that this chapter, for all its magnificence, is not the answer.

Theologically, also, chapter 28 is a pivotal one. The *kî*, as already noted, links it with chapter 27 and puts the passion of that and previous chapters into a calmer and more rational perspective. At the other end of the chapter, the words 'And he said to man' mark it off as a considered statement and contribution to the debate.

The 'debate', however, has ground to a halt, with the friends becoming ever more scurrilous and platitudinous. Job, on the other hand, has shown astonishing insight into the cosmic dimensions of his situation (anticipated, for example, in chapters 9 and 19), but in chapter 27 that insight has proved inadequate as a bulwark against depression, and that chapter shows an element of hubris in Job which vitiates the effect of that perception. Thus, here in chapter 28, a statement of the fundamental wisdom and order underlying the universe is necessary and provides a breathing space for passions to subside. Job's long speech (chapters 29 – 31) is a final summing up for the defence by outlining his reasons for claiming that he has in fact been characterized by 'the fear of the Lord', which is, of course, what the narrator had said in 1:1.

Chapter 28 is valid as far as it goes. We might characterize it by saying that it is the theologian's answer and as such is no mean theology. However, theology cannot provide the full answer, only an appearance of God himself can, and such an appearance and answer are not theology itself but the reality to which theology points.

A glance at Elihu's contribution is relevant at this stage. He, too, takes up the theme of wisdom in 32:7: 'I thought, "Age should speak; advanced years should teach wisdom".' Elihu, with brash confidence, virtually assumes the role of arbiter in the court – the arbiter Job had cried for – and seeks to expound wisdom. He, too, proves inadequate, and thus God's own intervention and the true perspective on wisdom is vital.

'The world is charged with the grandeur of God' (chs. 38 – 39)

God has not spoken directly since chapter 2, and Job (and the audience) is desperate to hear him. I shall comment very briefly on chapter 38, because I shall discuss it more fully in a later chapter on the raging sea (ch. 8). The wonders of creation are surveyed in a cataract of magnificent images from the depths of Sheol to the great constellations in heaven.

But chapter 38 is more than a series of vignettes of creation, it is a series of pictures of the creative act itself which contains within it the idea of continuing creation. Each of these pictures has mythological overtones that I shall examine in chapter 8.

Verses 4–7 deal with the foundations of the earth in relation to the heavenly court. As already noted in chapter 2, the parallelism between 'morning stars' and 'sons of God' suggests that on a mythological level these natural phenomena are visible symbols of the heavenly court. Also, on a literary level, it is a picturesque way of speaking of the great symphony of nature where, as in Psalm 148, all creation, including 'shining stars', praises Yahweh. This continues in the medieval idea of the 'music of the spheres', beautifully captured by Shakespeare in Lorenzo's words to Jessica:

> 'There's not the smallest orb that thou beholdest,
> But in his motion like an angel sings
> Still quirring to the young-eyed cherubins.'[29]

Verses 8–11 continue with the creating of the sea in a passage bristling with mythological language. I will deal with this language more

---

[29] *The Merchant of Venice*, Act V, scene i, ll. 60–62.

fully in chapter 8, but here I want simply to point out the vividness and exuberance of the words. The poet evokes powerfully the continual battle of the encroaching sea upon the land: the gnawing away of shores, cliffs, sands and headlands. Yet the ultimate restraining of the ocean is finely suggested.

We come next to the dawning of the day and indeed the morning of creation itself (vv. 12–15). Again this passage is replete with mythological allusions, but these are conveyed in images of great power. Night broods over the earth like a blanket underneath which various evils are perpetrated. Then, as dawn appears, all is revealed in vivid and stark contours as if clay were stamped with a seal.

The creation of the netherworld and the primeval ocean is alluded to in verses 16–18. To 'comprehend' this (v. 18) has the nuance of the wisdom by which creation came into being. These dreary realms are thus seen as part of the total picture and meaning of the universe.

From the depths we are led to the phenomena of the heavens. Light and darkness are the great primeval realities, not simply markers of time, and thus to 'know' them would be to have the Creator's power over them. Verses 22–35 link heaven and the deep in a panoramic survey and the focus is on areas of creation that are remote from human beings and their concerns. Verses 31–33 fill us with awe at the great constellations in heaven, and are a challenge to Job if he can control the great meteorological forces in verses 34–35. This section closes in verses 36–38 with an evocation of the mysterious cloud-covered heavens and the elusive wisdom required in that realm.

With verses 39–41 we come to a passage that bridges the cosmos and the animal world. Yahweh is depicted here as the provider of food, again a prerogative of the Creator.

Thus chapter 38, in its matchless and glorious detail, gives us an awesome series of glimpses of the divine wisdom which made and continues to make the universe. We shall return to the more particular evocation of supernatural realities in chapter 8.

Chapter 39

In this chapter, Yahweh shows Job something of the wonders of the animal kingdom. As in chapter 38, the theme is not simply the habits and haunts of animals, but creation itself. These creatures are remote from humans and not subject to their control. This, in itself, puts Job's problems in a wider perspective and shows the limitations of an anthropocentric view of the universe. In looking at this chapter and the further light it throws on the Job poet's theology of creation, three matters will be considered: the use of verbs, the structure and, finally, the theology of the passage.

The verbs

The striking feature of the verbs in chapter 39 is their association with creation. The opening word of the chapter, $h^a y \bar{a} \underline{d} a' t \bar{a}$ ('Do you know . . .?') controls the whole passage. The verb $y \bar{a} \underline{d} a'$ has implications not only of knowing but of the kind of insight already demanded in chapter 38 and earlier in chapter 28 which can belong to the Creator alone. In verses 1–4, the mountain goats give birth, and the picture of procreation, with its blend of pain and joy, is a vivid metaphor for creation itself and an implied criticism of Job for cursing the day of his birth. Then he had wished that his birthday should not come into the number of the months (a phrase echoed in v. 2). Verse 3 reminds us of the evocation of childbirth in Job's own case (3:11–12). There may be a glance at Canaanite myth: Aquhat is told by Anat that he shall 'count the months' (*tspr. yrhm*), which is a poetic description of immortality, a property of the gods alone.[30] Job has neither the knowledge or immortality of the Creator and therefore cannot fathom the mysteries of birth.[31]

This basic idea of knowledge is now illustrated by a series of specific actions and ideas. The vignette about the wild ass (vv. 5–8) echoes the '[loosing of] the cords of Orion' (38:31). Yahweh can set free and still retain control, for this government of the universe allows latitude within his overarching providence. This is a powerful hint of the ultimate solution he is to unfold in his second speech where Behemoth and Leviathan are subject to his power and yet have enormous freedom in their own domains.[32]

The opposite idea, that of servitude, is treated in the section on the wild ox or buffalo (vv. 9–12). This section recalls the binding of the Pleiades (38:31) and anticipates the impossibility of making Leviathan a slave for ever (40:28). Moreover 'servant' is the very word God has used of Job in 1:8, and the implication is that only the Creator can make a 'servant' of any creature and that Job's happiness depends ultimately

---

[30] *CML* (Aquhat) 17, col. vi, l. 28.

[31] The translations have, on the whole, obscured the force of v. 1 by leaving untranslated the word '*ēt* ('time', 'season') and replacing it with the colourless 'when'. '*ēt* has in it the idea of providence.

[32] Yahweh's control of the widest reaches of the universe is hinted at in some of the vocabulary used here. *Ḥopšî* in 3:19 has connotations of Sheol. *Miškān* (39:6) is often used of Yahweh's tent, which is sometimes the whole earth.

on his realization of this. Thus the verb *'āḇaḏ* has implications of creation and providence. Its further nuances of reverence and worship are significant in bringing Job to an appropriate frame of mind.

Of the next vignette, that of the ostrich (vv. 13–18), Andersen writes: 'It is hard to argue that this hilarious sketch of the ostrich serves any solemn didactic purpose.'[33] That is true, as far as it goes, but Andersen ignores the fact that a piece of literature can be entertaining and amusing and yet make a serious point.[34] The verb 'laughs' (v. 18) is probably the key to this section. Laughter is a sign of control; God laughs because he is in control: 'The One enthroned in the heavens laughs' (Ps. 2:4) The evocation of the grotesque here is amusing, but it is the amusement of the Creator who laughs with total knowledge and power. The ostrich, too, secure in her place in creation, can afford to laugh.

We move on to the picture of the war horse (vv. 19–25) introduced by the verb *nāṯan* ('to give') which has nuances of the bounty of the Creator; similarly, the verb *lāḇaš* ('to clothe') is used in a creation context in chapter 10:11 of God clothing Job with skin and flesh. Very significant too are the verbs *rā'aš* (v. 20) and *rāḡaz* (v. 24), both used of God shaking heaven and earth. Thus, here we have the idea of creation and providence intertwined and exemplified in the portrait of this magnificent creature whose appearance is like that of El himself.

The final vignette of the birds of prey (vv. 26–30) underlines the nuances of the initial *yāḏa'* by asking Job if the hawk pursues its unfettered flight by his 'understanding'. Indeed this serves to round off the whole speech, as Yahweh's first question in 38:4 is 'Tell me, if you understand.' Here wisdom is not simply to plot the flight of the hawk, but to control its path through the trackless heavens. Similarly, it is not information about the eagle but the power to control its predatory actions that is the issue.

The verbs employed in this chapter, then, have nuances of creation and providence. God is present and active in the most remote and uncongenial parts of the universe.

Structure

This chapter is very carefully constructed to highlight the themes of creation and providence. Not only are there the linguistic links already noted between the beginning and end of the chapter, there is

---

[33] Andersen 1976: 281.
[34] A good example of this is Byron's *Vision of Judgment* which is full of rollicking and scurrilous humour yet is a serious political statement.

also a thematic link: verse 1 begins with conception and verse 30 ends with death; death, moreover, which nourishes the lives of the young eagles. Thus the idea of a complete life-cycle is suggested. Moreover, both the first and last vignettes speak of the young of the respective creatures and the middle vignette about the ostrich speaks of the young too. There is also a progression of thought in the picture of the young. In the case of the mountain goat, it is the mystery of birth itself that is intensified by the further mystery of the young goats disappearing, led by instinct into the unknown. With the ostrich, natural instincts are abandoned and the young treated with neglect and cruelty. When we come to the hawk, we are confronted with the savagery of the young from their earliest days – 'His young ones feast on blood' (v. 30).

With this in mind, a pattern can be discerned:

39:1–4: fundamental mystery of birth and life:
    Example 1: vv. 5–8: mystery of freedom.
    Example 2: vv. 9–12: mystery of domesticity.
39:13–18: comedy: a *reductio ad absurdum* of the mystery of life:
    Example 1: vv. 19–25: magnificence of the wild.
    Example 2: vv. 26–30: cruelty of the wild.

In more detail, the structure can be seen to mirror and underline many of the main themes and motifs of the book. The portrait of the wild goat (vv. 1–4), with its depiction of the process of procreation and birth, reminds the hearer that it is the mystery of existence itself that lies at the heart of the book. It is a potent reminder that Job had cursed the day of his birth and has been unable to grasp the mysteries of his own existence, let alone those of such a remote and elusive creature.

The development of this also parallels Job's own experience. The next two vignettes (vv. 5–8 and vv. 9–12) explore the parallel themes of freedom and control, both of which have loomed large in Job's mind. Here the rhetorical questions and statements emphasize the fact that real freedom is the gift of God whose writ runs in the remote desert and steppe lands. The mirror image of this, the motif of servitude, is also a powerful factor in Job's experience. He has spoken of how humans experience 'hard service on earth' (7:1) and, in the grim parody of Psalm 8, beginning in 7:17, how they long to be free from the service of the 'watcher of men' (7:20).

The ostrich vignette (vv. 13–18) is a pause for comic relief in the flow of the chapter and of the speech as a whole, yet, as already noted, it makes a serious point. Like Job, the ostrich appears to be unaware of 'wisdom' and 'understanding'. Yet, like Job, she too has her place and abilities and gifts which are denied to other creatures. Moreover, and this is a point missed by many commentators, the theme of the book is startlingly brought to the surface in verse 17: 'God has made her forget wisdom and given her no share in under-standing' (RSV). God himself has been responsible for this lack of wisdom in the ostrich and this is another picture of his role in orches-trating the whole scenario in Job's life.

The reference to the horse (v. 18) provides a natural transition to the last two vignettes of the war horse and the birds of prey. These reflect, but also develop in a grimmer and darker way, the elements of freedom and control in the pictures of the wild ass and the ox. The theophany-like language both reflects earlier parts of the book (e.g. 9:4–10) and anticipates the Leviathan passage. A variety of vivid imagery is used: *visual*: 'leap like a locust' (v. 20), 'eats up the ground' (v. 24); *auditory*: 'striking terror with his proud snorting' (v. 20), 'the shout of commanders and the battle cry' (v. 25); *emotive*: 'catches the scent of the battle' (v. 25), 'spread his wings towards the south' (v. 26). All these create an eerie and haunting picture. It is here that imagery, structure and poetic technique merge into theology.

Theology

I shall consider the theology of chapter 39 in three mains ways: as it relates to the doctrines of creation and providence; as it addresses the problem of evil in nature; and as it relates to Job's own situation.

With regard to the doctrine of creation and providence, perhaps there is no part of the book which more clearly demonstrates their inextricable intertwining. The first feature worthy of comment is the sheer intricacy of detail with which the Creator plans the life-cycle of nature from conception and birth to death and decay. Yahweh ranges over the process of birth, the varied habitats of the wild animals, the corresponding picture of domestication, the exuberant evocation of the ostrich, the haunting cameo of the wild horse and the chilling habits of predatory birds. Not only does this raise in Job's mind the obvious question of his own lack of wisdom compared to that of the Creator, it implies another question. If God cares in such detail for the creatures of the wild in the midst of a world of cruelty and sav-agery, then is his care of Job less detailed and painstaking?

A further comment is necessary on this concern with detail. Part of worship, as already noted in commenting on the star passages, is a spontaneous delight in the 'manifold works' of God. Here this is carried a stage further. Having seen not only the majesty and beauty but also the savagery and bizarre nature of the universe, we are being forced to the conclusion that there is far more mystery at the heart of providence than we have yet understood and that this sense of mystery is fundamental to all true worship.

A further feature of the doctrine of providence implicit in this chapter is the subtle blend of control and freedom in creation. This is seen first in the picture of the mountain goat. Procreation is plainly a voluntary act, yet the 'number of the months' is not under their control, nor is the subsequent destiny of their offspring. Similarly, the wild ass is free to roam, yet certain habitats are 'given' to it; also the ostrich has been 'given' speed not wisdom. Even the horse, godlike in his pretensions, and the untameable birds of prey, are responding to instincts deeply implanted in their nature.

It is this matching of divine sovereignty and creaturely responsibility that is at the heart of the book's wrestling with the problem of meaning. Life itself – procreation, instinct, natural behaviour (including the callous indifference of the ostrich and the savagery of the eagle) – is the gift of God, which means that although he sets limits, the freedom is genuine.

This is related to the place of paradox in the universe, as is clearly shown by the combining of images of domesticity, of neglect, of peaceful remote places and of blood lust, of comedy and grimness. Habel expresses it thus: 'In this world of paradoxes Yahweh continues to operate with the opposites of life and death, chaos and order, freedom and control, wisdom and folly, evil and blessing.'[35] This means that the created universe in itself can provide no real answer to the problems of evil and suffering, a point to which I shall return. The main thrust of this chapter, like that of chapter 38, is to fill Job with wonder at the intricate planning and guiding of the whole vast cosmos and show him how inadequate has been his understanding of the ways of God. This is where Habel, I think, goes wrong when he argues: 'From these parallels in the natural world Job is left to draw the necessary conclusion relevant to his personal world.'[36] This is valid only if Behemoth and Leviathan are simply more of the same

---

[35] Habel 1985: 534.
[36] Habel 1985: 535.

and not a new development of Yahweh's argument. I shall argue in detail in later chapters that they carry the thrust of the book much further.

The second main theological issue is how evil relates to the natural world. The first point to be made is that evil is in some way integral to the structure of the living world itself. Moreover, the interrelationship of good and evil is too finely balanced to allow any mere tinkering with details. The young goat's freedom is at the cost of final separation from its parents; the young eagle's hunger is satisfied only by the death of another creature. These are merely illustrations with a much wider application of how good is not achievable for all life everywhere simultaneously.

Behind all this is the more fundamental interplay of life and death. Since this chapter is an evocation of the cycle of life, death is a fundamental factor in that cycle. The idea of death is more strongly present in verses 19ff., not least in preparation for Behemoth. Indeed, the cruelties and brutalities of the animal kingdom are manifestations of the power of evil and thus it is most effective to use monstrous creatures as metaphors of the gods of death and primeval chaos. The fact that the chapter ends not only with death, but with violent death, is a reminder of the disasters of the prologue.

The third main issue in the theology of this chapter is how it relates to the situation of Job himself. Many of the issues he has wrestled with (the mystery of life and the violence of the world, freedom and slavery, and the apparent anomalies in God's providence) are illustrated from the pattern of life in the animal world. This shows to Job that he is not unique; that the mystery he has wrestled with in his own life is also there in the daily experience of other creatures.

By the same token, Job is being shown that both his perspective and power of action are limited. His perspective is limited for he has not seriously looked at the animal kingdom; his power of action is limited for he cannot exercise the kind of control that alone would enable him to understand it. The animals, remote and uncongenial as they are, have their place within the divine providence.

This invites another observation. I argued earlier that chapter 28, while it anticipated Yahweh's speeches, did not make these speeches irrelevant but rather prepared the way for the definite statement he was to make. However, if chapters 38 and 39 were all that God had to say, then that criticism would be hard to refute. Yahweh does indeed, with breathtaking beauty and comprehensiveness, paint a panoramic view of the universe and its life in terms of his creation and providence. Nevertheless, if this remains the final answer, it stops short. It does not provide that final clue that makes all the rest of the images and intimations cohere. Thus, unless chapters 40 and 41 have a new element to contribute, we are indeed left gasping at the greatness of the universe and the intricate variety of life, but Job has already shown such understanding and emotion, not least in chapters 9 and 26. By contrast, the friends, despite occasional references to nature, use it mainly as a stick with which to beat Job. Indeed, in 12:7–9, Job had anticipated the theme of this chapter: 'But ask the animals . . . the birds of the air . . . the hand of the LORD has done this.'

What Yahweh has not yet answered is the pivotal question of 9:24: 'If it is not he, then who is it?' Indeed, the naturalistic interpretation of the second speech does not do justice to the biblical blending of creation and providence. It effectively drives a wedge between God and the world by postulating that a mere description of the wonders of nature is an adequate theodicy, rather than the realized presence of God grappling with evil powers active in both the natural and supernatural worlds.

Two more comments are necessary to sum up the thrust of this chapter on the tragic creator. The language employed in the imagery of nature is of some importance. The star imagery, couched in hymn-like language reminiscent of the Psalter, creates an atmosphere of worship that in itself establishes a true perspective from which the contours of the problem can be seen. The tree passages are more akin to the lament psalms and this provides the necessary balance by underlining the mystery that is at the heart of nature. Chapters 28 and 38 – 39 have the majesty of a psalm such as 104, with its tremendous sweep and breadth which range through the whole of creation.

Secondly, this is far more than beautiful nature poetry. At a deeper level, this is the theology of the Job poet, for only poetry of such splendour can embody the issues involved in the doctrines of creation and providence. I have already argued in my first chapter that myth is necessary not only to describe evil but to embody it in palpable form and allow it to be experienced as well as discussed. So it is with creation; in poetry of this kind we are not simply talking and thinking of the phenomena of heaven and earth; rather, as in Psalm 148, we are joining with 'sea monsters and deeps' and with 'sun, moon and shining stars' to praise God, and that alone is the basis on which real wisdom can be built.

Chapter Four

The raging sea

When the contemporary world fears disaster and destruction from beyond, this menace is usually associated with alien powers from space. This is evident in such recent films as *Armageddon*. In the Old Testament, however, the terror of the unknown is often seen as the raging sea, the great sea which appears to go on for ever, the watery chaos which threatens the ordered and good creation. This chapter's focus is on the imagery of the sea in Job, but first it will be useful to say a few words about its Old Testament context.

Genesis 1:8–9 tells us of how, on the second and third days of creation, God separated first the upper and lower waters and then land and water. That separation was good. The flood story tells of the 'uncreation', when those boundaries were broken and 'the springs of the great deep burst forth, and the floodgates of heaven were opened' (Gen. 7:11). Similar language is used in Exodus 15:5–8 and in Habakkuk 3:8–10 of Yahweh's victory over Pharaoh and the gods of Egypt at the Red Sea.

The Psalter has many references to the power of the raging waters (e.g. Pss. 18, 24, 29), none more striking, however, than 77:16:

> The waters saw you, O God,
> the waters saw you and writhed;
> the very depths were convulsed.

The praise of the Lord and his victory over the raging waters was an important part of Israel's worship.

The image is prominent in prophetic and apocalyptic texts: Isaiah 24:18–19 speaks of the floodgates of heaven being opened and an unnamed city devastated; then a few chapters later Isaiah refers to the smiting of Leviathan (Is. 27:1); Jeremiah describes the impending exile in imagery redolent of the flood (4:23–26); and Ezekiel writes of Pharaoh as 'the monster in the seas' (32:2). Perhaps most striking, however, is Daniel's reference to the four beasts that rise out the great sea (7:2). This has both a geographical and historical reference, but at the same time suggests the haunt of evil (as does the similar Revelation 13).

The reference to Revelation 13 is important. Two beasts are summoned by the dragon: one from the sea (v. 1) and one from the earth (v. 11). The watery chaos, the abode of evil, was often linked with Sheol. Jonah, in his prayer in chapter 2, describes his prison inside the fish as both 'the very heart of the seas' (v. 3) and 'the roots of the mountains' (v. 6). I shall be arguing in detail later that Behemoth and Leviathan represent the dark powers of earth and sea and this seems of a piece with these other passages.

These are only a selection of a great number of passages which show the menace of the sea and its untamed nature.[1] It is not surprising, therefore, that this is an important image in many parts of Job and an examination of its use forms the major part of this chapter.

Chapters 2 and 3 have examined the basic worldview of Job and shown how fundamental is the divine council and all that implies about the providential governing of the universe. The doctrine of creation has been explored, and now we turn to the discords that run through the fallen creation as it groans in frustration. Thus we examine the basic image of evil – the sea – before exploring in detail the figures of Behemoth and Leviathan.

The passages discussed will be Job 3:8; 7:12; 9:8, 13; 26:11–14; 28:11, 14 and 38:8–11. We shall also explore the image and its significance further in the gospel accounts of Jesus stilling the storm and walking on the water.

Job 3:8

The NIV reads:

> 'May those who curse days curse that day,
> those who are ready to rouse Leviathan.'

The MT reads *yôm* ('day'), but some, including Gunkel, emend to *yām* ('sea'). (See further discussion in ch. 7.) Gunkel may be right; the

---

[1] There are, of course, other passages where the sea is simply part of creation and part of the realm of the one true God: e.g., Ps. 95:5: 'The sea is his, for he made it'; also Ps. 98:7, where the psalmist calls on it to join in the symphony of creation to its Creator: 'Let the sea resound, and everything in it.'

words would often be identical in archaic Hebrew script. The point I want to make here is that in Job 3 the universe has become a most threatening and evil place. The sense of God's protecting presence has been replaced by images of terror and despair. This is more than distress and suffering, this is a world of cosmic evil and Job is at the centre of a colossal battle raging in the heavenly places.

Not only has Satan struck at Job's body and family, but he is subtly insinuating images of death and chaos into Job's mind. God had warned Satan 'You must spare his life' (2:6), and Satan, with characteristic subtlety, is observing the letter of the law. However, he is trying to get Job to do his work for him by allying himself with the magicians who call up the dark powers of chaos. He had already alleged that he could make Job curse God (1:11) and this is what he is attempting to do.

Job 7:12

Job here is at a low point, obsessed by the swiftness of life and crushed by a sense of futility: 'Am I Yam[2] or Tannin that you place me under guard?' (lit. trans.).

Tannîn, or sea monster, occurs in Genesis 1:21 as part of the denizens of the sea. In Psalm 148:7 the *tannînîm* are called to join in the universal chorus of praise to the Creator. The word is used in Exodus 7:9, 10 and 12 of the snakes which emerge from staffs in the confrontation between Moses and Pharaoh's magicians; in Deuteronomy 32:33 it is used of venomous snakes, as in Psalm 91:13 also.

The word *mišmār* ('guard') has attracted much comment. The meaning 'guard' is supported by the LXX; the Vulgate goes further and renders the phrase as 'that you have enclosed me in a prison'. This fits with the nuances of verses 17–21 which are a parody of Psalm 8 where Job castigates God for his persistent and unwelcome attentions. The passage has implications of the barracks, the parade ground and the prison.[3]

In any case there is a clear reference to the persistent Near Eastern myth of the battle with the dragon. In the Ugaritic myths Baal defeats Yammu, and in other texts his sister Anat claims to have dispatched various monsters, including Lotan (or Leviathan). This, for the

---

[2] 'Sea' here appears without the definite article.
[3] Dahood (1961: 270–271), citing an earlier article by Lowenstamm (1959), translates *mišmār* as 'muzzle' or 'silence' on the basis of both Ugaritic and Akkadian.

NOW MY EYES HAVE SEEN YOU

author of Job, is a profound metaphor for God's containment and eventual destruction of evil.[4] The many references to this in Job's own speeches and its confirmation in the divine speeches are one of the most significant factors in the book and link the prologue and the dialogue inextricably as we find Satan, in various guises, tormenting Job.

Job 9

We have two particular verses to examine here: 8 and 13, and it will be useful to say something about the context. Job's speech (chs. 6 and 7) has been replied to by Bildad (ch. 8). Bildad is blunt and aggressive; his view of justice is purely mechanical and there is no place for mystery in his deistic universe. Job's reply (chs. 9 and 10) becomes a profound exploration of God's power as Creator and Judge. God is warrior as well as Creator. The reference to Rahab (v. 13) makes more likely the interpretation of verse 8 in a cosmic sense and the discerning here of another allusion to the battle with the dragon.

So to verse 8.

Job 9:8

'He alone stretches out the heavens and treads on the back of Yam' (lit. trans.).

In this passage Job uses the language of doxology, but in a particular way. In Psalm 46 the psalmist writes that he does not fear though the earth is removed and the mountains thrown into the sea, but here that same activity is a source of mystery and terror. Yet the sense of wonder at the sheer immensity of God is powerfully conveyed, a sense totally missing in the speeches of the friends.

Verse 8 indeed foreshadows in miniature the structure of a number of later passages: chapter 26, where verses 5–10 are about creation, and verses 11–14, about smiting the monster; chapters 38 – 39, about the created order, and chapters 40 – 41, about the place of evil within it. Thus here in verse 8 we must look at 'stretching out the heavens' before we examine 'treading on the back of Yam'.

In an important article, Habel examines the phrase in some detail.[5] He looks particularly at its use in a number of passages in Isaiah

---

[4] See the Appendix: 'Job and Canaanite myth' for a further discussion of the Ugaritic texts and their bearing on the interpretation of Job.
[5] Habel 1972: 417–430.

which he sees as connected with titles or formulae 'designed to identify and magnify Yahweh as the unique living God of the entire earth who is in the process of revealing his magnificence'.[6] He further observes that the phrase is often paralleled by 'founded the earth', and thus brings together the ideas of pitching a tent and establishing a building. He therefore argues that this idiom probably derives from an ancient creation tradition and that similar deductions can be drawn from the phrase 'stretching out the heavens'. He maintains that this particular way of viewing the creation of the heavens is especially associated with theophany and is the prototype of the cultic tent-motif. Habel goes on to argue that the 'pitching' of the heavens by Yahweh is not only viewed as a past primordial event but also as a *revelatio continua* which is part of his *creatio continua* and his saving intervention through cult and history.[7]

If Habel is correct, this ties the passage neatly into Job's experience of God's providence. Job is feeling something of the anguish, the discord, that runs through the fallen creation, magnificent as it still is. It is these glimpses of the reality of evil and its presence in the universe that are part of Job 'speaking right' about God (42:8), something I will examine more fully in the final chapter.

The crucial question in 9:8b is the meaning of *bāmᵒtê-yām*, which the NIV, along with the RSV, translates as 'waves of the sea'. Dhorme argues: 'Our author, who is immediately inspired by Amos 4:13 or Micah 1:3, replaces the "heights of the earth" by the "heights of the sea", i.e. the waves which rear themselves so that their crests become as mountain peaks.'[8] Dhorme, here, makes two assumptions: (1) that Job is later than one or both of these prophets; (2) that the word means 'heights' or 'high places'.

A thorough study of the word was made by Patrick Vaughan.[9] He argues that its use in Job should be distinguished from *bāmâ* (pl. *bāmôṯ*), used in Kings of the notorious high places, sometimes cultic platforms, sometimes natural eminences, that were a major feature of idolatrous practices. It is dubious that such a rigid distinction can be made and it might be better to see them as different nuances in a semantic field rather than completely separate words. Indeed the different shades of meaning may be deliberately invoked by the author.

---

[6] Habel 1972: 417.
[7] Habel 1972: 430.
[8] Dhorme 1967:130.
[9] Vaughan 1974.

The nuance of trampling on the body of the sea monster[10] would anticipate the 'cohorts of Rahab' and would fit well with the chaos battle motif. However, the nuance of 'high places' or 'heights' also suggests control over the natural world and serves as a reminder that what we call the natural and supernatural worlds are ultimately one. The sea is the literal ocean as well as the symbol for the powers of evil which is to be made explicit in 38:8–11.

This great lyric of creation is rounded off in 9:13 with the first of the book's two references to Rahab:

> 'God does not restrain his anger,
>   even the cohorts of Rahab cowered at his feet.'

Rahab is another name for the sea monster and this is a good place to say something about the term which also occurs in Psalms and Isaiah. The world itself is quite obscure. BDB links it with the relatively uncommon verb *rāhab* ('to act boisterously, stormily, arrogantly'). The verb may well be denominative, that is, 'to play the part of a Rahab'. In Isaiah 30:7 and Psalm 87:4 it is a figurative name for Egypt, but here and in 26:12, as well as in Psalm 89:10 and Isaiah 51:9–10, it refers to the personified Sea.[11]

Here, as in chapter 7, Job is feeling crushed by that terrifying anger of God which subdued the sea monster and his cohorts. Job feels that in the cosmic battle he is on the wrong side, and, like Luther confronted with the righteousness of God, he sees God as angry and condemnatory. Characteristically, the psalm-like language, without any sense of incongruity, blends into legal language in verses 15–20 and there is the tantalizing brushing against the answer in verse 24c: 'If it is not he, then who is it?' This then leads to the agonized cry for an umpire in the heavenly court (v. 33).

There are many layers of significance in chapter 9, one of the key passages in the flow of the book, and here the blending of the language of liturgy and litigation is most evident. What produces adoring worship at the grandeur of God also leads to shrieking protest at his apparent savagery and vindictiveness. Satan is hard at

---

[10] In Ugaritic *bmt* sometimes means 'ribs' or 'sides' and is probably related to the Akkadian *bamtu* ('rib cage').

[11] The LXX in 88:11 (MT 89:11) renders it as *hyperthania* ('arrogance'), and in Isaiah 30:7 as *mataiotēs* ('vanity'). Jerome uses such words as *superbia* and *vanitas*. This is followed by the AV which renders Job 9:13 as 'the proud helpers' and 26:12 as 'he smites through the proud'. The name has not been found in other Semitic languages.

work. The friends have already impugned Job's righteousness and are about to become even more savage in their condemnation. Satan works to drive a wedge between Job and God, although in verse 24 Job is very close to perceiving the reality.

The reference in verse 13 is curiously oblique – Rahab's cohorts[12] rather than Rahab *per se.* Yet this contributes to Job's sense of loneliness and fear as he is surrounded by hostile powers. This elusiveness is, in itself, part of Satan's strategy, for if Job is unable to perceive Satan, the only one he can blame for his situation is God himself.

Job 26

Earlier I argued that, in spite of the views of many commentators, this speech is not a continuation of Bildad's words in chapter 25 but the beginning of Job's eighth response (see ch. 3, p. 68).

Chapter 26 is of the utmost importance in the flow of the book. Yahweh here is creator and warrior and the verses are full of vigorous verbs suggesting violent and warlike action and his power is awesomely displayed from the heights of heaven to the primeval deep. Our concern here is mainly with verses 11–13 which work a picture of universal dissolution (rather like Psalm 46 where God is Lord even though the created order dissolves). The language of theophany strongly recalls the terror of river and sea in Habbakuk 3:8 where they cower before God the warrior.

Our main concern here is verse 12 where Sea and Rahab appear in parallel:

> 'By his power he churned up the sea;
> by his wisdom he cut Rahab to pieces'.

These refer in different ways to the same reality and underline the identity of Sea and Rahab.

'He churned up the sea'; God has already 'stirred up' or 'roused' the Leviathan/Rahab figure and this may be a further reference to that.[13] This is a delicately nuanced verse. Unlike Babylonian and

---

[12] The 'cohorts' probably have echoes of Tiamat's forces who march against Marduk. Similarly, Canaanite myth knows of a number of sea monsters dispatched by Baal and Anat (*CML* 3D, ll. 34ff.).

[13] *rāga'* is fascinating: NIV follows Is. 51:15 and Jer. 31:35 where it clearly means stirring up the stormy sea. These, like the occurrence here, are the Qal Perfect. The meaning 'still', 'quiet' (supported by Habel, Hartley and Pope) makes the verb Hiphil.

Canaanite mythology, Yam/Sea is not the main antogonist of the chief god; this would veer too far in the direction of dualism. Thus 'the sea' is the haunt of the monster, the prince of the sea, here called Rahab.

It is by his 'wisdom' (*t^ebûnâ*, derived from the verb *bîn*) that he dispatches Rahab.[14] This is no mere brute power, this is part of his loving purposes for creation. Indeed, verse 14c has the same verb in the Hithpael, with the meaning of 'comprehend, understand fully'. This is a sharp reminder that the control of the sea and the smiting of Rahab are not the whole or even the most important truth about the universe and that in seeing God's control of evil we are glimpsing only the merest hint of his majesty. It is this insight of Job that anticipates the great treatment of creation and evil in Yahweh's speeches (chs. 38 – 41).

This is not the place to examine the references to Rahab in Psalms 87:4 and 89:10–14 or in Isaiah 30:7 and 51:9–10. Suffice it to say that the sea imagery, with allusions both to creation and exodus, occurs there. In Rabbinic legend this is also the case. Ginzberg, in his massive collection of these legends from rabbinic sources,[15] demonstrates the connection of Rahab with both creation and exodus. Rahab is 'the angel of the sea, who rebelled at the creation of the world' and 'the Prince of Egypt'.

Job 28

We have already examined the nature and place of this chapter, with its rich tapestry of allusions to earlier parts of Job as well as its anticipations of Yahweh's speeches (see ch. 3, pp. 65–70). Here, our concern is with the allusions to the rivers and sea in verses 11 and 14.

Verse 11 comes at the end of the section on mining which has overtones of the netherworld as well as Job's own sufferings. This is the place of 'the sources of the rivers'; also known in Ugaritic as *mbk.nhrm.* where El meets with the divine council. Again the link of this assembly with the mysteries of creation is underlined.

In verse 14 the sea and the deep say that they do not have wisdom

---

[14] Pope 1973: 185 renders it 'by his cunning' and draws attention to the strategems of Marduk as well as the magical weapons Kothar and Khasis give to Baal in his battle with Yam. This may be a secondary nuance but it misses some dimensions of *bîn*.

[15] Ginzberg 1909. The creation reference is vol. 1, p. 18 and the exodus reference is vol. 6, p. 8. It is also worth noting that in vol. 5, p. 26, Rahab, Leviathan and the Angel of Death are considered to be identical.

in them, which is tantamount to saying that they are creatures. They are merely part of the scheme of things and God's overarching wisdom contains them and has power over them. Similarly, both Behemoth (40:15) and Leviathan (41:33) are described as creatures. God alone has life in himself and the power to give that life to others.

In this chapter the references to the sea have Psalm 104:26 as their background. There the sea is part of creation and Leviathan is there only to frolic. This is not a contradiction of those passages where the raging sea is a menace but a necessary complement to them. The emphasis of chapter 28 is that the only real fear in the universe is the fear of Yahweh. So in Revelation 6:12–17, where there is the terrifying language of cosmic convulsion, earthquake and universal dissolution, what causes mad terror is the fear of God. Far better to die in a crashing avalanche than to face the wrath of the Lamb. So chapter 28 is an important stage on the journey to chapter 42, where all secondary figures fade away and Job is left alone before the Judge of all the earth.

Before looking at the treatment of sea in the divine speeches it is useful to make some observations about Job's allusions to the subject. First, in his many references to sea, Rahab and the like, Job has shown a deep consciousness of evil in the created order. He does not inhabit the flat deist universe of the friends, where suffering is an inevitable and mechanical result of wrong doing. Rather he is aware of a cosmic dimension to all that happens and his great fear is that in that battle he is on the wrong side.

Job has glimpsed the profound mystery that the good creation is suffering in anguish, and it is this insight that God is to build on and put in a wider context in chapters 38 – 41. Job is only too aware of the dark powers which sea represents.

Second, through it all Job has a consuming desire to see God. His language is that of one who desperately wants to meet God and speak with him. These are not the words of someone indifferent or unbelieving; rather these are the outpourings of someone surrounded by the grim lords of death and chaos and struggling to hold on to faith: 'you frighten me with dreams and terrify me with visions' (7:14).

Third, the imagery used by Job has the effect of drawing the reader into his experience. This is not an abstract dissertation on 'the problem of evil', this is a powerful dramatization of a man assaulted by the powers of the evil one. The deep imaginative associations of the raging sea link Job's sorrows with the great chasm of anguish and suffering which is part of the fallen creation.

Job 38

Before dealing with our particular concern here (vv. 8–11), something
needs to be said about chapter 38 as a whole. We have seen how chapters 38 and 39 are far more than 'nature poetry' (pp. 73–81). Rather,
the whole created order and the evil which stalks it are called to
witness as God gives Job an insight into his creation in stunning and
panoramic detail.

The structure of the chapter is significant. Yahweh speaks out of a
storm, probably the one gathering in chapter 37:2ff., and thunders
from his holy mountain. This is a fine dramatic touch and a palpable
reminder of the power and majesty of God. But there is more. Storms
and other violent natural phenomena are not self-evidently manifestations of God; indeed they seem more like a further outburst of evil.
It is this evil which Yahweh is about to unmask. What does God do
as he speaks from the storm? He 'answers'; this is now the authorita-
tive word from the heavenly court. He replies to Job's words beginning in chapter 26 and indeed all his previous speeches, not least in
chapter 3.

Looking more closely at the structure of the chapter, an interesting pattern emerges. It is possible to read verses 4–7 as a poetic
description of the creation of the heavens and the earth and the rest
of the chapter as examples of created phenomena. However, it is possible to see the chapter as a series of pictures of the creative act itself
viewed from different angles. Thus the curbing of the sea would be
parallel to creation itself, an emphasis to be explored in detail in the
study of Leviathan. Thus the unfolding theme of the chapter would
be as follows:

vv. 4–7:	Yahweh lays the foundations of the earth
vv. 8–11:	he creates the sea
vv. 12–15:	creation's dawn
vv. 16–18:	the place of death and the underworld
vv. 19–38:	the phenomena of the heavens
vv. 39–41:	Yahweh the provider

Thus in verses 8–11 we have the culmination of the sea imagery in
Job. Driver-Gray have a most interesting observation:

The original independence of the sea and the stern conflict
before it was subdued, which belong to the mythology lying

behind these verses, are blurred by the fundamental monotheism of the writer, who for purposes of poetry does not,
however, refrain from introducing traits that only receive their
full explanation from polytheistic thought; see on 7:12; 9:13;
26:12.[16]

The comment is shrewd but rather misses the point. The power of the
sea is used not to exalt the dark powers but to emphasize the unapproachable transcendence of God, while at the same time showing
the sheer power and scale of evil rooted in creation itself. Moreover,
since God himself speaks thus of the sea, he is placing his imprima-
tur on this supernatural dimension, a dimension entirely missed by
the friends. Job had already linked creation with the curbing of the
sea and the defeat of the monster but had not yet been given the revelation of its part in the whole created order.

Now to some of the details. There is a wonderful blend of menace
and playfulness in verse 8:

'Who shut up the sea behind doors
    when it burst forth from the womb?'

The terrifying chaos monster is seen as a baby but one, none the less,
with a vigorous and dangerous life of its own. This is both a parallel
and a contrast to the stories in Canaanite myth where Baal and Yam
are well-matched and the outcome of their struggle is doubtful. In the
Old Testament the incomparability of Yahweh makes no room for
dualism or polytheism. Yet the power of evil is immense and from the
human side the menace seems overwhelming. The curbing of such a
powerful monster is part of creation itself and this is a continuing
task. In one sense the restraining of the sea within strict limits refers
merely to the natural phenomena of shores, cliff, sands and promon-
tories which prevent the ocean overrunning the land. As the centuries
pass, there is a continual battle of sea and land, with the sea often
winning. Yet this is also a powerful metaphor for that great and elemental struggle of God with the forces of chaos which will end only
when the sea is no more. The verb *sûk* (translated as 'shut up' by the
NIV) is probably a deliberate echo of 1:10 and 3:23. In 1:10 Satan uses
the word in the sense of 'protect': God has put a hedge around Job
and through that hedge nothing evil can pass. In 3:10 Job complains

[16] Driver-Gray 1977: 328.

93

that the door of his mother's womb had not been blocked, and in 3:23 he uses the word negatively of how God has shut him in (much as he later complains in mythological language in 7:12). The use of the word here cleverly echoes and adds further nuances to its earlier uses. God has indeed, in spite of Satan and his minions, hedged Job in. Satan is unaware that this hedge is still intact and that just as the sea may batter, erode and inundate the land but eventually be forced to recede, so his attacks, ferocious as they are, will not finally overpower Job. The links with chapter 3 and the parallels with the womb and Sheol will be further explored in the discussion of death.[17]

In a further poignant metaphor in verse 9, darkness is described as its 'swaddling band' (NIV 'wrapped it in thick darkness'). In chapter 3, clouds and darkness were seen by Job, in his despair, as evidence of evil and 'uncreation'. However, here Yahweh is showing that these apparent harbingers of evil and disaster are in fact his gracious providence to curb the violent sea god. Thus even the darkest mysteries of the universe are part of God's plan to 'hedge in' the monster.

A number of textual points arise in verse 10a: 'I fixed limits for it' (NIV). The phrase reads literally 'and I broke my statute upon him'. The verb *šābar* ('to break') reads oddly in this context. E. B. Smick points out that the NIV, RSV and other English versions have probably connected it with the Arabic *sbr* ('to prescribe boundaries').[18] The word is used metaphorically in Proverbs 25:15: 'a gentle tongue can break a bone'. In Leviticus 26:19 the verb occurs: 'I will break down your stubborn pride.' This is probably close to the intended meaning here which could be paraphrased as 'and I broke him by imposing my limit on him' (a similar nuance can be found in v. 15). Thus the word need not be amended but rather seen as contributing an additional shade of meaning.

'Limits' is more exactly 'my limit' (*huqqî*) and has also been subject to emendation.[19] However, Habel sees it as a subjective suffix, 'the limit set by me', which fits well into the context.[20] It also recalls Job's use of the word in 26:10:

> 'He marks out the horizon on the face of the waters
> for a boundary between light and darkness.'

---

[17] See pp. 112–115 of this study.

[18] Smick 1988: 1040.

[19] Blommerde (1969: 133), following Dahood, argues that the MT i-suffix is third person (i.e. 'its limit'). The NIV's 'limits for it' is ambiguous.

[20] Habel 1985: 521.

That is another indication that God is addressing directly what Job has said and placing his insights in the wider context of creation and providence.

But perhaps the most striking detail in this pericope is the verb in verse 11a, *wā' ōmar* ('when I said'). This is outside the metre but should not be deleted and indeed (cp. Job 28:28) that fact draws attention to it. The emphasis on the creating word takes us into the world of Genesis 1 and underlines a fundamental difference between Hebrew and other Ancient Near Eastern views of creation. In Canaanite and Mesopotamian theology the smiting of the sea monster is the crushing of one immense and brutal power by another. Thus Baal fights Yam with clubs supplied by Kothar, a minor deity[21] and Marduk uses mace, bow and net, as well as 'the flood weapon, his great weapon' and smashes Tiamat to pieces.[22]

Here the word of God is the creative agent which both gives life and curbs chaos. It is by wisdom that God smites the monster. Job (v. 2) had spoken words without knowledge, but the words Yahweh speaks are those which create and destroy. The poetic language of Job here describes the same reality found in Genesis 1:9: 'And God said: "Let the water under the sky be gathered to one place, and let dry ground appear".' Similarly, in Revelation 19:15 the rider on the white horse destroys the beast and his army by a sharp sword from his mouth, a metaphor of his powerful word.[23]

Two main metaphors have dominated this pericope. The first is that of the sea as a lusty infant, similar to the description of Leviathan as a plaything in Psalm 104:26. This metaphor emphasizes the sole power of Yahweh as Creator. There are no co-creators, nor has he a rival.

The other metaphor is that of limits. God separates land and sea as well as light and darkness. In the words of Psalm 104:9:

> 'You set a boundary they cannot cross;
> never again will they cover the earth.'

But God also hedges humans; which both delights and dismays Job.

---

[21] *CML* (Baal and Yam) 2, col. iv, ll. 11–15.

[22] See 'The Epic of Creation' in Dalley 1989: 251–255.

[23] V. 11b has caused difficulties. It reads literally 'here will be set on the pride of your waves'. Blommerde (1969: 134) proposes *yišatab* as an infixed t-form from *šbb* which he relates to Ugaritic *tbb* ('to break'). The sense would then be that the waves are broken at a set limit. The NIV's 'halt', while a paraphrase, probably expresses the sense well. Again Lev. 29:19 supplies a useful parallel.

It is important now to examine more carefully the context of this pericope within chapter 38. The immediate context is the delight of the morning stars/sons of God, the members of the heavenly court, as they rejoice at the work of creation as he builds the earth and separates land and water. Their rejoicing is a powerful suggestion that creation is good and that the divine providence is a loving one. Further, in a way that preserves monotheism, powers other than God are seen to be part of the created order. This is part of the inner secrets of creation when no human was present, which can be known only by revelation.

The curbing of the sea is further paralleled by verses 12–15 where the dawning of the day and indeed the morning of creation itself is evoked. As God separated land and water, so first he separated light and darkness. Not only has the sea been restrained in its place, so dawn (*šaḥar*) is commanded by Yahweh alone. Isaiah 14:12–15 speaks of 'morning star son of the dawn', the AV's 'Lucifer, son of the morning' and his impious attempt to storm the holy mountain and sit on the throne of God. It seems reasonable to find mythological nuances here that parallel the sea passage. Thus Job is being asked if he has the power of the Creator not only to control and summon natural phenomena but also the supernatural powers behind these.[24]

Verses 16–18 return directly to the sea, here linked with the world of death. The emphasis moves from control to understanding the mystery of the sea, of Sheol[25] and the world of death. This emphasis recalls 26:14 about merely glimpsing the outer fringes of God's ways and understanding these only in part. Moreover, there is a subtle allusion to 3:11ff. where Job longs for Sheol which he sees as a place of peace and rest. We shall explore this further in chapter 5 (pp. 102–103).

---

[24] The mythological significance of all this may be further suggested if we follow a suggestion by Driver (1953: 208–212) for an alternative rendering of the difficult v. 15: 'The wicked are denied their light, and their upraised arm is broken'. Driver draws attention to the suspended *ayin* in *rᵉšāʿîm* ('the wicked') and argues that the copyists intended to denote some unusual significance for the word. He suggests it means evil constellations rather than evil men. He further identifies the 'upraised arm' with the arm of Leo (i.e. the stars of the Navigator's Line which extend across the sky from horizon to horizon). Thus he renders the verse:

'And the light of the Dog stars is withdrawn from it
and the Navigator's line is broken up.'

This is followed by the NEB, one of the many places where that translation reflects Driver's philological excursions.

[25] 'The vast expanses of the earth' probably refers here to the underworld, as this naturally follows from the gates of death. Andersen (1976: 276) demonstrates that *'ereṣ* can mean 'underworld'.

This theme of inaccessibility and mystery continues in verses 19–38 which explore the mysteries of the cosmos and the phenomena of the heavens, and in verses 39–41 which talk of Yahweh's providential care of the animal kingdom (developed in chapter 39). Detailed discussion of these verses would take us too far from the theme of the raging sea, but two points are worth making. The first is that the remotest parts of the cosmos are known to Yahweh and are under his control. Human understanding can only go a little way. This is particularly illustrated by verse 26:

> 'to water a land where no man lives,
> a desert with no-one in it'.

Humans are not the only objects of God's care.

The other noteworthy feature is that again much of the language has mythical overtones.[26] This does not (*pace* Gordis 1965) dilute the author's monotheism. Rather it shows (as the heavenly court motif supremely does) that no part of the universe, even that associated with pagan deities, is outside the control of the one true God. Since the sea is the most fundamental symbol of these hostile forces, it is unsurprising that we should find other such allusions in this chapter.

I shall try now to draw these various threads together by making five observations. The first is that the universe cannot be understood simply by observing natural phenomena nor adequately explained in physical terms. Thus references to the raging sea, while having a naturalistic dimension, have a supernatural meaning as well and that dimension must be recognized in the passages already discussed.

The second is that this dimension is gained largely in Job's words but is absent in the speeches of the friends. Job wrongly imagines that like the sea god he is the object of divine anger, but he is right to discern the supernatural and cosmic dimensions of his agonies. It is this insight that is put into true control in the divine speeches, and, as we shall see in chapter 9, is no small part of Job speaking what is right about God.

Thirdly, it is important to establish the supernatural dimensions of

---

[26] One such text (the subject of much comment) is v. 36: NIV translates it: 'Who endowed the heart with wisdom or gave understanding to the mind?' The margin expresses doubt as to this meaning. Dhorme (1967: 591–592) translates it: 'Who has imparted wisdom to the ibis, or who endowed the cock with understanding?' Pope (1973: 256) argues that *tuḥôt* and *śekwî* sound like Thoth, god of learning, and Souchi, the Coptic name for Hermes/Mercury. The text remains difficult.

the sea passages as a background for the detailed consideration of Behemoth and Leviathan. Much of the misunderstanding of these passages has come from a failure to discern the way the poet has built up the pattern of imagery that culminates in these figures.

Fourthly, the discussion of the heavenly court, of creation theology and the sea passages has suggested a profound underlying unity in the book. From apparently diverse materials the poet is weaving a tapestry of how the created order is both good and yet fallen. Job stands in the centre of biblical theology as we shall see further in chapter 9.

The fifth point is that these passages point beyond themselves, not only to a number of passages in the Old Testament but also to a significant number of New Testament passages where they are of vital importance. This introduces us to the final section of this chapter.

The sea stories in the gospels

If the above interpretation of the sea passages is correct, they add an extra dimension to a cluster of passages in the gospels where Jesus stills a storm and walks on water. There are two such clusters. First, Matthew 8:23–27, Mark 4:36–41 and Luke 8:22–25 describe how Jesus was asleep in a boat on the Lake of Galilee and then rose up to still the storm. In all three cases this is followed by the casting out of demons from the tormented man and the descent of the swine into the sea. These two stories further demonstrate the link of evil spirits and the sea.

The account in Mark is a good case-study for our present purpose and three particular points call for attention. The first is the use of the verb *epetimēsen* ('he rebuked') in 4:39a; a word also used in 1:25 of rebuking an evil spirit. In the LXX this verb (and the noun *epetimēsis*) is often used to translate *gā'ar*, as in Job 26:11. It is used in Mark 9:25 of exorcism and in Jude 9 of Michael's dispute with Satan over the body of Moses. Plainly the word has supernatural nuances.

The second is the verb *pephimōso* ('be still') in verse 39b, which also occurs in 1:25. Cranfield[27] points out that the form is perfect imperative passive, with the connotation of 'be silent and remain so'. Cranfield rejects the idea of a demon or personification of the sea here. However, the occurrence of the word in 1:25 as well as in the story of the demon-possessed man which immediately follows it in all

[27] Cranfield 1959: 174.

the Synoptic accounts suggests that here indeed we have a reference to an evil power.

These two observations lead to a third comment. The disciples' awestruck question in 4:41 gains even deeper significance: 'Who is this? Even the winds and the waves obey him.' This story comes at the climax of a series of mighty acts: healings, exorcisms and unprecedented authority in preaching. All of these have many Old Testament parallels: David driving the evil spirit from Saul by his playing; healings and even raising from the dead in the ministry of Elijah and Elisha; the inspired utterances of the prophets. Thus there was inevitable controversy (most of it reflected within the disciples themselves) about who Jesus of Nazareth was. If the prophets had shown similar powers, was he only a prophet? But surely there was only one who could say to the proud waves 'Thus far shall you come and no further'?

Yet more parallels emerge in the other cluster of passages about Jesus walking on the sea (Matt. 14:22–32; Mark 6:47–52; John 6:15–21). The twin elements of darkness and the raging sea show once again the battle with the powers of evil. In each of the gospels this miracle is associated with the feeding of the five thousand and there is plainly a connection being established between Jesus as curber of the sea and giver of food and Jesus the Creator.

Some specific points call for comment. Job 9:8, 'trampling on the back of Sea' (lit. trans.), was seen to be linked with the power of the Creator. There is an important detail emphasized in each of the accounts: 'walking on the lake' (Matt. 14:26; Mark 6:49), 'walking on the water' (John 6:19). Reductionistic accounts which allege that Jesus was wading in the shallow water on the lake's edge completely obscure the evangelists' concern to show that the Creator is present in his creation and showing mastery of winds and waves. Likewise Job 38:16:

> 'Have you journeyed to the springs of the sea
> or walked in the recesses of the deep?'

This verse shows that such activity is the prerogative of the Creator alone. A further striking parallel is found in Psalm 77:19:

> Your path led through the sea,
>   your way through the mighty waters,
>   though your footprints were not seen.

Another important detail in the sea stories is that Jesus himself sent the disciples into the storm. He went up the mountainside to pray, knowing well that the storm would come. Psalm 107:23–32 could almost be a commentary on this story. There Yahweh speaks and stirs up a tempest which imperils those who have gone down to the sea in ships. Just as here God has raised Leviathan, so in the gospel narrative Jesus sends the disciples into the storm and waits until it reaches a fierce pitch before intervening. Indeed, when he appears they look on him as an additional cause of terror: 'they thought he was a ghost' (Mark 6:49). Once again this reflects the experience of Job.

The raging sea is thus not merely a colourful backdrop but an indication of cosmic evil whose subduing is part of the new creation. I will conclude this chapter with three observations. The first is that both Yahweh's kingship and Christ's lordship are demonstrated by their control over the waves. A characteristic Old Testament expression of that faith is found in Psalm 93:4.

> Mightier than the thunder of the great waters,
>   mightier than the breakers of the sea –
>   the LORD on high is mighty.

We have already seen that the astonished question of Mark 4:41 makes a similar New Testament affirmation.

Secondly, both Old and New Testaments deal not with an abstraction but with a personal evil power. Here we have in time and space the reality which was partially glimpsed by the old myths.

Thirdly, the importance of the sea passages in conjunction with our study of the heavenly court and the creation theology of Job has now been demonstrated. This lays a foundation for the detailed consideration of the Behemoth and Leviathan passages which will form the subject of the next four chapters.

Chapter Five

The shadowlands

Pontifical death that doth the crevasse bridge
To the steep and trifid God.[1]

Thus wrote Francis Thompson, and his words might well also sum up the shrinking and the fascination Job feels at the prospect of meeting God and how inextricably this is bound up with death. Indeed few treatments of death and what lies beyond approach the profundity and complexity or the imaginative power of the Job poet. We have already examined the imagery of the heavenly court and of creation and seen how at various points death raises huge question marks over the whole concept of God's care and providence. It is therefore necessary now to examine the imagery of death and of supernatural evil as the poet presents these.

In exploring the imagery of death it is necessary to keep a number of levels of meaning in mind. There is first literal death: the process of dying and the state of being dead which is the immediate subject of the book. There is also death as a 'philosophical concept', examined in chapters 13 – 15. But parallel to these is the ambiguous relationship of God and Satan in the heavenly court, and a number of passages (e.g. ch. 18) which appear to suggest that Mot, the god of death, well known from the Ugaritic texts, is a 'character' in the story.[2] I shall return later to the discussion of the relationship of all this to the mysterious figure of Behemoth (see ch. 6).

We have already noted how the heavenly court metaphor unites the folk tale and the poetic dialogue, and it is interesting to see how the different levels of the reality of death are already established. From the ordinary viewpoint the calamities that rain down on Job are effected by a series of manmade and natural disasters: Chaldaeans, Sabaeans, lightning and storm are indeed the immediate agents. Yet

---

[1] Francis Thompson, 'Anthem of Earth'.
[2] By 'story' I do not simply mean the prose tale but the continuing activities of the heavenly court hinted at all through the poetic dialogue especially in Job's own speeches.

the reference in 1:16 to the 'fire of God' suggests more than lightning (there is, after all, a word for that purely natural phenomenon). In many ways, that phrase encapsulates the fundamental problem of the book: fire is from God just as Satan comes from God and with him the catastrophes. Job himself identifies God as the author of those awful events: 'The LORD gave and the LORD has taken away' (1:21), and 'Shall we receive good at the hand of God, and shall we not receive evil?' (2:10 RSV). Death, not just in the sense of an individual's passing but as the dark power which benights the universe, is the most obvious place where God's goodness is called into question, and thus the relationship of God and death is a fundamental issue in understanding the book of Job.

The significance of Job 3

As the book moves from narrative to dialogue, the sombre and deceptively simple story is paralleled by a poem of immense power and poignancy. Chapter 3 is a powerful evocation of the world of the dead and establishes many of the fundamental concepts and images which are to be developed throughout the dialogue. There are at least four major clusters of images of death which are related to each other and which establish much of the tone and atmosphere of the book.

The first image is that of the womb, already anticipated in 1:21: 'Naked I came from my mother's womb', which is one of the many links between the prologue and the dialogue. A comparison of verses 11–12 with verse 16 shows that the vague unsubstantial life in Sheol is compared to the mysterious life in the womb before birth, both equally unknown and unknowable to mortals. In chapter 3 the negative aspects are underlined when Job longs to have been a stillborn infant whose brief emergence from the womb would immediately have been followed by being 'hidden in the ground' (v. 16) along with all others who rest at peace in the grave.

Secondly, this image of the womb is developed by his picture of the world of the grave and the fundamental equality of all in death (vv. 13–19). The verb šākaḇ (v. 13), used here of lying down in death, is also used to mean this in 7:21 and 14:12.

The third cluster of images is that of shadows and darkness descending on the day of his birth. This is linked with the sinister world of Leviathan and possibly Yam (I shall discuss later Gunkel's reading of yôm in verse 8a as yām). The images of verses 5 and 6 (e.g. ḥōšeḵ and ṣalmāwet) occur later in connection with the netherworld.

So already, parallel to the escapist picture of the peace of the womb and the oblivion of Sheol, an altogether darker and more hostile universe peopled by sinister presences is being built up. Job has thus stumbled upon a profound truth.

This leads on to the fourth area of imagery in verses 20–26. Plainly the MT reading *yitēn* ('he [i.e. God] gives') has proved too embarrassing for many of the versions and translations which prefer to read the passive *yutan*. However, it is likely that 1:21, 'The LORD gave and the Lord has taken away', is being echoed in a negative way. Moreover, the phrase 'God has hedged in' (v. 23b) echoes the words of Satan in 1:9. There the 'hedging in' was positive; here it has become negative, thus illustrating the problem of distinguishing between God and Satan which lies at the heart of Job's agony.

This problem in effect means that in many passages God appears as tormentor, as a kind of demon who seems more like Resheph and Mot than Yahweh. Much of the book of Job's dynamic lies in this ambiguous area of the relationship of God and death.

I want now to examine these four clusters of images both separately and in terms of their interrelatedness. I shall deal with the first three in this chapter, and shall come back to the fourth area and its links with the figure of Behemoth in chapter 6.

The womb of the earth

This basic image will illustrate the fundamental polarity of reversal which lies at the heart of much of the poetry of the book.[3] The womb, with all its associations of new life, here becomes a prison which swallows the doomed mortal after his brief pilgrimage. Significantly, this image occurs first in 1:21, a poetic snatch in the prose tale anticipating the dialogue.[4] The imagery is characteristically ambivalent, recalling Genesis 3:19, 'for out of it you were taken; you are dust and to dust you shall return'.

Chapter 3 begins a great reversal of all values, which plainly indicates that the sinister power of chaos and uncreation has begun to infiltrate Job's mind. His strong faith begins to crack as malign forces start to grip him. Images of the womb of darkness and Sheol are at

---

[3] Robert Alter sees these 'binary opposites' as being at the very heart of the imagery of the book and makes a telling contrast between the images of chapter 3 and those of Yahweh's speeches (Alter 1985: 87).

[4] Pope (1973: 16), retaining the MT reading *šāmmâ*, sees *šām* as a euphemism for Sheol and cites an Egyptian text which describes the dead as *ntjw'im* ('those who are there').

once narrow and cramping and yet desirable. The climax of this comes in verse 19b: 'The slave is freed from his master.' The word *ḥopšî* has positive tones of freedom from slavery in a number of Old Testament references (e.g., Exod. 21:2 is about the Hebrew servant who is to go free in the seventh year). However, Psalm 88, the bleakest of the lament psalms, has the phrase 'free among the dead' (v. 6). Probably both these positive and negative nuances are present here. The womb and the netherworld are indeed in one sense 'the house of freedom', but Job will find that freedom to be increasingly illusory.[5]

A related image to that of the womb is used by Eliphaz in 4:19: 'those who live in houses of clay, whose foundations are in the dust'. The 'dust' is both literal dust and the netherworld and there is another possible echo of Genesis 3:19.

It is Job who returns to the image in 10:8ff. and turns it into a complaint against the seemingly gratuitous cruelty of God who moulds from dust, from the womb of earth, mainly with the purpose of destroying. Habel points out that 'the powerful threatening hands of the adversary (7b) are contrasted with the sensitive artistic hands of the creator (8a)'.[6] The verb often translated 'destroy' (v. 8) is *bāla'* (lit. 'to swallow') and may be comparing God to Mot, the Canaanite god of death, whose jaws encompass heaven and earth. Plainly the motif of being swallowed up in the womb of earth is becoming more sinister and less to do with a 'house of freedom'.

The theme of being taken from the clay or womb of earth is used by Elihu in 33:6, 'I too was formed from a piece of clay' (RSV), probably alluding to chapter 10. It is interesting that the verb used here for 'form' is *qāraṣ* whose Akkadian cognate *qaraṣu* is used in the Gilgamesh epic of the formation of humans by the divine potter. Behind all these images of clay and the womb is the positive image of the Creator which all the negative ones have been unable to crush.

The image of the womb (like all the other images) is taken up in Yahweh's speeches and given a striking new emphasis. In 38:8 the womb from which the sea bursts has cosmic dimensions. The word *gîḥ* recalls the river Gihon of Genesis 2:13 bursting out of the womb of earth. The womb here in chapter 38 is the primordial abyss. In chapter 3 Job had wanted the forces of chaos to curse the night of his

---

[5] The world also occurs in the Ugaritic texts. In two crucial passages Gupn and Ugar are sent to the netherworld (*Wrd. bt. hptt ars*). They are warned to avoid the jaws of Mot (*CML* 4, col. viii, ll. 7; 5, col. v, l. 15). These echoes of Canaanite myth would probably be familiar to the original audience.

[6] Habel 1985: 198.

birth because the doors of his mother's womb had not been locked. Now God, in no uncertain manner, is reminding Job of who opens and closes doors.

Finally, in chapter 42 the image of the womb returns in a positive sense with the birth of more sons and daughters. This image thus manifests on a domestic level the resolution of the conflict on the cosmic level. It is important to realize that this is not the simplistic happy ending some have alleged it to be. Rather, this is the public vindication of Job, who is already possessed of an immeasurably deeper faith than before, which is not dependent on, and indeed precedes, his increased prosperity.

The image of the womb and the related image of clay have demonstrated a developing pattern. They are enclosed between Job's great utterance of faith in 1:21 and Yahweh's vindication of this in chapter 42. The 'great reversal' in chapter 3 sees the womb and the grave as a desirable refuge. This illusion is speedily dissolved by the picture of a vengeful deity, and then the image is set in its cosmic context in Yahweh's first speech.

The vast reaches of the underworld

Moving out from the idea of the womb, the poet presents a related cluster of images about the world of the grave, the 'geography' and 'cosmology' of the netherworld. In analysing these images we have to be aware of the grey area where the physical merges with the mythical. Chapter 3 portrays Sheol as a realm peopled with every kind of person, and Job's longing for rest is vividly conveyed by the simile of the grave robber in verse 21.

The basic indicator of the netherworld is 'there' (šām, v. 19): 'the small and the great are there'. This strong local emphasis prevents us from thinking of death merely as a 'state'; it has solidity and dimension and this is of some importance in assessing the total impact of this imagery.

Job returns to the local emphasis on the grave in chapter 7, with the accent this time being on the grave as 'the land of no return' (vv. 9–10). That is one of its designations in Akkadian, especially in the myth of Ishtar's descent to the netherworld. Negative ideas have predominated in Job's speech; as in 6:14, for instance, where Job had compared his friends to desert streams which vanish in the heat of summer. Job here is numb rather than angry and this mood is reflected in his picture of Sheol as the land of final forgetting.

The local emphasis is of some importance in 7:21:

'For I shall soon lie down in the dust;
    you will search for me, but I shall be no more.'

The word '$\bar{a}p\bar{a}r$ ('dust') is ambiguous, referring both to the frailty of mortals and to the netherworld. This ambivalence and growing sense of hopelessness well fits Job's present mood. There is an additional ironical thrust in the use of the word *šiḥar* ('search, look for') which is used in Psalm 78:34 of the worshipper seeking God and in Psalm 63:1 of the soul longing and thirsting for God.

The image of the land of no return is developed in 10:20–22 (which I shall discuss later in connection with the images of shadow and darkness). The point here is that Job's thinking has come full circle from chapter 3 and now the world of death seems singularly bleak, nor is there any mention of inhabitants.

These images of the mystery of the world of death are conveyed particularly powerfully in chapter 14. Dhorme expresses this well: 'Confronted by the corpse we wonder whither has fled the life which animated it.'[7] Once again we find the image of lying down in the grave, which helps to create the all-pervading atmosphere of melancholy. In verse 14 the intriguing irony occurs again. Sheol is seen as a hiding place where Job would be free from God's anger until that time has passed and then he would have a fair hearing in the heavenly court. This reminds us forcibly of the importance of the events in heaven which have set this whole train of circumstances in motion.

With a new depth of pessimism, Job returns to this image in his speech in chapters 16 and 17. In 16:22 the idea of the 'journey of no return' is again prominent in Job's mind and he faces this with a crushed and broken spirit. The context is the second of the 'witness' passages already discussed, where Job, while unaware of Satan's role as accuser, nevertheless feels the need for an intercessor. The local reference continues in 17:1–2 where the land of the dead again looms before him.[8] This land is no longer a 'house of freedom' but of cor-

---

[7] Dhorme 1967: 199.
[8] Pope (1973: 128) translates 17:2 thus:

'The mounds loom before me,
    On the slime pits my eyes dwell.'

He construes *tulîm* as 'mounds' and *merôṭām* as 'slime pits' and sees these as referring to the Canaanite myth of the twin hills bordering the netherworld. However, the normal rendering of 'mockers surround me, my eyes dwell on their hostility' makes perfectly good sense.

ruption and decay (vv. 13ff.). The companion is not 'the small and the great' of chapter 3, but the worm, and we are in the nightmare world of Edgar Allan Poe.

As we approach the second part of the book and Yahweh's speeches, images of the land of the dead are seen less in individualized and more in cosmic terms. For example, one interesting image occurs in 24:12: 'From out of the city, the dying groan' (RSV). Bearing in mind that Job is describing life at its most exposed and miserable and that such a life is itself a kind of death, it is at least possible that the 'city' may be the infernal city.

Chapter 26 is of great importance in this connection, especially verses 5–6:

> 'The shades below tremble,
>   the waters and their inhabitants.
> Sheol is naked before God,
>   and Abaddon has no covering' (RSV).

The major issue here is the mysterious word $r^e\bar{p}\bar{a}'\hat{i}m$ ('Rephaim'), usually translated as 'shades' or some such word. We have moved far beyond the world of domestic or even communal grief to the world of cosmic evil, of Rahab the chaos monster. We have travelled from images of the netherworld common to all cultures, such as 'the house of the dead' and 'the land of no return', to the thought-world and imaginative atmosphere of Ancient Near Eastern mythology.

In examining the use of the word $r^e\bar{p}\bar{a}'\hat{i}m$ we have two main sources: other passages in the Old Testament and references to the *rpum* in the Ugaritic texts. BDB, not with entire conviction, connects the word with the verb $r\bar{a}\bar{p}\hat{a}$ ('to sink, relax') and suggests the meaning of 'sunken and powerless ones', thus alluding to the dim, insubstantial existence of the 'shades' in Sheol. The word also refers to the old race of giants, the ancient inhabitants of Canaan, especially Og, King of Bashan (Deut. 3:11).

Some of the other Old Testament passages are particularly significant. The word occurs in Isaiah 14:9. The 'shades' here are neatly paralleled by 'the kings of the earth'. The significant point is that, as here in Job 26, there is turmoil in the underworld and the mysterious figure of Helel is connected with it. In Psalm 88:10, 'Do the shades rise up to praise you?' (RSV), it occurs with emphasis on the dreary insubstantial nature of the world of death. This is one of the passages where 'shades' is probably the nearest English equivalent. In Proverbs 2:18 it is parallel to death and there refers to the adulteress, the dark mirror-image of Lady Wisdom. Thus it is far more than domestic sin, as death here in Job 26 is far more than individual death. Again it is used in Proverbs 9:18 as a warning that straying from the 'path of wisdom' will lead to the house of the Rephaim. Finally, in Isaiah 26:19, again in a passage referring to the pains of childbirth, the 'shades' are seen as coming to life and shouting for joy. The simile of the morning dew recalls the tree and water imagery of Job 14:7–12.

The above (with Job 26:5) are the passages where BDB recognizes the first meaning of 'shades' as 'ghosts'. The word has connotations of sterile cosmic presences as opposed to the life-giving principle of wisdom. The difficulty arises in trying to link these with the passages where the meaning 'giants' is more appropriate. Some of these are very brief: for example, in Genesis 15:20 in a list including the Hittites; also in Joshua 17:15. In Deuteronomy 2:11 and 3:11 they are identified with the Moabite Emim and Anakim, and Og, King of Bashan, is described as the last of the Rephaim. His mysterious iron bedstead would make better sense if we adopted Craigie's rendering of 'sarcophagus'.[9]

The use of the word by such a consummate literary artist as the Job poet is plainly of significance and is no mere synonym for 'the dead'. The dating, not only of Job but of all the passages, is problematic and thus we cannot say with any certainty who influenced whom. What we can say is that all these passages give the strong impression of handling a concept already well known. This is perhaps especially the case in Deuteronomy 2 where the Emim and Anakim are explained in terms of the Rephaim. The Isaiah passage, as well as Job 26, associates them with cosmic powers. The Proverbs passages emphasize the connection with creation as well as the underlying moral connotations that accord with Job's anguished plea for justice in chapter 27. So the word is most apposite here in chapter 26, linked as it is with creation and the world of primordial evil.

The connection of the meaning 'shades' with that of 'ancient giants' is unclear, but some points can be noted. There may be a characteristically subtle nuance here. The Rephaim were the pre-Hebrew inhabitants of Canaan who are not only dead but trembling in Sheol before God. Gigantic and terrifying as they once appeared (like the

[9] Craigie 1976: 120.

King of Babylon in Isaiah 14), they are now impotent and terrified before Yahweh. Indeed this may throw some light on the puzzling word *ḥᵉrābôt* in 3:14 – 'the ruins' which the 'kings and counsellors of the earth' built. These, though powerful and impressive, are doomed to end in insubstantial ruin like their builders. This same idea occurs often in Old English poetry, especially in the beautiful but anonymous lyrical elegy 'The Ruin'. In it a city (probably Bath) is described as 'the old work of the giants', a common way of referring to Roman remains which were believed to be the haunt of demons. A further link may be discerned with Job 27:14–23 on the instability of the houses of the rich and the great.

It is now necessary to examine the Canaanite evidence. A number of the Ugaritic tablets mention the *rpum*. For example, *Šps. rpim. thtk* ('Shaphash, the shades are under you') (*CML* 6, col. vi, ll. 46ff.). Here we have a close parallel to Job 26:5. Moreover the parallel words are *ilnym* ('ghosts'), *ilm* ('gods') and *mtm* ('the dead'). The passage further mentions the demonic 'Arsh and the dragon'. The whole passage parallels Job 26 in a remarkable way and both appear to reflect a tradition where the Rephaim belong in the context of cosmic battles and primordial chaos.

Much controversy centres around the 'Rephaim texts' which are fragmentary and difficult (*CTA* 20, 21, 22). The *rpum* are invited to a feast at the *grnt-mt't* (usually understood as 'threshing floors' or 'plantations') where they spend seven days eating and drinking. A number of studies have been made of these puzzling texts, the most thorough of which is probably that of Conrad L'Heureux.[10] L'Heureux gives a useful summary of the different views regarding the identity of the *rpum*, which fall into three broad categories. The first is the view of Virolleaud who, in *Les Rephaim R.E.S. Babylonaica* (1940), suggested the meaning of 'healers' or 'healed ones', based on the fact that their leader is called *rpub'l*, which Virolleaud understood as 'Baal has healed' or 'Baal the healer'. The meaning 'shades' is regarded as derivative, referring to the role they played in ceremonies commemorating Baal's death. This view is espoused by Gaster[11] among others. The second view, held by Dhorme, Driver, Gibson, Pope and Gordon, to name a few, is that they are 'shades of the dead' because of the parallels with *ilnym* and *mtm* already noted, as well as the evidence of Hebrew and Phoenician

[10] L'Heureux 1979.
[11] Gaster 1966.

cognates. The third view, advocated especially by Gray,[12] is that these are cultic functionaries who accompany the king to the 'threshing floors' or 'plantations' in order to promote fertility.

Virolleaud mentions a god named *rpu mlk'lm* who may be identical with *rpub'l*, but certainty is impossible.[13] Plainly, the Canaanite material, like the Hebrew, bristles with problems but some potentially illuminating points emerge. L'Heureux argues vigorously that their presence at a banquet precludes the possibility of their being shades. But L'Heureux ignores the possible irony of the passage, as well as, more significantly, the fact that in Proverbs 9:17–18, the $r^e\bar{p}\bar{a}'\hat{\imath}m$ feast on 'stolen bread' in the house of the adulteress, which is in fact Sheol.

The issue is exceedingly complex and dogmatism is unwise. However, in the light of both Hebrew and Canaanite material certain observations can be made about the Rephaim in this context in Job 26. The word was presumably chosen to show the world of the dead against its cosmic background and thus, like other details in the chapter, anticipate Yahweh's speeches. There may be a further relevant interplay of ideas in the Ugaritic texts. L'Heureux argues cogently that the status of El is linked with that of the Rephaim. He is *rapiu* ('the Hale one') *par excellence*. However, this occurs only in the title of Daniel in *Aquhat* (*CML* 17. col. i, l. 19) and *passim* elsewhere, but it is difficult to avoid a link between this and *rpub'l*. If we accept the rendering 'shades' it may be that the nuance 'healthy ones' is in fact a euphemism in the context of mourning for a kind of death (i.e. the failure to have offspring). In a Hebrew context Yahweh is both El and Baal, in the sense that not only does his providence direct, but his activity is involved in the process of creation. Gibson argues that Rapiu or 'the shade' is 'apparently a title of Baal associated with his summer stay in the underworld'.[14] Now that stay in the underworld is linked with his temporary defeat at the hands of Mot in which El appears to play an inglorious part. It may be, therefore, that behind verses 5–6 is a veiled allusion to the battle of Baal and Mot. Job is in the same situation as Baal, 'the shade', the power of death is gripping him, and Yahweh in his role as El seems to be the real attacker.

This linking of the world of the dead with the furthest reaches of Yahweh's power is perhaps continued in the puzzling chapter 27. I

[12] Gray 1952: 39–41.
[13] *Ugaritica V*, 2.
[14] In *CML*, p. 26, n. 4.

shall discuss this chapter more fully in connection with the chaos monster in chapter 26, but one point is worth making here. It may be that the latter part of this chapter (vv. 13ff.) is a significant bridge by which the metaphors of the world of the dead cross over from chapter 26 to chapter 28. Indeed, perhaps even the first part of the chapter may be linked with this if the 'enemies' of verse 7 are more than human. In the latter part of the chapter, verses 18–19 may refer to the opening of the eyes in Sheol when all earthly things have vanished. Moreover, the picture of the desolate ruins recalls 3:14 already mentioned in connection with the Rephaim.

However, the chapter also looks forward. The last words, especially 'his place', anticipate the significant use of place (*māqôm*) in 28:1, and there is irony in the differing nuances of the words. Chapter 28, with its opening description of mining, uses imagery which powerfully evokes the underworld and thus suggests the impossibility of finding out the secrets of that land because they are the secrets of the Lord of Wisdom himself. Verse 22 is particularly significant, for there Abaddon and Mot are said to have some inkling of God's purpose. Thus, in similar vein to chapter 26, they are relegated to their place in the cosmic scheme.

These soaring speculations are not contradicted by the gloomy picture of Job 30:20ff. Job's sudden reversal to extreme pessimism and despair is the result of his reliving the happy past in chapter 29, and the grim contrast with the bleak present is underlined by the opening 'But now' of chapter 30. The words, 'I know you will bring me down to death, to the place appointed for all the living' (v. 23), fuse together many of the earlier pictures of the netherworld.

The geography of the underworld is touched on by Elihu in chapter 33:12ff. Verse 18 is interesting: 'To preserve his soul from the pit, his life from perishing by the sword.' 'By the sword' (*baššelaḥ*) is perhaps more naturally translated as 'crossing the river'. Andersen points out that *'ābar* usually means 'pass through' rather than 'perish', which makes 'river' rather than 'sword' more appropriate as well as a more natural parallel to 'pit'.[15] Dhorme provides supporting evidence for this meaning.[16] The word is used in the plural in Song of Songs 4:12 of the waters irrigating the gardens of the lover, and as a proper noun in Isaiah 8:6 as a metaphor of the overwhelming power of the king of Assyria. Dhorme also cites the Akkadian *šilihtu*, which means

[15] Andersen 1976: 249.
[16] Dhorme 1967: 496–497.

'channel' or 'canal'. Thus it is probable that here we have a reference to the mythological river of the underworld.[17]

The world of the grave is taken up in a particular way in Yahweh's first speech in 38:16–18. First of all, the grave is seen in cosmic dimensions, already suggested in chapter 26. It is connected with 'the springs of the sea' (v. 16), the primeval ocean, which is also *Šelaḥ*, the river of death, and an echo of 'the sources of the rivers' in 28:11. In Canaanite myth, El's abode is at 'the confluence of the rivers' (*mbk.nhrm*). This powerfully underlines the fact that only God himself understands the world of the dead, rooted as it is in creation itself. Leaving aside verse 17 for consideration in the next cluster of images, I would suggest that 'the vast expanses of the earth' are not the visible globe but the realms of the underworld. This is a fitting culmination of the earlier images of the netherworld. It is a wasteland of mystery and not the confined space where the dead lie in eternal slumber as Job had imagined in chapter 3. The verb 'comprehend' is very significant. This is the power by which God smote Rahab in 26:12 and it is regularly used in the Wisdom literature of God creating the world. Thus God is asking Job much more than if he 'understands' the world of death. He is challenging him to assume the powers of the Creator, and thus anticipating the challenge of 40:13 to humble the proud by binding them in the netherworld, a fact of crucial significance in interpreting the Behemoth passage. The thrust of the passage is that death, like the stars, sea, plants, weather and animals, is part of the cosmic design partially adumbrated in chapter 28. This placing of the netherworld firmly in the grand cosmic design contains hints of the solution to the problem.

The powers of darkness

So far we have attempted to establish that the basic image of death in the book is that of the womb and that a further level is the world of the grave, the 'geography' and 'cosmology' of the netherworld. Behind these lies a third area of imagery where death is given a more personal and even overtly mythological emphasis. This is suggested

[17] Tsevat (1954: 41–49) argues that it is in fact the name of a god, attested in the name of the patriarch Methuselah, which he explains as 'man of Salah'. His linguistic evidence comes from the royal archives of Mari where names occur with the element 'man of . . .' plus a divine name. Tsevat further argues, disagreeing with Dhorme, that the word does not mean 'channel' (i.e. vertical shaft leading from the grave to the underworld), but 'ocean currents' (i.e. the primeval ocean).

by a number of passages where the netherworld appears to be filled with shadowy and menacing figures which embody its darkness and mystery.

The imagery of shadows and darkness is introduced in 3:4ff. where a veritable cataract of pictures create a cumulative sense of menace. The nouns ḥōšeḵ ('darkness') and 'opēl ('gloom') are not mere rhetoric but sinister and shadowy presences. Ḥōšeḵ is used both of the primeval darkness in Genesis 1:2 and of the darkness over Egypt in Exodus 10:21–22. It is also used in an eschatological sense of the Day of the Lord in Amos 5:18 and 20 and in Zephaniah 1:15.

Also, for the first time, the word ṣalmāweṯ occurs (v. 5). Traditionally translated 'shadow of death', it is best known from its use in Psalm 23:4, 'the valley of the shadow of death'. Its use here in 3:5 suggests that the poet sees it as one of the powers of darkness that Job is summoning.[18] It would be possible to render the word 'shadow of Mot' to bring out the mythological nuances of the word.[19] However that may be, the powers of darkness have been presented in a sinister and personalized manner. What emerges is a cry for an 'uncreating act' which will return the universe to primordial chaos; an altogether more sinister picture than the deep peace of the grave.

The text returns to these images of sinister presences in chapter 10:20–22 where Job plumbs the depths of depression. Again the sinister 'Darkness and the shadow of death' (RSV) occur, and here they form a pair, the presiding genii of Sheol. Moreover, the idea of 'uncreation' continues, for Sheol is not only a 'place of no return' ruled by darkness and 'Mot's shadow' but identical with the primeval chaos before creation: 'land . . . of disorder' (v. 22 RSV). So there is no escape that way; Sheol is no resting place but a deep pit haunted by menacing presences.

The image probably recurs in 12:22:

'He reveals the deep things of darkness
and brings deep shadows into the light.'

[18] Many scholars argue that the word should be vocalized as ṣalmûṯ ('darkness'), deriving it from a Semitic root ṣlm ('to be dark, black'). But the traditional understanding must be early because the LXX renders it as skia thanatou.
[19] This may receive confirmation from the third part of the verse. The phrase kimᵉrîrê yôm is often emended to kamᵉrîr, thus 'blackness of day'. Early Jewish commentators such as Rashi and Ibn Ezra link it with Deuteronomy 32:24 which refers to plague, pestilence and demonic spirits. They further link it with Psalm 91:6 and see there a reference to noontide demons.

Both Pope[20] and Dhorme[21] regard this verse as misplaced in a catalogue of earthly people and events. However, Habel sees it as 'an ironic allusion to Zophar's assertion that the mysteries of God's wisdom are "deeper than Sheol"'.[22] There is an almost identical statement in Daniel 2:22, and indeed the underlying thought of both passages may be similar. That passage is expounding the belief that behind earthly rulers and events there are spiritual powers and conflicts that shape the destinies of rulers and the outcome of events. This would also make good sense here, but there is an additional layer of meaning, for this is one of the places where Job glimpses the reality of the situation. In an encapsulated form it points to chapter 26 with its powerful picture of Sheol naked before God and to chapter 38 with its declaration of Yahweh's control over the underworld and the primeval darkness. Moreover, the association here of the earthly and supernatural reminds us of the prose tale and the heavenly orchestration of earthly events.

In chapter 24 the images of darkness and shadow occur in a passage reminiscent of Proverbs 7:27 already cited as identifying the house of the adulteress as the gateway to Sheol. So here in verses 13ff. we have the idea of the murderer and adulterer not just in league with darkness in the abstract sense of evil, but with Sheol itself. This idea also occurs in Isaiah 28:15 where Ephraim is condemned for making a covenant with Mot and Sheol. This would gain additional import if, as I have already suggested, the city of verse 12 is Sheol itself. At this point we must face an exegetical issue of some importance. Chapter 24:1–17 paints a vivid picture of human misery and wickedness which is Job's bitter riposte to the friends' platitudes on the triumphs of the righteous (e.g. Eliphaz in 5:19ff.; Bildad in 8:16ff.; and Zophar in 11:5ff.) as well as to their assertions that the wicked will be destroyed. Yet in verses 18ff. Job appears to contradict this and speaks of the ultimate punishment of the wicked. What we must keep in mind is the increasingly choric nature of the speeches in this part of the book as the poetic dialogue draws to a close, and I have already argued in more detail in chapter 3 that these speeches, especially chapters 26 – 31, are a kind of assessment of, and commentary on, various viewpoints and images, and thus need not be rearranged. Thus here Job may simply be presenting a balance sheet for and

---

[20] Pope 1973: 94.
[21] Dhorme 1967: 178–179.
[22] Habel 1985: 221–222.

against God's justice.[23] In any case, Job has never disputed that God will judge the wicked, what he has maintained is that he is not of the wicked. This is the thrust of verse 25:

> 'If this is not so, who can prove me false
> and reduce my words to nothing?'

That said, verses 13ff. can be seen as another example of the imagery of hostile shadowy powers. Here the wicked make friends with the demons of darkness and death (v. 17). The theme of 'uncreation' is again emphasized.

Yahweh's speech returns to this image in 38:17:

> 'Have the gates of death been shown to you?
> Have you seen the gates[24] of the shadow of death?'

Since this particular image of the 'shadow of Mot' has been especially associated with the sinister presences of darkness, the verse is of some importance in the final solution of the book. Yahweh is here establishing that not only does he control the realm of the underworld, as in verse 18, but that he rules the powers and presences of that realm.

The Job poet has explored many images of death and the underworld, and these have contributed to the atmosphere of blackness and desolation. However, we have still to see if he is to go further and face the embodiment of death itself. This will be explored in the next chapter.

---

[23] Andersen (1976: 213–214) discusses this question.

[24] Some emend the second *ša'ªrê* ('gates') to *šo'ªrê* ('gatekeepers'); this is the LXX reading. This is not intrinsically impossible (cp. Sin and Death at the gates of hell in John Milton's *Paradise Lost*, book 2), but is hardly necessary.

Chapter Six

Yahweh, Mot and Behemoth

The title of this chapter reminds us that we are wrestling with the problem of the relationship of God and death. We have seen already that behind the basic images of the womb and the netherworld is the imagery of darkness and shadow where the physical and the supernatural merge into each other. This has prepared the way for the fourth and most fundamental image of death, found in those passages where God appears as tormentor and is described in terms reminiscent of an underworld demon. There are two further issues to be addressed; namely, is there a figure, like the Canaanite Mot, god of death, who is not simply a rhetorical figure but a real actor in the drama, and if so, how does it relate to the mysterious figure of Behemoth?

God as tormentor

The starting point for our investigation is 3:20:

> 'Why is light given to those in misery,
> and life to the bitter of soul?'

This is amplified in 3:23:

> 'Why is life given to a man
> whose way is hidden,
> whom God has hedged in?'[1]

It is important here to keep firmly in mind the basic image of the heavenly court that is behind the action of the entire book. Job and his friends do not know of the events in heaven in chapters 1 and 2 and

---

[1] The translations usually gloss over the starkness of 3:20 by using the passive *yutan*, rather than following the MT *yitēn* ('he gives') which attributes the calamities directly to God.

thus they attribute what is happening directly to God. So it is that death and related powers appear to take on a sinister life of their own. On one level, these images can be seen as rhetorical devices showing the power of death, but behind the rhetoric and giving it extra depth stands the 'mythological' figure.

In particular there follows a series of images where God is seen as a warrior, especially an archer, shooting his arrows at Job. We may cite, for example, 6:4: 'The arrows of the Almighty are in me'; and 7:20: 'Why have you made me your target?' This image, however, probably occurs first in 5:7 in Eliphaz's opening speech: 'Yet man is born to trouble as surely as the sparks fly upwards'. The beautifully picturesque and expressive 'as the sparks fly upwards' obscures the fact that the Hebrew reads 'as the sons of Resheph fly upwards'. Is this then a reference to the god of plague and pestilence widely wor- shipped and feared throughout the Ancient Near East? Resheph is often spoken of in terms of archery. In the fragmentary Ugaritic tablet 1001:3 he is described as *b l h z ršp* ('Resheph, lord of the arrow'). In *KTU* the phrase '(May) B' a lu stop the arrows of Resheph' occurs. In Psalm 91:5–6, plague (*deber*) is paralleled by 'the arrow that flies by day', probably a veiled reference to Resheph. Thus Job here sees God as a vengeful malevolent deity like Resheph, who sends not only calamities but 'terrors' (*bi'ûtê*) (6:4), anticipating 'the king of terrors' in 18:14.

The most recent study of this god is the work of William J. Fulco,[2] which conveniently assembles a mass of scattered references and much material not readily accessible elsewhere. Fulco demonstrates the extensive occurrence of the god's name in Egyptian iconography (about fifty stelae, ostraca, papyri, amulets and scarabs relate directly to him). As noted, his name is found in the Ugaritic tablets as well as in Phoenician and Aramaic inscriptions, and is apparently contained in a proper name from Ebla (*eb-du-d Rs-ap*), where apparently one of the city gates was called 'the gate of Rasap'. He is generally identified with Nergal, the Mesopotamian god of pestilence, who sends up plagues and destruction from the netherworld. Thus the name would be recognized by the audience and its resonances appreciated.

Indeed, in context, the reference to Resheph becomes a tantaliz- ingly elusive clue to the reality of what is happening; the grim under- world deity is indeed attacking Job, but God is in ultimate control. Chapter 5:19 reads:

[2] Fulco 1976.

'From six calamities he will rescue you;
in seven no harm will befall you.'

It may well be that the audience would remember the Canaanite story
of Keret's misfortunes and his subsequent happiness. In *CML* 14 a
series of devastating blows befalls Keret and in rapid succession he
loses seven wives (col. i). The fifth of these is carried off by Resheph
(*yitsp ršp*), who also occurs as 'Prince Resheph' in *CML* 15 where
Baal stands up in the divine court and asks El now to bless Keret (col.
ii, l. 6). Resheph is under the control of El and is allowed to carry out
his deadly work. Thus at a deep level of poetic imagery we can sense
the presence of a power associated with pestilence and death.[3]

Once this atmosphere of dread and terror and the presence of sinister, shadowy figures is recognized, the depths and resonances of the
text become apparent and the patterns of imagery become clearer. In
7:12ff. Job speaks of how, at the subconscious level of dreams and
visions, he is terrified. The grim parody of Psalm 8 which follows sees
God as a Resheph-like figure with Job as his target (v. 20).[4]

It seems reasonable, therefore, to find embedded in this imagery a
reference to the activities of Resheph. The 'personality' of this god
remains unclear in spite of copious textual and iconographic references, probably because we have no primary texts about him, unlike
Baal, Yam and Mot. Nevertheless enough has been said to suggest
that such an allusion as that in 5:17 would be recognized.

The following chapters contain many images of God as the violent
tormentor carrying on a Resheph-like pursuit and harassment of his
helpless victim (see especially 9:17–24). Job 10:16, with its reference
to God stalking Job like a lion, is associated with God displaying his
awesome power against Job. The verb *pl'* used here is more often
employed about the 'mighty acts' of God in rescuing his people (e.g.
Exod. 3:20 and Ps. 139:14). For Job these mighty acts are now hostile
and he is being attacked by armies: 'your forces come against me wave
upon wave' (10:17).

---

[3] There may be a further reference to this power in 5:21: 'You will be protected from
the lash of the tongue.' This may allude to the tongue of Mot which reaches to the stars
(*CML* 5, col. ii) and may also anticipate the ravenous appetite of Mot in 18:13.

[4] Andersen (1976: 137–138) translates v. 15a: 'and selected Strangler my neck, Death
my bones'. The trouble is that the verb is feminine, which suggests *nepeš* ('my soul' or
simply 'I') as the subject. The allusion would still be there, with some such translation as
'I have to choose the Strangler.' Michel (1987: 155) takes this line and translates 'So my
soul might choose the Strangler.' The basic problem is to find textual evidence for Mot
being a Strangler. Andersen cites iconography but without precise references.

Job's next speech in chapters 12 – 14 marks the end of speeches and contains much on death, but the particular passage relevant for this part of the study is the famous crux in 13:15a: *hēn yiqtᵉlēnî lō' 'ᵃyahēl*. The splendid AV rendering, 'Though he slay me, yet I will trust in him', is based on the Qere reading which substitutes *lû'* for *lō'*, and is followed by the NIV: 'Though he slay me, yet will I hope in him', although that version draws attention in a footnote to the MT reading: 'He will surely slay me; I have no hope.' Indeed this phrase encapsulates many of the problems of the book of Job. Here in a few words is concentrated the ambiguous relationship of Yahweh and Mot, yet another example of the difficulties of translation which confront the commentator on the book. Here also the work of Dahood and his followers is seen at its most controversial.[5]

A point which must be made is that, whether we accept the Ketiv or Qere reading, blame is laid squarely at God's door and what is in dispute is Job's reaction to that fact. The mystery of the apparent violence and aggression of God is underlined in verses 20ff. with a renewed reference to God's terrors, and verse 27 with its reference to the prison house recalls Sheol with its confinement and misery.

The next cycle of speeches takes up many of the images of death and terror but at a more intense and frightening level. A violent, sinister figure whom Job identifies with God becomes more and more evident. Eliphaz's speech in 15:17ff. once again mentions visions, and this time they are no vague spirits or mere metaphors of death, but horrifying presences which torment the living. Clines makes this point in relation to verse 21: 'The "terrors" (*pᵉḥāḏîm*) are not simply the plural of the abstract noun "terror", but the personified spirits of vengeance, denizens of the underworld, whom we meet at 18:14 ruled over by "the king of terrors".'[6] Eliphaz's vision of the spirit in 4:14 was heralded by a *pahaḏ* and this gives further weight to Clines' argument. Moreover the use of the word 'darkness' (*ḥōšek*) recalls chapter 3 with its evocation of the sinister powers of the netherworld. In verse

---

[5] Michel (1987: 297) is the most effective exponent of the Dahoodian position. He translates 13:15a: 'If the Victor slays me I must be silent.' Michel's argument begins with the LXX rendering, which reveals that the subject *ho dunastes* has been added Michel argues further 'with the recognition of the Ugaritic root *l'y* "to prevail, be strong" and the divine appellative *'lyn b'l* "the Victor Baal", it becomes possible to suspect the Hebrew *l'* in a number of texts to be the divine appellative *le'*, "the mighty one, victor".' He also says that Dahood has found the root *l'y* ('to be powerful') in the Ebla tablets. The problem in all this is to try to discern a link between the *l'* of the MT of Job 13:15 and the rool *l'h* as it would be in Hebrew.

[6] Clines 1989: 357.

30, the consuming flame (*šalhāḇeṯ*) is probably no ordinary fire but a devouring judgment (the word is used of the fires of love in Song of Songs 8:6). In chapter 16:9ff. this violence is attributed directly to God by Job; and God is both Resheph the archer and Mot the mauler. The violence of the verbs in verse 12 is well brought out in Habel's translation:

> 'I was at ease but he smashed and smashed me;
> Seized my neck, then bashed and bashed me.'[7]

The verb *pārar* is also used of Yahweh smiting the sea in Psalm 74:13 and conquering the earth in Isaiah 24:19. Job is here turning the arguments of Eliphaz on their head, and by alleging that this frightening violence is from and not against God he underlines his plea for an advocate in heaven (v. 19). God here is a deadly adversary, but the audience, remembering the scene in the heavenly court, realize that the dark powers who attack Job are permitted to do so by God who is protecting him with the very hand that smites him.

All these images are focused in a vivid passage in Bildad's speech in chapter 18 as part of his discourse on the fate of the wicked. Bildad uses these powerful images in ignorance of the full implications of what he is saying. In his opening words in verse 4 he scornfully demands 'is the earth to be abandoned for your sake? Or must the rocks be moved from their place?' These words recall 9:4ff., where in a passage of immense grandeur, God's awesome power to remove mountains and shake the earth is evoked. Moreover, in the 'Song of the Sea' in Exodus 15 and in the 'Song of Deborah' in Judges 5 God does exactly these things on behalf of his people.

Then Bildad proceeds to give a chilling catalogue of the punishments awaiting the wicked man caught in a trap and noose of his own devising. But in 18:11ff. the picture grows darker as the demons of the netherworld and their grisly lord wait to seize him. There are three particular articles by Sarna,[8] Burns[9] and Wyatt[10] which deal with this passage in detail and to which I shall refer in the following comments.

---

[7] Habel 1985: 263. He says 'The pilpel forms *yᵉparpᵉreni* and *yᵉpaspᵉseni* exhibit a striking assonance and a forceful intensity.'

[8] Sarna 1963: 315–318.

[9] Burns 1987: 362–364.

[10] Wyatt 1990: 207–216.

The first word which calls for attention is 'terrors' (*ballāhôṯ*), alone in verse 11 and in the phrase 'king of terrors' (v. 14). It is also significantly paralleled with 'shadow of death' in 24:17. It occurs in 27:20 in a powerful passage reminiscent of this one: 'Terrors overtake him like a flood'; and again in 30:15 of God's violent attacks on Job: 'Terrors overwhelm me.' The singular form occurs in Isaiah 17:14 of the 'sudden terror' mentioned in the oracle against Damascus. In Psalm 73:19 it is used of the 'terrors' which sweep away the ungodly; in Ezekiel 26:21 (also 27:36 and 28:19) it is used of the terrible end of the Prince of Tyre, once again with 'mythological' connotations because it is not merely the earthly ruler but the more sinister power behind him.

Next we are given a picture of the insatiable appetite of this underworld deity. Roeb can be seen as an epithet of Mot, 'the ravenous one'. This ravening appetite of Mot is attested in *CML* 5 (col. i, ll. 15ff.); in lines 18–19 he boasts of his appetite for clay: 'if it is in very truth my desire to consume clay'. 'Clay' there is metonymy for human bodies, which exactly parallels what the ravenous one is said to do there.[11]

Let us look now at the interesting phrase *beḵôr mawet* (v. 13) which is often taken as 'the first born of death', that is 'the son of Mot', who was probably the grim herald ushering souls into the netherworld.[12] Burns, in the article already cited, supports this view and argues that 'death's first born' can be identified more clearly from Mesopotamian than from Canaanite sources. Thus he identifies 'the first born' as Navitar who drags the wicked before Nergal that grim lord of the underworld. This god of plague and pestilence, the *sukallu irsiti* (the 'Vizier of the underworld') is also described as *ilitti dereškigal* ('offspring of Ereshkigal'), who was the queen of the underworld.

[11] A more problematic link may exist between v. 13 and *CML* 5, col. i, ll. 19–20. The problem centres around *baddê* ('limbs'). Some want to emend to *bidway* ('by a disease'). Sarna, however, draws attention to the Ugaritic text cited above: '*pimt bkl (a) t ydy ilhm*' ('then in truth by the handfuls I must eat [it]'). Gordon (1965: 47) points out that the noun *yād* ('hand') has been fossilized in the frequent combination *bd* ('in, from the hand(s)'). Thus it is possible that *baddê* could mean 'with two hands' and that *baddiu* could mean 'with his two hands'. This would yield excellent sense for v. 13 without the need for emendation and could be rendered: 'The first born of Mot [or first born Mot] will devour his skin with two hands (i.e. tearing off handfuls to eat); yes devour [him] with his two hands.' This may be given some support in one of the El Amarna letters where the Akkadian *ina qâtisu* ('in his hands') is glossed by the Canaanite *ba-di-u*.

[12] This is the view of Dhorme (1967: 265) who cites the Akkadian *bukru* and identifies him with the plague god Namtaru.

However, Wyatt, in his article, points out that Burns has failed to exhaust the possible allusions in the Ugaritic texts. He further argues that it is the plague god Resheph who is identified with Nergal, the Babylonian equivalent of Mot. Resheph is nowhere called Mot's son. More important is his suggestion that *mawet* and $b^e \underline{k} \hat{o}r$ are in apposition to each other and mean not 'death's first born' but 'first born death' (i.e. Mot himself, 'the king of terrors'). Pope[13] points out that $b^e \underline{k} \hat{o}r$ is used as a royal title in Psalm 89:27: 'And I will make him the first-born, the highest of the kings of the earth' (RSV).

The whole thrust of the imagery of the passage is considerably reinforced if the virtually meaningless $mibb^e l\hat{\imath} - l\hat{o}$ (lit. 'things of what are not his') of verse 15 is read with Dahood[14] as *mabbel* ('fire', cognate with Akkadian *nablu* and Ugaritic *nblt*). In Numbers 16:31–35 fire from the netherworld destroys Korah, Dathan and Abiram and this is seen as a direct judgment of Yahweh. The translation 'Fire resides in his tent' would well convey the idea of divine judgment devouring in its intensity. Bildad then presses remorselessly on in verse 16 with what is probably a savagely ironical evoking of Job's great image of the tree in chapter 14. There it was used with wistful longing, here with savage vindictiveness. Indeed, Bildad throws off all pretence in verse 21 by describing Job as an 'evil man'.

Plainly Bildad's speech is of crucial importance in the developing imagery and theology of the book and it well illustrates the ambivalence of the poetic technique. It can be read on one level as hyperbole; poetic rhetoric about the terrors of disease and death. However, the whole movement of the book suggests a more personal and mythological meaning as well. What is plain is that Bildad has totally misread the situation. God has indeed unleashed the powers of death on Job, but as a means of proving in the face of all these attacks that his servant is a man of integrity.

Job responds to this in the passage leading up to the famous crux about the *gô'ēl* in 19:25 which I have already discussed (see pp. 43–52). The context of that passage is a series of images where the Resheph-like character of God is emphasized. He is the hunter and besieger; the siege imagery carrying on from chapter 16. He blocks Job's way (19:8), recalling the 'hedging up' of 3:23. He uproots hope (19:10) 'like a tree', again recalling the image of the tree and mortal life in chapter 14.

[13] Pope 1973: 135.
[14] Dahood 1957: esp. 312–314.

As the book approaches its second half, the images of this terrifying and aggressive deity proliferate. Zophar's words in 20:24 develop the picture of the archer god:

> 'Though he flees from an iron weapon,
> a bronze-tipped arrow pierces him.'

Here the arrows are linked with the terrors of darkness and consuming fire. Job 30:11ff. provides a further cluster of images which are relevant for this part of the study, but some background from chapter 29 will help to put this in sharper focus. In that chapter Job reviews his past life as lived under the blessing of El, the antithesis of the grim world of Mot. This former life is characterized in a vivid metaphor in verse 6:

> 'when my path was drenched with cream
> and the rock poured out for me streams of olive oil.'

This recalls the blessings of the promised land in Deuteronomy 32:13:

> 'He nourished him with honey from the rock,
> and with oil from the flinty crag',

and the blessing of Asher in 33:24: 'and let him bathe his feet in oil'.

These were to be the physical manifestations of the blessings of God. Similarly, the Canaanite story speaks of the world where Mot has been destroyed as:

> the heavens rained oil,
> the ravines ran with honey.[15]

By contrast, in chapter 30, Job finds himself harassed by 'a base and nameless brood' (v. 8) and once again siege imagery is used.

The language here is strikingly similar to some of the lament psalms, for example, Psalm 44:17:

> All this happened to us,
> though we had not forgotten you
> or been false to your covenant.

---

[15] *CML* 6, col. iii, ll. 12–13.

It is possible that the enemies here (as often in the Psalter) are not mere human enemies but the evil powers haunting Job. These 'terrors' (*ballāhôt*) described in verse 15a have already appeared in chapter 18 as emissaries of Mot. This confusion of God and Mot is underlined in 30:21 where God is described as *'akzār* ('the cruel one'), a word also used of Leviathan in 41:2 (Eng. 41:10). Job's pessimism is embodied in verse 26:

> 'Yet when I hoped for good, evil came;
> when I looked for light, then came darkness.'

It is probable that 'good' and 'light' and 'evil' and 'darkness' are not abstractions but symbols of God and his adversary.

How the images relate to each other

Before turning to the crucial question of the implications of this fourth area of imagery for Yahweh's speeches, I want to say something of how these four areas (womb, grave, darkness and shadows and God as tormentor) relate to each other.

On the poetic level these images balance and help to define each other. Images suggesting the confinement and deep peace of the womb, as in chapter 3, are balanced by those evoking vast spaces and endless horizons, as in chapter 38:17–18. The hostile presences filling that land vividly dramatize the fear and pain of death, while the bleak nihilism of chapter 14, with its cold clarity, encapsulates a mood of melancholy. In other words, the differing, often simultaneous emotions with which the fact and reality of death are confronted are vividly portrayed. The poet is trying to make the audience not only think about death but feel its power and suffer with Job as he is driven almost beyond endurance.

On the theological level, the combination and cumulative power of these images is far more effective than a series of systematic statements. To attempt in philosophical propositions to state that God made everything including death, that death is attacking Job, and that God has unleashed the power of death on Job is to show the inadequacy of such statements, as well as the impossibility of avoiding metaphor, especially personification. My argument is that personification is necessary because it corresponds to a profound reality. The reality is that the universe is not a mechanical system as envisaged by a rationalistic deism (which, incidentally, is as metaphorical a view as any other) but a vast series of complex relationships involving not only God but other powers. It is, in other words, the metaphor of the heavenly court that brilliantly embodies this idea.

Moreover, such images of power as those employed by the Job poet force the hearers or readers to re-examine their beliefs. It is one thing to theorize about faith and the challenge posed to it by death, it is another thing to experience that dark power in all its ferocity.[16] It is not that the experience will necessarily require a radically different systematic and propositional formulation but that the content of that formulation will be immeasurably enriched. That is why the faith of chapter 42 is incalculably deeper than that of chapters 1 and 2.

The argument has already been advanced that each of the first three levels of imagery is taken up and given definitive comment in Yahweh's first speech. The womb becomes the cosmic womb in 38:8; the land of the dead is seen as 'the wide expanses of the underworld' (my trans.) in 38:18, the land of shadows likewise in 38:17. Nevertheless, the cluster of images just discussed, relating to the hostile presence of Mot, god of death, does not appear to be addressed in this speech at all. This provides a convenient introduction to the next major part of this study.

The figure of Behemoth

There is a double question involved here. The first is, can the Resheph/Mot figure be discerned in the speeches of Yahweh? The second is, what is the relationship, if any, between this figure and Behemoth (40:15–24)? It has already been argued that it is possible (and indeed probable in the light of the Canaanite stories and motifs) that the vivid descriptions of the terrors of death are not simply metaphors but references to Mot and related deities such as Resheph. Wakeman[17] indeed has argued that just as Leviathan is equivalent to Yam so Behemoth is equivalent to Mot. She refers to *CML* 3D (l. 40): *mdd.ilm. ar(s)* ('Arsh the darling of the gods') and to *CML* 6 (col. vi,

---

[16] Cp. the academic treatment of suffering (helpful and cogent as it is) in C. S. Lewis, *The Problem of Pain* with the searing honesty of *A Grief Observed* written after the death of his wife. Although the latter does not mention Job, its picture of desolation and dismay at the apparent cruelty of God is a powerful evocation of the same kind of atmosphere.

[17] Wakeman 1973: 113–117. This study has been rather neglected and often assumed to be superseded by Day's work (see next note). However, although Day's study is more detailed, Wakeman often shows greater sensitivity to the nuances of the text and a more integrated approach to the material.

l. 50): *bym. arš. wtnn.* ('In the sea are Arsh and the dragon'). 'Arsh' she identifies with Mot (*'ereṣ*) and, ultimately, with Behemoth.[18] Gibson argues that Wakeman's theory is an attractive one and that 'there is a whole area here which merits fuller investigation'.[19] It is to such an investigation I now turn.

Before examining the Behemoth passage in detail, it will be necessary to say something about the naturalistic interpretation which sees Behemoth and Leviathan as the hippopotamus and the crocodile (or various alternatives such as the buffalo and the whale). This is a widespread view, also reflected in the footnotes of many of the translations. Generally speaking, older commentators such as Driver-Gray and Dhorme, and, in more recent times, Andersen, do not argue in detail for the naturalistic interpretation but assume it and use that assumption as a basis for their arguments. However, Gordis,[20] in a lengthy excursus argues powerfully for this interpretation and it will be necessary to close with the issues he raises. What is said here will also be valid for the interpretation of Leviathan, and the arguments will be assumed in the later discussion. Gordis has five main arguments and I shall deal with each of these in turn.

First, Gordis argues that the first speech of the Lord deals with 'flesh and blood animals' and that the second 'heightens the impact of God's argument'. However, this would make the second speech rather tedious and repetitive and Job's reaction to it difficult to explain. This has been expressed cynically but none the less effectively by George Bernard Shaw who insists that God, when challenged about his justice and providence, really needs to do better than retort: 'You can't make a hippopotamus can you?' A more significant point is that Gordis forges a radical disjunction between the natural and supernatural worlds. Behemoth and Leviathan belong to both. It is not that they *are* the hippopotamus and the crocodile, but that these beasts in their size, ferocity and untameable nature are evidence of that dark power rooted in the universe itself which shadows all life.

Secondly, Gordis argues that 'Hyperbole, including the possible utilisation of traits from mythology', is normal poetic technique especially in Job. This is true, but it does not follow that hyperbole is mere poetic flourish. The purpose of imagery, as already discussed,

---

[18] Day rejects Wakeman's identification on three grounds: *ars* is feminine whereas *arš* is masculine; there is the discrepancy of *š* for *s*; also Arsh is plainly a marine monster.

[19] Gibson 1988.

[20] Gordis 1965: 569–572.

is to help understanding and to attempt to express what cannot otherwise be expressed. All imagery about the divine must be in terms of analogies drawn from the natural world.

Thirdly, Behemoth, he argues, is not 'horrendous and predatory', and Leviathan may be taken captive (vv. 25ff.) and eaten by mortals (vv. 30–31). However, in the case of Leviathan, the rhetorical questions have the opposite effect from what Gordis suggests and rather underline the sheer impossibility of doing these things. Moreover, the colossal strength of Behemoth is emphasized in 40:16–17; he is seen as a creature assailable only by the Creator (40:19); and the impossibility of his capture is emphasized (40:24). However, Gordis's arguments lay insufficient weight on the cumulative power of imagery such as that of chapter 18 which now reaches its climax.

Fourthly, he argues that the poet is describing 'present creatures' rather than 'cosmic events in the past, such as are the subject matter of the Babylonian and Ugaritic epics of creation'. This assumes what has to be proved and takes insufficient account of many passages (e.g. chs. 9, 26 and 38) all of which show that creation is not simply a primeval event but a continuing process. In any case, Gordis, like all other commentators, finds it impossible to argue that the reference to Leviathan in 3:8 is other than mythological. Once this is conceded, there is no *a priori* reason for rejecting a mythological interpretation here.

Gordis's fifth argument is in many ways the crucial one: that primeval monsters would be out of place in a universe governed by 'the exalted monotheism' which rejects the reality of these creatures. The issue is central to this whole study and a word of reminder on the general approach is necessary at this point. The whole burden of my argument has been the tension between the incomparability of Yahweh and the existence of other gods whose power is real and menacing, a tension captured in the basic image of the heavenly court. What is even more striking is the way this tension is implicit throughout the Old Testament even in such sober passages and the *Shema* in Deuteronomy 4:4. This has been cogently argued by Gibson: 'The desire to contrast Yahweh with other Gods so that he may be seen incomparably superior to them is endemic to Old Testament religious language in all its stages.'[21]

Thus I shall regard Behemoth and Leviathan, while containing elements drawn from physical characteristics and habits of animals, as

[21] J. C. L. Gibson, 'Language about God in the Old Testament' (unpublished lecture given to the Traditional Cosmological Society).

embodiments of the powers of death and evil. I shall begin with a translation of the Behemoth passage (40:15-24).

Translation

[15]Look now[a] at Behemoth whom[b] I made; there he is in front of you[c]; he eats grass as cattle do.

[16]Look at him: his strength is in his loins and his potency[d] in the muscles of his belly.

[17]He is able to stiffen his tail like a cedar, the sinews of his thighs are knotted together.

[18]His bones are tubes of bronze, his limbs like bars of iron.

[19]He is first of the works of God, even his Maker has to bring his sword against him.[e]

[20]For the mountains bring him their tribute[f] and so do all the living things of the steppe[g] who sport over there.[h]

[21]Under the lotus plants he lies, in the hidden place[i] of reed and swamp.

[22]The lotus plants conceal him in their shadow, the poplars of the stream surround him.

[23]When river swells violently he is not alarmed; he is confident even when Jordan surges against his mouth.[j]

[24]Is there anyone who can capture him by his eyes[k] or pierce his nose with hooks?

Notes on the translation

[a]'Look now' is an attempt to bring out the force of *hinnēh*, on which I shall comment later (pp. 130-131).

[b]'Whom' for *'ašer* indicates a personalized meaning.

[c]'There he is in front of you' is a paraphrase of *'immāḵ*, and an attempt to indicate that what is happening here is in some way analagous to prophetic vision.

[d]The translation 'potency' is an attempt to capture the sexual innuendo that many commentators have discerned here with its implications of Behemoth glorying in his creative potential.

[e]This line is notoriously difficult. Dhorme (1967: 621) reads it as *nogeš haḇeraw* and translates it 'He who was created a tyrant to his companions'. However, the MT can yield good sense and I shall discuss its possible significance.

[f]This takes *bûl* as *yeḇûl* ('produce', 'tribute'), and I shall refer later to some parallels in the Ugaritic texts; note also Akkadian *biltu* ('tribute'). Pope (1973: 325-326) follows Tur-Sinai and sees *bûl harîm*

as equivalent to Akkadian *būl-ṣēri* ('beast of the steppe'); he further reads *yiśᵉ'û* ('they lift up, bring') as *yišlāyû* ('they are at ease'), and translates the phrase 'the beasts of the steppe relax'. This, however, involves an unnecessary emendation of the MT.

ᵍThe rendering of *haśśadeh* as 'steppe' is of some importance in the interpretation offered below.

ʰThe rather periphrastic 'over there' for *šām* is to indicate the associations of the word with the netherworld.

ⁱSimilarly *sēter* ('the hidden place') is frequently a synonym for Sheol, as abundantly demonstrated by Tromp.

ʲ'River' and 'Jordan' suggest personalized entities.

ᵏ'By his eyes': Habel (1985: 553–554) suggests transferring *'el pîhû* to verse 24 and taking the repointed *'l* as subject (i.e. 'El takes him by the mouth with rings and pierces his nose with hooks'). I have preferred the MT because the Job poet characteristically is implicit rather than explicit.

Context

Consideration must now be given to the context of the passage. Yahweh, in chapters 38 and 39, had conducted Job on a tour of the marvels of the universe, taking up and focusing all the scattered hints in key passages such as chapters 9, 26 and 28. Chapter 38 has not been merely poetry about the universe but rather on unfolding of the mysteries inherent in creation itself. Chapter 39 especially deals with untamed nature and shows not so much that animals are evil, but that animal life is shot through with a savagery which mirrors ultimate cosmic evil.

The immediate context is Yahweh's challenge to Job in chapter 40:1–14. The first four verses use law-court imagery and Job is challenged to assume the attributes of God. The specific way Job would demonstrate that power would be to command the underworld and more exactly dispatch the wicked there. The word *ṭāmûn* ('hidden place') in verse 13 is probably an allusion to Job's use of the word in 3:21, and the reference to bringing them together in the grave is possibly also an allusion to Job's picture of the whole of humankind united in Sheol. God is challenging Job to behave as ruler of the universe, because if he does, he has Behemoth and Leviathan to contend with. Thus it is their role in the ultimate significance of the created order that is now addressed.

Thus when in verse 15 the phrase *hinnēh-nā' bᵉhēmôt* occurs we can see immediately that whoever or whatever this creature is, it is linked in some way with the netherworld. Moreover, *hinnēh*, not infrequently, as in the Elijah stories,[22] introduces a new and decisive stage of the action which reflects on what has happened and points to the next stage. So Behemoth's appearance here heralds the final stage of the action.

Turning now to structure, we can find some interesting pointers in the same direction. The passage can be divided into four useful parts:

1. *The challenge* (v. 15): There is no rhetorical question, unlike chapters 38 and 39. The use of the word *hinnēh* connects Behemoth with the world of the dead and leads us to expect further revelations about that world.

2. *The creature's appearance* (vv. 16–19): This builds up the suspense and excitement implicit in the challenge. The fact that there has been little in the way of description of the animals in chapter 39 strengthens the impression that here we are on a different level of meaning.

3. *His habitat* (vv. 20–22): Here numerous details which will be examined in the exegesis build up a picture of Behemoth's true identity.

4. *His invincibility* (vv. 23–24): This sums up the Behemoth passage and provides a natural transition to the Leviathan passage.

Plainly the structure has been crafted carefully to connect Behemoth both with the world of the dead and that of Leviathan. We must now face the crucial question: is Behemoth the same as Mot, god of death; is he the 'king of terrors' presiding over the netherworld?

Before turning to more detailed exegesis of the passage, I want to examine some comparative evidence, especially the Baal/Mot battle known to us from the Ugaritic texts. But some more fragmentary evidence needs to be looked at first. The myth of a fierce bovine creature killed, or at least subdued by a god, appears to have been widespread throughout the Ancient Near East. Pope, in a long and interesting discussion,[23] suggests a connection with the Sumero-Akkadian story of the 'bull of heaven' killed by Gilgamesh and Enkidu in the *Epic of Gilgamesh*. In Egyptian mythology there is the battle of Seth and Horus to which I shall return. More important for this study are the Canaanite versions of the story which we can glimpse only partially because of the broken and fragmentary nature of the tablets.

---

[22] Some examples in the Elijah stories are Elijah's meeting with Obadiah (2 Kgs. 18:7); the cloud rising out of the sea (2 Kgs. 18:44); the angel appearing to Elijah in the desert (2 Kgs. 19:5).

[23] Pope 1973: 320–323.

The first passage is *CML* 3D (ll. 40–41) where Anat boasts of her conquest of a miscellaneous collection of monsters. The relevant lines are:

> [40]*mhst. mdd. ilm. ar(š).*
> [41]*smt. 'gl. il. 'tk.*

Gibson renders these lines as:

> 'I did destroy Arsh the darling of the gods,
> I did silence Atik the calf of El.'[24]

There is a further fragmentary text (*CML* 12, col. i, ll. 25ff.) where two minor goddesses in the desert give birth to creatures called *aklm* ('eaters') and *'qqm* ('devourers'). That these were bovine creatures is attested by lines 30–32:

> *bhm. qrnm.*
> *km. trm. wgbtt.*
> *km. ibrm.*

which translate: 'on them were horns like bulls, and humps like oxen'.

These monsters are also the creation of El, and Baal contends with them; but it is by no means certain because of the broken nature of the tablet whether Baal is worsted by them or not.

These texts are fragmentary and too much cannot be built on them. What is more significant for the study is their possible connection with the major Canaanite saga of the battle of Baal and Mot and here a number of interesting points emerge. First, Atik (*CML* 3D, l. 41) is described as calf/bullock of El. Some argue that *il* here (cp. Hebrew *'elōhîm*) can have a superlative sense and thus the phrase would mean 'monstrous, ferocious bullock'. However, in a passage specifically about theomachy, it is more natural to suppose that the high god himself is meant. And, as already noted, in *CML* 4, col. viii, l. 23, Mot himself is described as *mdd.ilm* ('darling of the gods') here used of Arsh. Moreover, another of these monsters is *zbb* ('flame'), cognate with *šᵉbîb* (Job 18:6) in the 'king of terrors' passage. In the other fragmentary text (*CML* 12), Baal is felled in a miry swamp and it may not be unreasonable to suggest that here we may have another allusion to Mot's fiery city.

[24] *CML*, 50.

The main conflict between Baal and Mot is related in tablets 5 and 6. While many nuances suggest that Mot is responsible for the summer drought that consumes heaven and earth, there is little doubt, especially in the closing sections of tablet 6, that Mot is, as Gibson argues, 'quite explicitly what he is elsewhere implicitly, the personification of death simpliciter, humanity's ultimate enemy, a primaeval earth monster every whit as dangerous to mankind as the primaeval sea monster Yam Nahar'.[25]

We can probably assume the original audience were familiar with such stories, and we must now turn to an exegesis of the passage bearing in mind the suggested fourfold division.

The challenge to Job is given in 40:15. Commentators such as Dhorme[26] make great play of the fact that Behemoth is the 'beast *par excellence*' (the plural of *bᵉhēmâ*) and that therefore the portrait of the animals continues from chapter 39. However, the evidence does not inexorably point in a naturalistic direction. Rather, instead of generalizing about the links with the beasts of chapter 39, we must ask in what precise way that link is established. Now, as already noted, the last mentioned beasts, the horse and the hawk, are linked especially with death. Indeed in 39:30 the hawk is said to feast *šām* ('there'), a word already seen to be associated with the netherworld. 'Now', the poet says, in effect, 'here indeed is the "beast *par excellence*" not simply associated with death, but death himself'. Yet for all that, like the fearsome Leviathan, he is a creature (*'aśîtî*, 'I made').

The phrase 'he eats grass as cattle do' seems irrelevant and commentators have made little of it, but there may be a very significant nuance of meaning there. The verb *'ākal* has not only the connotation of 'eating' but also of 'devouring', and as such is used in Deuteronomy 5:22 of the fire at Sinai and in Nahum 1:10 of the fire which consumes Nineveh. In Ugaritic, in the fragmentary tablet already cited (*CML* 12, col. i), the creatures who confront Baal are called *'aklm*, and the result of their overthrow of Baal (if indeed they do) is a devastated land where the grass is consumed. This is also the case when he is dispatched by Mot (see *CML* 6, col. iv). Thus behind this seemingly innocent phrase is a sinister figure whose consuming of the vegetation suggests the devouring rapacity of Mot. Thus this brief line of challenge (v. 15) already is full of suggestiveness about Behemoth's true identity.

[25] *CML*, Intro., p. 18.
[26] Dhorme 1967: 619.

When we come to the description of the creature in 40:16–19, we find a number of pointers in the same direction. Verses 16–17 are an evocation of the creature's strength and indeed potency as suggested in the translation. The Canaanite stories refer to this attribute of Mot, *mt. 'z* (*CML* 6, col. vi, ll. 18–20)[27] and indeed he and Baal are described as going like wild oxen, a reminder that eating grass is not necessarily the sign of a peaceful creature.

In the next few phrases mythological details multiply and these have a cumulative effect. In verse 18 the creature's limbs are described as *kimṭîl barzel* (lit. 'like rods of iron'). Bernhard Lang argues that the conflict of Yahweh and Behemoth reflects that of Horus and Seth because Seth is often pictured appearing as a red hippopotamus.[28] Moreover, there is a play on the mythical description of iron as 'the bones of Seth' which appears in the Pyramid Texts and Manetho. This, if valid, would be another sign of the influence of Egyptian mythology, second only perhaps to Canaanite in Job. Seth or Setekh, in later mythology, becomes identified with evil, and an allusion to the god here would be entirely appropriate. The hippopotamus then becomes a symbol of evil, just as other animal symbols are used freely of God.

This brief and highly symbolic description of the creature's appearance has been variously rendered and is of crucial significance. Like Wisdom in Proverbs 8:22, Behemoth is called 'the first of the ways of God' (lit.). These two references are in fact parallel to Genesis 1 where a lurking menace is in some way embodied in creation itself. Moreover, in chapter 28:22 there is an enigmatic passage where Abaddon and Mot are said to have a knowledge of wisdom. If Behemoth is indeed to be identified with Mot, that would be no idle boast. Also relevant is Genesis 3:1, where emphasis is laid on God's creation of the serpent. The critical question is in what sense God 'created' evil. We will return to this question later in the chapters about Leviathan and Sea.

The second half of the phrase (40:19b) is difficult. Dhorme renders it 'He who was created a tyrant to his companions',[29] identifying the 'companions' with the wild beasts of verse 20. This rendering,

---

[27] The expression ('as strong as death') also occurs in the Song of Songs 8:6, a fascinating verse which also contains a reference to Resheph.

[28] Lang 1980. Egyptian iconographic evidence of crocodile and hippopotamus hunts are now realized to be mythological: i.e. they represent the battle of Seth and Horus. This area has been especially investigated by Keel 1984.

[29] Dhorme 1967: 621. He emends the line to *He'aśû yaggēš harbô* and justifies the passive *he'aśû* by the LXX rendering *pepoimenon*.

however, spoils the careful symmetry of the passage and sees verse 19 as primarily an introduction to verse 20, rather than the summation of verses 16–19. The MT, however, yields excellent sense as 'Even his Maker has to bring his sword against him', neatly balancing 19a and 19b. Evil is indeed rooted in creation and has real power; only God can control it. The image of the sword is an important one: in Revelation 19:15 a sharp sword comes out of the mouth of the rider on the white horse to destroy the beast and the false prophet. Now the sword is in fact the word itself, the creative word and the word of rebuke. (See earlier discussion on pp. 95–96).

The description of Behemoth's habitat in verses 20–22 has a dual purpose. On the one hand, the details are vivid and realistic and evoke a marshy scene (such as Lake Huleh) which firmly roots the creature in the natural world like the animals of chapter 39. On the other hand, the words resonate with deeper meanings which point with increasing clarity to the creature's real identity and the true location of his haunts. This is a supernatural creature who nevertheless manifests himself very palpably in the natural world.

Earlier (p. 130) I commented on the textual problems in verse 20a and justified the translation 'For the mountains bring him their tribute'. In the Ugaritic texts *ybl* occurs in a number of significant contexts. In *CML* 5 (col. ii, l. 5), Mot is said by Baal or one of his lackeys to have scorched *ybl. ars*; in *CML* 2 (col. iii, ll. 37–39), El says that Baal must bring tribute to Yam: *hw. ybl. argmnk kilm* ('Even he must bring you tribute like the gods'). So in the Canaanite story the word is used of bringing tribute to the gods of the netherworld and the primordial deep. The mountains may allude to the twin peaks bordering the netherworld. These hints are amplified in Job. The phrase *wᵉkol-ḥayyat haśśadeh* is obscured by the RSV's 'all the wild beasts' and the NIV's 'all the wild animals'. The AV's 'all the beasts of the field' points in the right direction by drawing attention to the importance of *śadeh*. The word is cognate with the Ugaritic *šd.* ('field', 'steppe'). This occurs in a significant context in *CML* 5 (col. vi, ll. 4ff., also 29ff.):

(n.' m ly). ars dbr.
ysmt. šd. (šhl) mmt.

There *šd* appears in a list of synonyms of Mot's abode along with *ars*. This is significant for both Wakeman and Day. There is no need to try to prove, as does Wakeman, nor to disprove, as does Day, that Behemoth is an earth monster. The identity of Behemoth is neither established by the assertion nor repudiated by the denial. The reality of the situation is apparent when we look at the previous lines where Mot's abode is described as *mhyt* ('watery place'), which in the parallel text is said to be at 'the edges of the earth' (*CML* 5, col. vi, ll. 3–7). This is the primeval ocean wherein is Mot's city *Hmry*. In other words, Mot's dwelling is both dry and wet; the arid steppe and the miry swamp represent extremes of unpleasantness. We may compare Jonah 2, where Jonah calls from Sheol which is also the primeval deep. This feature is found in other mythologies: the Old English tradition of hell, a form of old Germanic legend, was of a place where the damned were alternatively scorched and frozen. This is yet another link between Behemoth and Leviathan and between the two primal enemies, Yam and Mot, and a reminder that the battle with these is ultimately one.

Some further details call for attention. *yᵉśaḥᵃqû* (in the Piel) is also used of Leviathan in Psalm 104:26: 'There is that Leviathan whom you have made to sport in it.' Also the word *šām* makes the line very long, probably deliberately, to emphasize its importance. By translating it 'over there' I have tried to convey the nuance of the netherworld which it probably carries, as in 1:21 and 3:17. The LXX in fact uses the phrase *en tō tartarō*. Thus verse 20 introduces us to the land of Behemoth in words which are heavily freighted with allusions to the land of death.

Verses 21 and 22 create a vivid little vignette which on the natural level is drawn from the habitat of the hippopotamus and the water buffalo. However, some of the expressions are plainly intended to echo the water references of earlier passages. The word *taḥaṯ* may have connotations of 'beneath' in the sense of the underworld; and *yiškāḇ* can have the nuance of lying down in death, as in Isaiah 14:8 in the taunt song against the king of Babylon. This meaning is reinforced by the word *sēter* ('the hidden place'), one of the words used of Sheol, significantly in a passage already alluded to where the adulteress's house is identified with the underworld (Prov. 9:7). The word *qāneh* occurs in Psalm 68:31 (Eng. 30) of 'the beast among the reeds', which some identify with Behemoth. Combined with *biṣṣāh* ('swamp'), *qāneh* suggests the marsh where the hippopotamus lives, but also has nuances of Mot's miry city. Thus the very heart of the creature's abode is exposed now as Yahweh leads Job through the 'gates of death' and the 'broad spaces of the underworld' (Job 38:17–18). Moreover, verse 22a, 'For his shade the lotus trees cover him' (RSV), reminds us of many passages dealing with darkness and the shadowland. The RSV translation cited here is literal and brings out a nuance missed by more idiomatic translations of the word ṣil'ᵃlô ('for, as his shadow'). Gordis describes this as 'an adverbial accusative of specification'.[30] 'His shadow' (i.e. that of Behemoth) is almost certainly 'the shadow of Mot' (ṣalmāweṯ) so often met already.

Habel takes 'el in verse 23c as 'ēl and attaches it to verse 24, making El the subject. He translates it as 'El takes him by the mouth with rings'.[31] Habel may be right, although what he does is simply to make explicit what is already implicit in the MT. For that reason I believe the MT should be retained. It is characteristic of the poet to imply rather than state directly and the implied question (i.e. 'Who can do this? Not you, Job – only El?') leads neatly and directly to the series of questions about Leviathan.

I would submit, then, that these contextual, linguistic and structural considerations make the identification of Behemoth with Mot, the god of death, a very strong probability. If, as I shall argue, Leviathan is the power of evil, the Satan, then who but the figure of death could provide a parallel? Our discussion of Leviathan will develop and illuminate many of the arguments advanced here. The Hebrews had a profound knowledge of the mythological language of their day and they used it in a powerful and creative way to express their new revelation of a transcendent deity, his power as Creator, his providence and his battle with evil at both a cosmic and an earthly level.

---

[30] Gordis 1965: 478.
[31] Habel 1985: 554.

Chapter Seven

The ancient prince of hell

We have already noticed the intimate connection of the world of death with that of the primordial sea, and now we turn to a fuller exploration of the sea imagery. This chapter and the next will examine the depiction of Leviathan, for the Leviathan passages raise in the most acute form the problem of the relationship of God to evil and the underlying question of creation. Moreover, the issue of whether the Job poet lapses into dualism must be considered.

The scope of the study

Interest in the sea monster imagery of the Old Testament has been fairly continuous since the publication in 1895 of H. Gunkel's seminal work *Schopfung und Chaos in Urzeit und Endzeit*. This interest has quickened since the deciphering of the Ugaritic texts from 1929 onwards, which revealed, in a language more closely cognate to biblical Hebrew and a milieu closer to ancient Israel, stories and motifs that challenged comparison with the Old Testament, not least with many passages in Job. By no means all scholars, however, have agreed that the mythological references indicate a non-naturalistic interpretation, as evidenced early in the century by Dhorme, and more recently by Gordis, both of whom argue for a naturalistic interpretation of the crucial passages in Job 40 and 41.[1] Likewise, from a different perspective Andersen[2] plays down the significance of the mythological elements. Pope and Habel, each with a wealth of detail, demonstrate connections between the Old Testament and Canaanite myth, although the former merely catalogues the parallels, and the latter does not have the space to draw together the implications of his many penetrating comments on individual texts.[3]

---

[1] Dhorme 1967: 625–644; Gordis 1965: 569–572.
[2] Andersen 1976: 288–291.
[3] Pope 1973: 320–346; Habel 1985: 557–574.

The detailed studies of Wakeman (1973) and Day (1985) contain much crucial material, and indeed the value of another treatment of the subject might be questioned. However, Wakeman's study, while particularly strong on comparative and structuralist matters, leaves many theological and literary issues unexplored. Day's study requires somewhat fuller mention. The dust jacket (rather unfairly to Wakeman) describes the book as 'the first major study of the subject since Gunkel's classic work of 1895'. The book is indeed full of useful ideas and information, comparative, philological and mythological and is an indispensable work of reference. Nevertheless, there are at least three areas in which I believe the work needs to be supplemented.

The first area is theological. Only in his last paragraph does Day seriously begin to address the implications for Old Testament faith of the influence of Canaanite myths which he so abundantly demonstrates. He raises the issue of the transformation of polytheistic images in a monotheistic faith and asks how far this was a living image for old Israel. To answer that question fully would require another book, so there is certainly room to explore that area further.

The second area is literary. I am not convinced that Day gives sufficient weight to the sheer poetic and dramatic power of the Old Testament text and, indeed, parts of the Ugaritic texts. His interest is primarily philological, a necessary basis for any serious study, but on its own incapable of appreciating the nuances of the words used. This one-dimensional approach is seen, for example, in his description of Yahweh's control of the waters as 'a job of work'.[4] This rather mechanical approach to language often prevents him from addressing the question of how words and syntax create their impact.

The third area is exegetical. It has already been argued in the analysis of the Behemoth figure that the crucial passage in chapter 40 can be understood fully only if the reader is aware of images and illusions in the earlier part of the book. A similar case will be made about the Leviathan passages, and it will be argued that this dimension is present in other parts of the Old Testament. Day's overview of these motifs does not take this sufficiently into account, and thus his comments on individual passages lack certain dimensions.

After a brief comment on the prose tale we will go on to examine the reference to Leviathan in chapter 3 and comment on the sea monster references in the poetic dialogue. In the following chapter I

---

[4] Day 1985: 49.

shall translate and comment in detail on the major Leviathan passage (40:25 – 41:26) and examine the other Old Testament references to Leviathan. Building on my general argument already expounded, that Behemoth is Mot, god of death, I shall argue that Leviathan is a guise of Satan and that the prose tale and chapter 3 are essential foundations for understanding the allusions in the poetic dialogue.

A note on the prose tale

The analysis of the imagery of death has already indicated the importance of the prologue with its picture of the heavenly court and finely nuanced relationship of Yahweh and Satan. Earlier I gave somewhat fuller consideration to the role of Satan (see ch. 2), and here I want simply to make two further comments of some significance at this point.

The first is that Satan alone among the assembled court speaks. Moreover, the interplay of the dialogue suggests that Satan has already 'considered' Job, so prompt are his replies and speedy his action; action already being carried out by chapter 3.

The other significant point is that here we have established the identity of the main actors in the drama. Job, while he sometimes suspects the presence of a hostile power, notably in 9:24, 'If it is not he, then who is it?', can see only one author of his calamities. The unmasking of the real enemy makes the two scenes in heaven a vital part of the book and gives depth and power to much that is otherwise obscure in the poetic speeches.

The significance of chapter 3

We have already examined this chapter's imagery of death and seen how it is seminal in Job, and vital for a proper understanding of the chaos monster. No study of this chapter can neglect a long and important article by Michael Fishbane.[5] As I shall refer frequently to this article, a short summary of its argument is appropriate. Fishbane writes of both Jeremiah and Job: 'The movement in Genesis 1:1–10 from the void to the lights to heaven and earth with prominent features of mountains and hills is here reversed.' He further argues that Job 3:1–13 'is nothing less than a counter-cosmic incantation', pointing out that both in Akkadian and Egyptian

---

[5] Fishbane 1971.

literature the magician/priests wished to channel the creative forces of the primordial event to assist in their incantation. Thus in black magic the reverse incantations would summon the presence of ancient chaos. Fishbane sees verse 8 as crucial, with its mention of Leviathan and the ambiguity inherent in Yam/Yom which preserves the mythologies of both darkness and the primordial ocean. Thus there are strong grounds for seeing this chapter as an incantation and verse 8 as crucial for its understanding, a view supported by Hartley, who suggests the term 'curse-lament'[6] and argues that this is not so much a speech addressed to the friends as a statement of Job's deepest feelings.

Clines has a salutary warning on the importance of attending to the emotional and dramatic power of the chapter: 'The restraint that makes this a poem of world status is the exclusive concentration on feeling without the importation of ideological questions.'[7] This comment underlines why it is so important to be aware of the nuances of meaning and the power of imagery.

The earliest direct reference to Leviathan in the book is in verse 8: *yiqqᵉ buhû 'ōrᵉrê-yôm, ha'ᵃṯîḏîm 'ōrēr liwyāṯān*. The first point which calls for attention in verse 8a is the MT *yôm*, which Gunkel and others have amended to *yām*.[8] Morphologically this would be possible given the fact that vowel letters were not used in the older Hebrew script. Indeed Dahood argued that it was not necessary to revocalize *yôm* to *yām* since there is philological evidence that *yôm* may have been the Phoenician pronunciation of *yām*.[9] However, Dhorme makes the valid point that it is the 'supporters' not the 'cursers' of the sea who are enemies of the day.[10] Perhaps, however, a more subtle word-play is involved. Plainly, not only is *yôm/yām* parallel to Leviathan but *'ōrᵉrê* is parallel to *'ōrēr*, and given an oral reading, especially an incantatory one, the two would sound alike. Thus the possibility of the sound of *yôm* suggesting the similar sound of *yām* is very high.

Be that as it may, there is no doubt of the significance of Leviathan in verse 8b. Even commentators who are most convinced of the naturalistic interpretation in chapters 40 and 41 find it impossible to

---

[6] Hartley 1988: 89.
[7] Clines 1989: 104.
[8] Gunkel 1895. He translates 3:8 as: 'Die das Meer bezaubert halten, mogen sie verfluchen, Die macht haben, Leviathan zu erwecken.'
[9] Dahood 1957: 306–320.
[10] Dhorme 1967: 29–30.

avoid a supernatural meaning here. Thus it seems more natural to see the two appearances of Leviathan in chapters 3 and 41 as forming an 'inclusio', and so, in conjunction with the cumulative evidence presented here and in my next chapter, the case for regarding Leviathan as the crocodile is difficult to sustain. The verb *'ōrēr*, used here (in the Polel) of Leviathan, also occurs in that theme in Isaiah 14:9 of the rousing of the Rephaim in Sheol. In that passage the 'rousing' is to 'greet' Helel ben Shachar, cast out of heaven for overweening pride. That passage has many links with Job and I shall examine these in chapter 8.

Basically my argument is this: the total effect of the language and atmosphere of the chapter is to suggest that not only has Satan struck at Job's family and body, but is subtly insinuating images of death and chaos into his mind. When Job speaks of consulting the magicians who can summon the dark powers of chaos, these are in the last analysis irrelevant, it is the powers themselves which fill his mind. Thus early on he is identifying the real cause of his tragedy without realizing it. He is unaware of Satan and his activities, and, while familiar with stories of the chaos monster, does not apply these to his situation, except ironically in 7:12.

Fishbane draws detailed comparisons between the creation story in Genesis 1 and the 'uncreation'[11] of Job's cry of black despair, pointing out the power of speech both to create and uncreate and to unleash the power of 'inner paradox'. What is more dubious is his suggestion that 'this passage can only make sense for a magical *sitz im leben*'. For reasons suggested above it is, I think, the substance of Job's lament (the powers of chaos), and not the manner (an incantatory curse), which is basic to understanding the passage. Fishbane does not take sufficient account of the influence of Satan himself, defeated in the primeval battle, but now fighting it again and using Job as the scene of that battle.[12]

---

[11] There is an interesting parallel and indeed the use of the actual word in Pope's 'Dunciad':

> She comes! the cloud-compelling power behold!
> With night primaeval and with chaos old.
> Lo! the great Anarch's ancient reign restored,
> Light dies before her uncreating word.

(John Butt (ed.), *The Poems of Alexander Pope* (Methuen, 1963), pp. 424–425).

[12] This effectively links the cosmic and human and shows the battle to be one of crucial significance for human life. We may compare the situation in Shakespeare's *Macbeth* where the witches are both elemental powers and also at work in Macbeth's consciousness and experience.

A further comment is needed on Fishbane's argument that the days of creation are here shown in reverse order to demonstrate the process of creation running backwards to primeval chaos. He argues: 'The sevenfold knots, the charms which bind the days of creation, one to another, are, to use the language of magic, "loosed, banished and set free".' The correspondences he notes are as follows:

1st Day	Gen. 1:3–5: light and separation from darkness	v.	Job 3:4a: light turned to darkness
2nd Day	Gen. 1:6–8: firmament of heaven	v.	Job 3:4b: light not to shine
4th Day	Gen. 1:14–19: lights in sky	v.	Job 3:6: darkness seizes night
5th Day	Gen. 1:20–23: fish and birds	v.	Job 3:8: Leviathan
6th Day	Gen. 1:26–31: making humans	v.	Job 3:11: perish at birth
7th Day	Gen. 2:1–40: Sabbath rest	v.	Job 3:13: 'peace' of Sheol

He says 'Every day is represented except the third, unaccountably'.[13] Perhaps Fishbane may be overemphasizing the seven-day scheme rather than the more general process of uncreation we have here. What he has established beyond doubt is that there is an atmosphere of evil and menace surrounding Job which cannot simply be explained away as a reference to his particular calamities, of which he makes no mention. The problem is a cosmic one related to the very nature of creation itself.

Another significant point is the importance of the word both in creating and uncreating. Both Yahweh and Satan have spoken words in chapters 1 and 2 which have themselves brought about events. The fundamental issue is that Satan, within strict but wide limits, exercises some of the powers of God himself, and indeed this is what lies at the heart of the biblical doctrine of creation. God creates powers other than himself and thus gives them life, which means that if they choose they can rebel and disobey. That is why grappling with the issues raised by Behemoth and Leviathan is essentially a discussion of the biblical doctrine of creation from which every other doctrine of biblical theology flows.

[13] Fishbane 1971: 154.

A second area of imagery associated with the monster is that of shadows and darkness, the netherworld already discussed (see pp. 112–115). This will be seen to be significant especially in our consideration of chapter 26.

We have already noted the importance of a third area, that of stars and cosmic forces. The implications of *šaḥar* ('dawn') will be further examined. Finally, in this connection the role of God is vital. God has 'roused Leviathan' as Job had wished someone would. Job, however, is unaware that God has done so and his agony stems from that ignorance. Attention has been drawn to the fact that Satan, like Yam and Mot in the Ugaritic texts, does not appear to be a 'member' of the heavenly court *tout simple*, and indeed a parallel can be found in Yam's sending to El's court messengers of fearsome aspect (*CML 2*, col. i, ll. 23ff.). The scene is thus set for a great conflict in the 'heavenly places', mirroring and echoing the conflict within Job and raising the profoundest questions of creation, evil and the nature of the God who presides over such a universe.

The significance of the rest of the poetic dialogue

We turn now to the development of the theme in the rest of the poetic dialogue, leaving the major Leviathan speech for consideration in the next chapter.

The first of these passages centres around 7:12: *hᵃyām-'ānî imtannîn kî-tāśîm 'ālay mišmār*. This speech of Job is less an address to the friends than a kind of soliloquy in which God himself is arraigned. With a savage irony he asks if God regards him in the same way as the personified sea or as the monster itself. As in chapter 3, there is an atmosphere of dread and menace which is especially prominent in verse 14 with its reference to terrifying dreams and visions. Here, at a profound level, the vision and insight associated with knowing God have been paralleled sinisterly by a subtle adversary who can wear the form and assume the style of the Almighty. Shakespeare presents a similar situation in *Macbeth* where Macbeth speaks of 'the affliction of these terrible dreams that shake us nightly', and that too is set against the background of universal dissolution: 'let the frame of things disjoint, both the worlds suffer'.[14] So here, the evil power has infiltrated Job's whole mental and emotional landscape and filled him with a nameless dread.

[14] *Macbeth*, Act III, Scene ii, ll. 18–20.

The context of 7:12, with its reference to God 'frightening' Job with dreams and 'terrifying' him with visions, makes it probable that Job is referring directly to Eliphaz's vision in 4:12–17 because of the similar imagery. That particular passage with its powerful and eerie evocation of the 'spirit' in the night is often taken as a description of inspiration. But what if the 'spirit' is not God, but the enemy skilled in deception and raising the most disturbing of questions? Indeed Habel argues that 'the poet's bizarre collage of disparate allusions border on a parody of traditional modes of revelation'.[15] I want to develop this and try to demonstrate that it is in fact the Satan/Leviathan figure that Eliphaz has experienced.

We can, of course, identify certain features which suggest that this is of a piece with visions and revelations in the prophets. The dread (*pahad*) which Eliphaz experiences in 4:14 can be paralleled by Isaiah's 'Woe to me!' (Is. 6:5) when he sees 'the LORD Almighty'; and by Daniel: 'So I was left alone, gazing at this great vision; I had no strength left, my face turned deathly pale and I was helpless' (10:8). The 'deep sleep' of verse 13 is echoed by Elihu in 33:15–18 as a circumstance in which God speaks; it is also used in Genesis 15:1–2 of the revelation given to Abraham, as well as in Daniel 10:9 before the revelation is given.[16] The other comparison with prophetic inspiration is that the spirit leaves a message and a 'theological' one at that. The essence of the message is the impurity and vulnerability of human beings before God:

'Can a mortal be more righteous than God?
Can a man be more pure than his Maker?' (4:17)[17]

However, there are other considerations which I believe point in the opposite direction and suggest a brilliant deception of the enemy. The *pahad* (v. 14) foreshadows the dismay that is the harbinger of Leviathan in 41:14 (Eng. 41:22), as well as the fear associated with

---

[15] Habel 1985: 121.

[16] Clines (1989: 129), however, makes the interesting point that it may be the sleep of others, and cites Byron, 'Deep sleep came down on every eye save mine.' This is a fascinating suggestion and may, if correct, be another indication that this vision is not all it seems.

[17] The comparative *mîn* in *mē'elôah* can be: (1) The straight comparative, i.e. 'more in the right with God'; (2) 'From the standpoint of, with regard to, before' – not such a common meaning, but attested occasionally. Neither meaning alters the basic sense of the argument nor invalidates the view suggested here. Either would be unexceptionably orthodox but for that reason would not require a special revelation.

Mot in chapter 18.[18] But more important is the effect this fear has on Eliphaz. The fear and trembling that come on the true prophets of the Lord at once convince them of God's greatness and their own unworthiness and give them a specific message. But here Eliphaz (like Bildad later in chapter 25) legalistically condemns the whole human race and slams shut the door of hope. In other words, unlike a genuine prophetic message, which does indeed condemn human sinfulness but also calls attention to the remedy and provides the strength to carry it out, this 'Message' induces paralysing fear and subtly exploits Job's growing alienation from God whom he had regarded as a friend. Indeed, throughout the poetic dialogue, especially here and in chapter 18, Satan is using the friends as his instruments to torment Job by giving him sinister images of those powers attacking him, while they themselves remain in bland ignorance of their reality.

As the dialogue develops, a veritable cascade of images follows relating to the netherworld and primeval deep. Some of these have been discussed already in the chapters on death (chs. 5 and 6) and others will be looked at later in the chapter on sea imagery (ch. 4). What I want to do here is to mention briefly a number of passages where God is seen as someone of frightening savagery. Then, in the next chapter, I will comment on how similar images are used of Leviathan in Job 41.

Job takes up his lament in chapter 9, where God again is a figure of terror and blatant injustice. This image of terror is found again in 10:16ff. where God is seen as a savage animal stalking his prey. In Job's reply to Eliphaz in chapters 16 and 17, he uses even more violent images. Indeed, Eliphaz has used these images himself and inverted them to represent Job as the arrogant warrior attacking the Almighty.

However, in chapters 25 and 26 many of these mythical allusions and images are gathered together and point forward to Yahweh's speeches. Many commentators (e.g. Dhorme and Habel) see chapter 26 as part of Bildad's speech, arguing that if this chapter is from Job's mouth it reveals a positive note that is absent from the cynical

---

[18] Michel goes further and sees *pahad* as 'Dread', an epithet of Mot; his evidence is based on Dahood's identification of the personal name *li-pa-ad* ('Dread is powerful') in the Ebla tablets and further argues that here we have a composite divine name *pahad ure adah* ('Dread and Trembling'). This may be overstated. I would prefer to see it as a nuance under the surface, like the reference to Resheph already discussed (see pp. 117–119).

comments in chapters 10, 12, 16 and 19.[19] A number of points, however, can be made against this view. The first is that in spite of Eliphaz's vision in chapter 4 and Bildad's blundering against part of the solution in the 'king of terrors' speech in chapter 18:11ff., the friends have shown a bland ignorance of the cosmic forces behind the situation. On the other hand, Job's speeches (e.g. 7:12 and 9:8–13) have repeatedly shown awareness of the cosmic dimension. Thus as the book approaches its climax it is entirely proper that a number of these images should come together in Job's words. What Yahweh finally says reveals the innermost significance of many things Job had glimpsed. This is confirmed in 42:7 when God says that Job has spoken 'what is right', not in the sense that everything he said was true, but in his continual awareness of a cosmic and supernatural dimension to his sorrows. Moreover, the 'positive' note is scarcely evident in 26:1–4 with their cynicism, and in verses 5–14 it is the unfathomable greatness of God rather than the human response to this which is emphasized. Commentators too seldom give weight to the fact that Job is oscillating through a whole gamut of moods. From a literary viewpoint there has been little trace of the majestic, even Miltonic poetry of chapter 26 in Bildad's speeches; whereas 9:1–13, and in different ways, chapters 14:7–12 and 19:23–27 strike the same note as this passage. These considerations point strongly to chapter 26 being the words of Job himself.

Indeed, unless we see the contrast between chapters 25 and 26 we will not fully appreciate the underlying thrust of the imagery. Chapter 25 is not so much wrong as shallow and banal. Andersen rightly comments 'Bildad's feeble ideas, most of which we have heard before, are the platitudes of theology, common to all the protagonists.'[20]

The structure of Job's reply in chapter 26 is significant, for in a striking way it points to that of Yahweh's speeches. The chapter can be divided as follows:

vv. 1–4:   Job's probing questions.
vv. 5–11:   The mysteries of the universe.
vv. 12–14: The smiting of the chaos monster.

---

[19] Habel 1985: 366. His argument on the length of the speeches is unconvincing and has already been touched on in the comments on ch. 28. Moreover, his argument that ch. 26 responds to specific elements in Job's speech in ch. 23 could just as easily be a reason for maintaining that here Job is developing his ideas further. Dhorme also transposes the order of some of the verses and attaches 26:1–4 to ch. 27.

[20] Andersen 1976: 214.

This structure reveals a number of fascinating parallels with chapters 38 – 41. (1) Verses 1-4, with their searching questions, anticipate those of Yahweh in chapters 38 and 40. (2) The reference to powerlessness in verse 2 reminds us of Yahweh's challenge to Job to be a man in 38:3 and 40:7. (3) The insight and advice of verse 3 parallels 38:2:

'Who is this that darkens my counsel
with words without knowledge?'

(4) Verses 5–11, like chapters 38 and 39 probe the recesses of the cosmos. (5) Verses 1–14 introduce us to the supernatural world of chapters 41 and 42.

At the heart of the chapter is the issue of creation and the evil which appears to be rooted in the universe itself. My concern here is to explore the implications of *nāḥāš barîaḥ* of verse 13b and how it fits into the context. Verses 5–10 speak of creation in a series of vivid and awe-inspiring pictures. The uncharted universe is heavily freighted with mythological associations which prepare us for the appearance of Leviathan/Rahab. Clouds likewise are among the most frequent images used by the Job poet, and these both conceal God and often indicate his immediate nearness. The waters and light and darkness are the great elemental powers prominent in the creation account in Genesis 1.

Verse 7 reads: *nᵒṭeh ṣāpôn 'al-tōhû tōleh 'ereṣ 'al-bᵉlîmâ*. The connection with *tōhû*, the sinister abyss of Genesis 1, is apparent. Saphon in Canaanite myth is the mountain of Baal, victor over Mot, Yam and Leviathan. In some sense creation itself is a saving act, and the establishment of the cosmic mountain over the void is analogous to the smiting of Leviathan. In Isaiah 14:13, Helet ben Shachar wishes to lord it over the heights of Saphon, there parallel with *har mô'ēd* ('the mountain of assembly'?). Indeed, that passage and some references in the Ugaritic tablets appear to place the battle in Saphon itself. In *CML* 6, Baal and Mot fight like savage animals in the recesses of Saphon (col. vi, ll. 12–34). The cryptic passage *CML* 3D, where Anat recounts her part in a struggle with a variety of monsters, appears to speak of Baal being vanished from the heights of Saphon (*bmryn. spn*) (ll. 29ff.). Interestingly enough, Bildad uses that very word *bim-rômay* in 25:2 of God's establishment of order in the universe – 'he establishes order in the heights' (perhaps another allusion to the chaos battle which he failed to perceive). Moreover, the mountain appears to be defined as *il. spn.* (*CML* 3C, l. 26), where it is also called *g'r. nhlty.* ('rock of my heritage') and *gb. tli yt.* ('hill of my victory'). Thus the word *ṣāpôn* has rich associations which are not fully captured by the translation 'north'. Also, in the Ugaritic tablets these lines follow the 'tale of woodland and the whisper of stones' which suggests that the stability of the creation is parallel in some way to the victorious outcome of the fight on Zaphon. The phrase *har naḥᵃlāṯᵉka* ('the mountain of your inheritance') occurs in Exodus 15:17 where the creation of Israel is established as a result of the victory over Pharaoh at the Red Sea. In Job itself the word *ṅaḥᵃlat* is used by Zophar in 20:29, but there the heritage provided for Job is destruction by the waters, and indeed this is echoed by Job in 27:13 and 31:3 where it is applied to the fate of the wicked.

In the light of this discussion it seems reasonable to suggest that an atmosphere of primeval conflict is fundamental to this chapter, confirming what has already been discussed in the section on the Rephaim. This means that verses 12ff. are not so much a change of subject as the same reality from a different viewpoint. So we need to examine verse 13: *bᵉruḥo šāmayim šiprâ ḥōlᵉlâ yāḏô nāḥāš bāriaḥ.* Chaim Rabin, in a detailed discussion, surveys the problematic meaning of *bāriaḥ.*[21] Does it mean 'to twist' or 'to be harmless, smooth, bright'? The first meaning is mainly found in Arabic, where it always has connotations of pain. The second is wider and can approximate to 'slip away' (i.e. to become smooth and not easily gripped). Rabin rejects 'slippery' as the basic meaning here and opts for 'tortuous' or 'convulsive' as the best translation, alleging that the constellation Draco is intended. Rabin gives no real evidence for this view, and it is difficult to see in what sense God can be said to 'pierce' a constellation. Moreover, this translation would destroy the parallel with the dismembering of Rahab. Habel mentions that in one of the bilingual texts from Ebla the word *barih-um* appears as equivalent to the Sumerian *hul* ('evil').[22] We cannot, of course, be certain of that word's identity with *bāriaḥ.*

The Ugaritic form of this word occurs in *CML* 5 (col. i, l. 1) – *Ltn. btn. brh.* Here Mot attributes the smiting to Baal, although this is claimed by Anat in *CML* 3D. The parallel *'qltn* ('twisting', 'wriggling') gives support to the idea of 'slippery'. Indeed the translation 'gliding' or 'slippery' may have the nuance of 'difficult to hold down', defeated in the primeval battle but still active. The book of Revelation may allude to a similar idea when it mentions 'the beast who was

[21] Rabin 1946: 38–41.
[22] Habel 1985: 365.

wounded with the sword and yet lived'; and even more strikingly in 17:8 when it refers to the beast who 'once was, now is not and yet will come'. At the heart of creation is an enormous struggle, the implications of which Job is now beginning to see but only Yahweh's speeches will put into true perspective.

The verb *ḥālal* ('to pierce') suggests a victory rather than complete destruction, and this is significant for the overall theology of the book. Creation in the sense of the primal act was parallel to the defeat of evil, but that defeat did not eradicate it and it still manifests itself in the world. Further, the word 'hand' is important. We have already noted the significant interplay in chapters 1 and 2 between the hand of God and the hand of Satan. In 19:21 Job exclaims 'Have pity on me, my friends . . . for the hand of God has struck me'; and in 23:2: 'his hand is heavy on me.' Now the fact that Job here is able to see that hand smiting Leviathan is one of his leaps of faith and provides a basis on which God can build when he finally reveals to Job the identity of his adversary.

Finally, the word *nāḥaš* itself draws clear attention to the nature of Job's sufferings and, as in its use in Genesis 3, it is more remarkable for its powerful connotations than precise definition. This is probably deliberate, for a precise picture can be given only by Yahweh himself. Job can suspect and suggest, but Yahweh alone can 'rouse' and expose. I have discussed Rahab and the sea already (see pp. 86–87), but it is clear that this word is a particularly rich and definite allusion to the chaos battle. Chapter 26 ends with Job's awed reference to the majesty and mystery of God's ways, thus providing a starting point for Yahweh's rhetorical questions in chapters 38 and 39 and serving as a rebuke to the conceit of the friends.

Before we look at a further possible reference to Leviathan in chapter 28, a word is necessary about chapter 27. Job has asserted the awesome power of God and now he turns to his justice. He is not so much denying that justice as castigating the glib orthodoxy which speaks of it as something self-evident. The use of the oath formula in verse 2 is virtually a challenge to God to explain his ways (*dᵉrāḵāw*: 26:14) which indeed he is shortly to do:

'As surely as God lives, who has denied me justice,
    the Almighty who has made me taste bitterness of soul.'

The power of God is not in doubt, rather it compounds the mystery, indeed it *is* the mystery. What is the relationship between God's power and his justice, and what part do those other sinister powers play in the universe?

We have already discussed chapter 28 in the context of chapters 26 – 31 (see pp. 68–81), but I want to look at a probable further allusion to the world of Leviathan in 28:8. Chapter 28 is profoundly concerned with creation, because *ḥokmâ* ('wisdom') is the principle which holds the universe together. The poet here is showing that God alone controls the universe, but, unlike the friends, he gives due weight to other powers lurking in the cosmos, such as Abaddan and Mot (v. 22). There is also a reference in verse 8a to *bᵉnê šāḥaṣ* ('the sons of pride'); these also occur in 41:26 (Eng. 41:34) where Leviathan is described as their king. There may be a deliberate ambiguity between the zoological and mythological, for the bird of prey and the falcon may then perform the same function, as in chapter 39 where they provide a bridge to the world of Behemoth and Leviathan.

Also significant is the word *šāḥal* (v. 8b). Mowinckel, in a long and interesting study, argues that the usual meaning of 'lion' is inappropriate here as what is alluded to are narrow crevices passable only by serpent-like creatures.[23] He further compares this to the Norse myth of Odin changing himself into a serpent, and argues that 'the "sons of pride" belong not so much to zoology as to mythology'. He suggests the translation 'lizard' here and in Psalm 91:13 (Norwegian *ögle*). Since Semitic languages have words which can mean 'lion' in one dialect and 'serpent' in another, Mowinckel draws attention to the Mesopotamian *musruššu* on the Ishtar Gate in Babylon, the serpent griffin of Marduk's temple at Nippur and the figures on Gudea's vase from Lagash. Thus the word may have been chosen deliberately to indicate the mythical serpent dragon, one of the many manifestations of Leviathan.

Now this possible allusion to Leviathan may be confirmed by the phrase in verse 11a, *mibbᵉkî nᵉhārôṯ* ('the sources of the rivers'), with which we may compare *nibkê-yām* in 38:16, which probably alludes to El's abode at 'the confluence of the rivers' (*mbk. nhrm.*). This is also the meeting place of the heavenly court where the 'sons of pride' cannot come. Nor indeed has the serpent penetrated there in the sense of fully understanding it. Indeed, this whole chapter, in more restrained and less flamboyant language, is emphasizing the transcendence of God over creatures both human and supernatural, just as chapter 26 has done in more overtly mythological language.

[23] Mowinckel 1963.

I want briefly to highlight some other significant allusions in chapters 29 – 31 to the world of Leviathan in this final testimony of Job. In chapter 30:11ff. the images of violence and especially of siege return with great force, recalling particularly 19:7ff. In 30:21 the word *'akzār* ('fierce', 'cruel') occurs, here used of God, but used later to describe the 'rousing' of Leviathan (41:2). Also, in 30:21, Job again sees the hand of God turned against him. Worse still, the rider on the wind, who is usually the deliverer of his people (e.g. Ps. 18:10: 'He mounted the cherubim and flew; he soared on the wings of the wind'), is using his power to destroy Job (vv. 22–23). In chapter 31, Job's great cry of innocence is one of the signs that the end of the book is approaching, for it harks back to the narrator's description of him right at the start: 'This man was blameless and upright' (1:1), words confirmed by God in 1:8. Indeed, Job's summoning of God in verse 35: 'let the Almighty answer me', is what God responds to in chapter 38.

The Elihu speech

Throughout the book we have noticed the skilful build-up of the 'mythical' dimension, with powerful echoes of the Canaanite stories. It is not my purpose at this point to discuss the authenticity of Elihu's speech, but to find if there are further evidences of this developing imagery and theology.[24] Whatever may be made of the earlier part of the speech, chapters 36 and 37 are a fine and powerful poem of the greatness of God in nature, both recalling chapters 9 and 26 and looking forward to chapter 38.

In 36:22ff. Elihu extols the greatness and unsearchableness of God and uses, by way of illustration, the coming of a storm, an integral theme in theophany passages. God's approach is described in 36:33 as 'thunder' (lit. 'roaring') and again in 37:2–3 as 'thunder and lightning'. The most obvious comparison is with the theophany psalms (e.g. Ps. 29, 'the psalm of the seven thunders'). Elihu, of course, is simply using theophanic language to back up his argument but, without knowing it, he is at the same time announcing the actual coming of God.

Evidence of a similar emphasis is found in Canaanite story: 'He uttered his holy voice and the earth quaked' (*CML* 4, col. vii, ll. 30ff.),

---

[24] If the view advanced here is accepted, the speech is likely to be genuine for it shows evidence of substantial poetic power. The allusions to the imagery of death noted earlier in ch. 33 may give further support to the authenticity of this speech.

referring to Baal thundering from Zaphon. There the context is Baal's challenge to Mot, and thus again the motif of cosmic conflict is underlined. Here in Job 36:22 the storm is the visible manifestation of the mighty convulsions in the spiritual realm whose inner meaning is to be unfolded in chapters 40 – 41. Probably, as Elihu speaks, the storm of 38:1, out of which Yahweh's voice is to be heard, is already breaking around them.

We need to examine the precise significance of this theophanic language. Pope, as so often, makes a telling observation: 'It is possible that incongruous features of El and Baal are mixed in Yahweh who absorbed elements of both.'[25] This implies a random and fortuitous mixing of traditions without any clear intention on the part of the poet. My argument, however, is that the poet is deliberately blending traditions for his own purpose.

This conscious blending of traditions is seen particularly clearly in 37:22: *miṣṣāpôn zāhāḇ ye'eteh 'al-'elôah nôrā' hôḏ.* Earlier commentators tended to take this phrase in a meteorological sense. Thus Driver says 'the allusion may be to the Aurora Borealis, the streaming rays of which, mysteriously blazing forth in the northern heavens, may well have been supposed to be an effulgence from the presence of God Himself'.[26] Dhorme's view is similar: '. . . describes the state of the sky when the golden rays of the sun border the clouds which are being dispersed by the wind'.[27] Pope, on the other hand, argues that it refers to Baal's palace on Zaphon:

> A major motif in the Baal cycle of myths is the building of a splendiferous palace of gold, silver and lapis lazuli on the heights of Mt. Zaphon. The rendering 'golden splendour' may be appropriate as suggesting the glow of the lightning which comes from the mythical golden palace of the storm-god on Mt. Zaphon.[28]

Once again, we are not forced to choose between two incompatible ideas. Rather, this is a continuation of theophany language and a direct transition to the appearance of God himself. When Elihu speaks of Shaddai coming from Zaphon, a ripple of excitement would have run through the original audience. Moreover, the cosmic

---

[25] Pope 1973: 275.
[26] Driver-Gray 1977: 323.
[27] Dhorme 1967: 572.
[28] Pope 1973: 287.

imagery powerfully reminds us that this is the God of heaven and earth whose glory is seen in creation. Thus again the twin notions of creation and the smiting of the monster come together.

There are a number of other passages, both Canaanite and Hebrew, which have a bearing on this. In *CML* 3C, ll. 19ff. we find the hauntingly beautiful lines about Baal 'understanding' or even 'creating' lightning (if *ahn* comes from the root *bny*). With this we may compare 36:30: 'he scatters his lightning about him', and 38:35: 'Do you send the lightning bolts on their way?' Both passages see the possession and deployment of lightning as a prerogative of God. Now the Ugaritic line occurs in a passage where Baal is described as 'mightiest of waters' (*CML* 3C, l. 11); an epithet also significantly applied to him in *CML* 5 in his challenge to Mot, when the latter sneeringly dismissed his despatching of Leviathan (col. ii, l. 11). The power of the warrior god is thus closely linked to, indeed manifested by, these elemental powers of nature.

The psalms likewise contain a number of striking examples. Psalm 93 celebrates Yahweh's cosmic and everlasting kingship which has subdued Yam and Nahar: 'mightier than the thunder of the great waters' (v. 4). Then comes the apparently irrelevant 'holiness adorns your house for endless days' (v. 5). But surely the point is that the establishing of the holiness of Yahweh's house, which is the holiness and incomparability of Yahweh himself, is the sign that he has been victorious. Similarly Psalm 29:9 says 'in his temple all cry, "Glory!".' Also, the Zion psalms, such as 46 and 48, are in the last analysis not about Zion, but about God: the 'house' is not about Zion, but about God; it is not simply the earthly temple, but the whole universe. A similar emphasis can be found in the 'Song of the Sea' in Exodus 15. There an integral part of the victory is

'the place, O LORD, you made for your dwelling,
    the sanctuary, O Lord, your hands established' (Exod. 15:17).

Another important Canaanite passage is *CML* 3D, already referred to in relation to the crushing of the monsters. Its context is the long poem describing the construction of Baal's palace which is the symbol of his accession to the kingship. The Job poet is using, for his own purposes, motifs and images which were part of the currency of thought and imagination in the Ancient Near East. Thus, as we approach God's speeches, the implicit theology of the link between the nature of evil and creation itself is made explicit. God's coming from Zaphon, in terms reminiscent of the language of Psalm 18 and Habbakuk 3, is a demonstration of his kingship.

None of this means that God's speeches are in any sense unnecessary. No-one in the book so far has fully appreciated the significance of these images and motifs, nor their part in the total picture of creation. Elihu's words here in chapters 36 and 37 draw heavily on the language of the Psalter, and his evocation of the grandeur of God paves the way for the final act.

Chapter Eight

Drawing out Leviathan

We come now to the climax of the second divine speech and to a full-blown picture of the fearsome Leviathan. The argument so far is that, if the basic premises of the previous discussion are accepted, when Leviathan fills the picture he is no newcomer, nor is he simply an inflated picture of the crocodile. Rather, along with Behemoth, he is the embodiment of cosmic evil itself, that power ceaselessly opposed to God and his purposes. As Behemoth probably is to be identified with Mot, god of death, so it appears that in Leviathan we have another guise of Satan. Interestingly these two figures are brought together in Hebrews 2:14 where the author speaks of Christ's victory, 'that by death he might destroy him who holds the power of death – that is, the devil'.

Not all scholars, however, are convinced of the importance of the second divine speech. Driver-Gray state, 'It seems probable that the description of these two animals was not written by the author of 38ff.'[1] They argue that questions are less frequent, that description is longer and less vivid and that there is no challenge at the close. Westermann dismisses most of the passage as 'mere description' and categorizes it (along with some other parts of the book) as 'passages [that] betray the tendency, visible at several places, of passing over from praise of the creator to description of what has been created'.[2] However, this approach ignores the gradual accumulation of themes and images already traced in the build up to the Behemoth passage. This is now crystallized as the more sinister power behind death; the Satan/Leviathan figure is unmasked as the climax of the imagery and theology of the book.

Before looking in detail at the passage it would be useful to mention another chapter which shows similar characteristics. This is Ezekiel 28:1–19 where the prophet announces judgment on the prince of Tyre

---

[1] Driver-Gray 1977: 351–352. They include the Behemoth passage in their strictures.
[2] Westermann 1981: 109.

for aspiring to godhead, the hubris which characterizes Leviathan. That this may tell of the fall of Satan as well as of the actual prince of Tyre is a very old view.[3] Neither understanding excludes the other, rather, the historical setting, in Ezekiel's day, is both a dateable event and a window into a deeper reality. So here, we have descriptions which echo the crocodile and the whale but go far beyond them.

Most of this chapter will be devoted to translation and exegesis of the Leviathan passage, followed by briefer comments on the other Old Testament references to Leviathan and concluding with some general comments on the overall significance of the material. Structurally the passage falls quite easily into four sections:

The challenge (40:25–32; Eng. 41:1–8).
Overwhelming fear (41:1–4; Eng. 41:9–12).
Description of the monster (41:5–21; Eng. 41:13–29).
His habitat (41:22–26; Eng. 41:31–34).

The challenge (40:25–32: Eng. 41:1–8)

Translation

25Can you draw out Leviathan with a fishhook or press his tongue down with a cord?
26Can you put a rope through his nose or pierce his jaw with a hook?
27Will he beg endlessly for favours from you or speak to you with gentle words?
28Will he make a covenant with you to take him as your lifelong servant?
29Will you play with him as if he were a bird or will you put him on a leash for your little girls?
30Will traders bargain over him, dividing him up among the merchants?
31Can you fill his hide with darts or his head with a fishing spear?
32If you lay a hand on him, you will remember the battle, and you will not do it again.

Contra Driver-Gray (1977), the rhetorical questions here link this passage closely with the first divine speech, and their intensity points

---

[3] This interpretation is found in Tertullian, *Against Marcion* (5:11, 17) and *2 Enoch (Slavonic)* (29:4–5).

to the approaching climax. Their theme is the awesome power of Leviathan and human impotence before him. The 'fishhook' presumably refers to the totally inadequate criteria which Job has used to try to understand the mystery at the heart of creation. The criteria are given solidity and definition by being compared to drawing in a monster as if it were a small fish. Moreover, by implication the sinister powers that had plagued Job are given a palpable reality; they are not figments of his imagination. The natural imagery does not imply that Leviathan is a natural creature, rather it shows the palpable nature of the evil he embodies. Moreover, the physical blends almost imperceptibly into the theological and the literary in verse 27 (Eng. 41:3) with the picture of the monster refusing to beg for mercy or speak in honeyed tones. This is reinforced in verse 28 (Eng. 41:4); *berît* inevitably reminds us of God's covenant. The 'lifelong servant' recalls Exodus 21:5–6 and Deuteronomy 15:17 where it is one of the covenant provisions. In verses 29 and 30 (Eng. 41:5–6) the domestic and commercial images form an incongruous picture with grim humour and uneasy laughter. These are, of course, the very aspects of Job's life which had been invaded and disrupted and thus form another of the many links that bind the book together.

In verses 31–32 (Eng. 41:7–8) we find resonances that take us out of the world of humour and irony and into the realm of cosmic conflict. Commenting on verse 31, Habel refers to the battle of Horus with Seth during which Seth assumes the form of a hippopotamus.[4] In the earlier comments on Behemoth (see pp. 130–131) we noted another possible allusion to that contest which is an important motif in Egyptian mythology. If this echo of the story is indeed to be discerned here and in the Behemoth passage, it increases the probability that *milḥāmâ* (v. 32) refers to the cosmic battle and not simply to a crocodile hunt. That battle has been alluded to in 26:12–13 as cutting Rahab to pieces and piercing the serpent. There Job perceived something of its meaning, and now God is putting that into perspective.

Overwhelming fear (41:1–4; Eng. 41:9–12)

Translation

[1]Look now,[a] there is no hope of your subduing him,[b] even the mere sight of him is overwhelming.

[4] Habel 1985: 570.

²No-one is fierce enough to arouse him, and who is there who can stand and face me?ᶜ

³If anyone tries to outface me I will pay him back; everything under the heavens is mine.

⁴I will silence his boastingᵈ and his mighty words and his fine argument.ᵉ

Notes on the translation

ᵃ*hēn* I have paraphrased as *hinnēh* in the Behemoth passage; just as Behemoth was unmasked, so now the more fearsome Leviathan is to be.

ᵇAn attempt to indicate both the MT 'of him' and the 'of you' of some mss.

ᶜMost translations follow some Hebrew mss. and the LXX in reading 'him'; however the MT reads 'me'.

ᵈTaking *baddāyw* as 'idle, vain talk' rather than 'limbs'; *ḥîn* is taken as 'argument' rather than a by-form of *ḥēn* ('grace').

ᵉTaking *hēn* in the sense of 'appealing, persuasive'.

These textual points indicate something of the obscurity of the passage, but these problems are at the very heart of teasing out its meaning. But first some general comments about this section. We have already noted Westermann's view that this little pericope is the culmination of what God has to say (p. 157); a view that could still be true without adopting his dismissive attitude to the rest of the chapter. Elmer Smick argues that 'It is perfectly good Hebrew style to put such a climax in the middle of the poem.'[5] This section provides the necessary groundwork for understanding the resonances of the description which follows. God has been emphasizing that Job is ignorant of much of this marvellous universe and cannot thunder with a voice like God. Now he is showing Job that it is unthinkable that he could confront Leviathan much less God.

Chapter 40:7–14 has been particularly concerned with the divine power and its relationship with evil and with challenging Job about whether he has the power to confine the proud and wicked in Sheol. Job's sorrows are thus placed in their widest context. What Yahweh is doing is revealing to Job the innermost secrets of creation and providence. Just as Job cannot create the frost, bind the stars or cause the hawk to fly, so he cannot curb Behemoth and Leviathan.

[5] Smick 1988: 1051.

Nevertheless, God can, and as often noted, especially in chapters 9 and 26 and in a different way in chapter 28, creation and providence, or nature and history, are fundamentally one and under the control of God. All is under God's will in spite of the dark mystery that often surrounds his ways. God is about to unmask this fearsome creature who terrifies even the angels (41:17; Eng. 41:25). Thus it is imperative that his own incomparability be underlined; Leviathan is so fierce that even a glimpse of him would be overwhelming.[6]

Verse 2a (Eng. v. 10a) reads like a contrast between Leviathan and Yahweh. If no-one is fierce enough to rouse Leviathan then certainly no-one can face God. The verb 'arouse' (*'ur*) is the one used in 3:8 of the rousing of Leviathan and so forms yet another link between the beginning and end of the poetic dialogue. Verse 2b (Eng. v. 10b) is fascinating; Satan/Leviathan has indeed stood in the presence of God, imagining in his arrogance that he came of his own volition rather than under control of the Lord's overarching providence.

Verse 3 (Eng. v. 11) may then be more than an implied rebuke to Job for his temerity in imagining that he could outface Yahweh in the heavenly court. Rather, this is a blunt statement of Leviathan's inferiority. Satan had tried to outface him in the divine council and had used 'everything under the heavens' to break and destroy Job and thus discredit him. Satan's attempt had failed and the moment of reckoning had come.

This helps to make better sense of the puzzling verse 4 (Eng. v. 12). The NIV, in attaching this to the third part of the passage thus makes it the beginning of the description of Leviathan: '*I will* not fail to speak of his limbs, his strength and his graceful form.' This position is supported by Hartley. However, *baddāyw* could as well mean 'idle talk', 'boasting',[7] a word already used in 11:3 where Zophar accuses Job of boasting. A similar use occurs in Isaiah 16:6 where Moab's pride is shown in her extravagant boasts. This would be a better parallel with 'his mighty words' which here must have the nuance of bragging.

Ḥîn is associated with *ḥēn* ('grace', 'favour') by BDB,[8] but without much conviction. They say (quite correctly) that it is not very appropriate in a description of the crocodile. The final word in the line – *'erkô* (lit. 'his form') – can be used for the form or arrangement of words (e.g. 32:14: 'Job has not marshalled his words against me'; see

---

[6] The verb here is the Hophal of *ṭûl* (lit. 'to be hurled, flung down').

[7] Hartley 1988: 527.

[8] See BDB, p. 95.

also 13:18; 23:4; 33:5; 37:19). A nominal form occurs in Proverbs 16:1: *ma'arkê-lēb* ('plans of his heart'). If we are curious about what his fine arguments were, we need only look back to 1:11: 'But stretch out your hand and strike everything he has, and he will surely curse you to your face.' (See also 2:5.)

It is difficult to imagine a more effective way of both showing the power of Leviathan and at the same time demonstrating his complete inferiority to God. The fear of God, which is the beginning of Wisdom, is powerfully underlined. The thrust of this passage is: 'Fear him, ye saints, and you will then have nothing else to fear.'[9]

Description of the monster (41:5–21: Eng. 41:13–29)

Translation

[5]Who can strip off his outer clothing or burst through his coat of double mail?[a]

[6]Who can burst open the doors of his mouth as terror surrounds his teeth?

[7]His back[b] is like a row of shields, closely joined by a seal.

[8]Each is so firmly linked to the other that not a breath can pass between them.

[9]They adhere to one another, they are interlocked and cannot be separated.

[10]His sneezings flash as light, his eyelids are like the rays of Shachar.[c]

[11]Firebrands pour from his mouth, sparks of fire shoot out.

[12]Smoke billows from his nostrils as if from a boiling pot over a reed fire.

[13]His breath sets coals ablaze and flames burst from his mouth.

[14]Strength lodges in his neck; dismay leaps in front of him.

[15]The folds of his flesh are close-knit so that they are firm and immovable.

[16]His breast is as hard as a rock, as hard as a lower millstone.

[17]When he rouses himself the angels cringe in fear, they retreat before his billowing power.[d]

[18]If a sword touches him it has no effect, nor does spear or dart or javelin.

---

[9] From the hymn 'Through all the changing scenes of life' by Nahum Tate (1652–1715) and Nicholas Brady (1639–1729).

[19]He treats iron like straw and bronze like rotten wood.
[20]Arrows do not make him flee, he turns stones from the sling into chaff.
[21]A club seems to him like a piece of straw; he derides the whirring of the javelin.

Notes on the translation

[a]Here the MT *risnô* (lit. 'his halter', 'his bridle') is puzzling. The LXX reads *thurakēs autou*, probably from the Hebrew *siryôn* ('coat of mail').

[b]Reading *gēwô* ('his back') (as LXX and Vulgate) for MT *ga'awâ* ('pride').

[c]'Shachar' to denote mythological reference.

[d]'Billowing power' attempts to bring out the underlying reference to the waves of the sea.

Now God goes on to give a detailed description which expresses with stunning clarity who Leviathan really is. Job had been tormented by shadowy and nameless terrors but now Yahweh has named and exposed the real enemy. Already, in many allusions, including references to Rahab and the dragon, Job had glimpsed something of this reality, but only God can place these allusions in a true and full perspective.

One other general point should be made before turning to the details of this section. The language is very similar to, and indeed a parody of, the style of theophany passages. If Leviathan is the great enemy who aspires to Godhead, then his coming must be eerily like that of God himself. Arguably the most significant verse in Job is 9:24c: 'If it is not he, then who is it?' That question is now being answered here. By bringing together a mass of allusions from earlier in the book, God is revealing to Job the nature of his adversary. We shall draw attention to some parallels with two theophany passages (Ps. 18 and Hab. 3) and comment on these more fully as occasion arises.

Job	*Psalm 18; Habakkuk 3*
41:11–12 (Heb.): Smoke from nostrils and flame from mouth.	*Psalm 18:8*: Almost identical with minor variations.
41:14 (Heb.): Strength before and dismay behind	*Hab. 3:5*: Pestilence before and plague behind.

163

41:17 (Heb.): Angels cringe in fear.   *Psalm 18:7*: Earth reels.
Hab. 3:6: Mountains crumble.

41:23–24 (Heb.): Deep stirred up.   *Psalm 18:5*: Deep laid bare.

These quotations are a most effective way of describing a creature who throughout the book has so successfully imitated God that Job has mistaken him for the Almighty. Job would recall his own references to the monster in chapter 26 and elsewhere and would now realize with awe the true identity of his tormentor.

Verses 5–9 concentrate on Leviathan's impregnable armour. The atmosphere is one of great conflict, comparable to the war in heaven in *Paradise Lost*, where, speaking of Satan's shield opposing Michael's sword, Milton writes:

> . . . opposed the rocky orb, of trifold
> adamant, his ample shield, a vast
> circumference.[10]

In Revelation 9:9 the trumpet of the fifth angel causes locusts to pour out of the abyss. They 'have breastplates like iron' and have as their king 'the angel of Abyss'. Job 41 leaves us in no doubt who that 'angel of the Abyss' is. Similarly in 'Ein Feste Burg', Luther appears to echo this passage:

> The ancient prince of hell,
> has risen with purpose fell;
> strong mail of craft and power
> he weareth in this hour,
> on earth is not his fellow.

This creature is a warrior, which is what Job had complained of God being earlier (e.g. 16:14: 'he rushes at me like a warrior'.)

Verse 6 speaks of the creature's teeth and their attendant terror. Very significant in this connection is 16:9 where Job complains:

> 'God assails me and tears me in his anger
> and gnashes his teeth at me'.

[10] John Milton, *Paradise Lost*, book 6, ll. 253–255.

Now Job is being shown whose teeth these really are. The poet is describing a supernatural creature which none the less manifests itself in physical violence and awesome force in the natural world. This parallels Job's physical and emotional calamities in the loss of his family, his health and his possessions, as well as his spiritual sufferings.

Verses 7–9 (Eng. vv. 15–17) emphasize the impenetrability of Leviathan's armour and the absence of any point vulnerable to attack. The physical nature of this description would not push us into a naturalistic interpretation any more than the physical attributes ascribed to God in earlier passages would. Rather it makes palpable the reality and power of this creature.

In the next few verses, however, supernatural elements begin to proliferate, with the emphasis on fire with its theophanic associations. 'The eyelids of Shachar' remind us of the connection of 'Shachar' ('Dawn') in 3:9 and there may be a link with Isaiah 14:12 where 'Helel ben Shachar' (AV: 'Lucifer, son of the morning') attempts to storm the abode of God, a connection that has been explored in chapter 4. In the natural world the red eyes of the crocodile are a fearsome sight, but the next verses go far beyond the crocodile.[11]

This proliferation of supernatural elements is amplified in verses 11–13 (Eng. vv. 19–21) by the images of fire. Fire is a common symbol of the power of God. For example, the flaming sword at the gates of Eden (Gen. 3:24); the burning bush (Exod. 3:2–3); and the river of fire from God's throne (Dan. 7:9–10). The fire from Leviathan's mouth would also probably remind Job of the bitter words of Eliphaz in 15:30:

> 'He will not escape the darkness;
> a flame will wither his shoots,
> and the breath of God's mouth will carry him away'.

The word 'smoke' (v. 12) is used as a theophany term in Exodus 19 and Isaiah 6:4, and is used of God's anger in Psalm 18. Thus in vivid imagery the god-like pretensions of Leviathan are delineated.

Verses 14–17 (Eng. vv. 22–25) take this to another level. Yahweh, in the theophany passages is accompanied by his entourage; so Leviathan has his entourage. 'Strength' and 'Dismay' help to intimidate any who would oppose him. Verse 17 (Eng. v. 25) in particular

---

[11] Pope (1973:341) refers to the Ugaritic Baal/Yam myth: 'In the Ugaritic myth of the conflict between Baal and Prince Sea, the terrible messengers of the sea god intimidate the entire divine assembly, except Baal, by their fiery appearance. Though the text is broken, the fire probably comes from their eyes.'

calls for comment. I think that here we have a reference to the fear that Satan instils even among other supernatural beings.[12] The early versions support the NIV translation 'the mighty', and my own translation of 'the angels' is supported by the Vulgate. The *ēlîm* are probably members of the heavenly court, and the fear aroused among these 'sons of God' or angels is evidence of the great conflict raging in the heavenly realms. A further vivid illustration of this occurs in Daniel 10 where Michael is said to have been involved in conflict with the angel prince of Persia. Jude 9 speaks of Michael 'disputing with the devil about the body of Moses'. There, the significant detail is added that in the battle Michael invoked the name of the Lord. Only God himself can ultimately subdue Leviathan.

In verses 18–21 (Eng. vv. 26–29) the emphasis is on the futility of weapons against Leviathan. Here no weapons can prosper against him; whether those suited for close combat like a sword, or for distance fighting like an arrow, dart or sling, or for crude violence like a club. Here indeed is an adversary whom no-one can tame and whose description is lavish in its use of superb and vivid imagery. Is then Westermann right in the contention that indeed the poet has simply lapsed into over extravagant praise of a creature?[13]

Three things can be said. The first is to note the pervasive use of irony and macabre humour; a point established in the rhetorical questions of 40:25–32 (Eng. 41:1–8). It may be that Job is no match for this fearsome adversary, but the ironic tone shows that the speaker is not fooled or intimidated. Indeed, Leviathan may deride the whirring of the javelin, but ultimately that will do him no good – he who sits in the heavens will have the last laugh.

The second observation is that this lengthy description develops the implied theology of the rhetorical questions in chapters 38 and 39. There Job was challenged to show if he understood the created universe. The impossibility of Job (or any other human) replying in the affirmative shows the gulf between the Creator and the created. To understand is to have the power and knowledge of the Creator. So

---

[12] The MT reads *miśśētô yāḡûrû 'ēlîm miśśᵉbārîmₐ yithattā'û*. Dhorme (1967) reads *gallîm* ('billows') for *ēlîm* and emends *miśśᵉbārîm* to *miśbᵉrê-yām* ('the waves of the sea') and translates the line:

'The billows are afraid of his majesty,
The waves of the sea draw back' (639).

This creates a neat parallelism and is part of his overall contention that Leviathan is a natural creature.
[13] Westermann 1981:109.

here God unfolds and exposes that part of creation at the heart of the book: the place and power of evil. By doing so God is underlining that he is in charge. Much mystery remains, but any idea of Satan being a kind of equal and opposite force is ruled out of court. So it is that the New Testament is to celebrate the victory of the Lord Jesus Christ over the devil and his angels and the availability of that victory to believers.

Thirdly, this passage demonstrates that Leviathan is no newcomer tagged on to the first divine speech by an inferior redactor. Rather the images of fire and lightning reveal this figure as the adversary who has been masquerading as God throughout the book.

His habitat (41:22–26: Eng. 41:30–34)

Translation

[22]Underneath him are sharp potsherds; like a threshing sledge he makes his mark on the mire.
[23]He makes the deep boil like a cauldron, he makes the sea like a point of ointment.
[24]Behind him he leaves a luminous path; you would imagine that the deep has a hoary head.
[25]On earth there is not his equal, created as he was without fear.
[26]He looks down on all the arrogant; he is king over all the sons of pride.

This final section of the Leviathan poem brings together a number of images relating to the monster's haunts and these echo many of the earlier ideas. 'Mire' in verse 22b (Eng. v. 30b), on one level refers to the mud of the river bank. However, in the Behemoth passage (40:21) we noticed that the references to marsh and swamp have nuances of the miry city presided over by the god of death in Canaanite myth, and that allusion is probably intended here as well.

A further indication that Leviathan is more than a natural creature is given in verses 23–24 (Eng. vv. 31–32) where we move from the river world of the crocodile to the open sea which is the haunt of the whale. Two words here have significant implications. First, there is $m^e s\hat{u}l\hat{a}$ ('the ocean deep') which occurs in Exodus 15:5 as the place where Pharaoh's army was destroyed; in Psalm 107:24 it occurs with reference to the wonderful deeds of God seen by those who do business 'in the great waters'; in Psalm 88:6 it is used figuratively of deep distress and in Jonah 2:3 of the place from which Jonah prays. Secondly, there is *t^ehôm* ('the deep or abyss is his haunt') in verse 24, previously used in Genesis 1:2 as the place over which the Spirit hovered at creation.

But the final touches to the picture come when Yahweh establishes beyond doubt Leviathan's place in the created order: 'On earth there is not his equal' (v. 25a; Eng. v. 33a). This is a creature of uniquely formidable potency and one who cannot be dismissed lightly, indeed cannot be dismissed at all except by the Almighty himself. And it is the word 'created' (v. 25b) that most underlines the significance of Leviathan. He is not self-existent, he is part of the created order and thus is not beyond divine providence. Moreover, there are mysteries in which Leviathan has no place, for the awesome power of the Creator is only partially demonstrated in the created order and the smiting of the monster, as Job himself realized in 26:14: 'These are but the outer fringe of his works.'

This section concludes with an underlining both of Leviathan's power and its limitations: 'He is king over all the sons of pride' (v. 26). Just as God has his court ('the sons of God'), so Leviathan has his ('the sons of pride'). We may compare this with John 14:30 where Jesus describes the devil as 'the prince of this world'. The phrase 'sons of pride' has already occurred in 28:8 where the way to wisdom is not theirs. Leviathan knows much, his power is awesome, but ultimately he is only a creature and it is God, not he, who 'views the ends of the earth and sees everything under the heavens' (28:24).

Theologically and thematically it would be impossible to find a more fitting conclusion. The echo of chapter 28 reminds us that the Creator is in charge and indeed he is about to demonstrate this in giving to Job a new family and even greater prosperity.

The evidence, then, identifies Leviathan with Satan, the culmination of various guises in which he has appeared, for example: Leviathan (3:8); Yam and Tannin (7:12); Sea (9:8 and 38:8–11); Rahab (9:13 and 26:12); the gliding serpent (26:13). Much mystery remains, but for Job the power and providence of the Creator have been demonstrated beyond dispute.

The other Leviathan passages

Although this is a study of Job, it is useful to look at the three other passages in the Old Testament where Leviathan appears: Psalm 74:12–17; Psalm 104:26 and Isaiah 27:1. These will further demonstrate the importance of this theme in different types of literature and reinforce the thrust of the Job passage.

Psalm 74:12–17

This psalm is a communal lament which evokes the devastation of the land and in particular the vicious destruction of the temple by foreign invaders. Most commentators associate the psalm with the destruction of the temple in 587 BC and the subsequent bitter experience of exile. The lament for the lack of prophets (v. 9) is paralleled in Lamentations 2:5–9. The four-point structure of the psalm underlines the message: (1) verses 1–9 describe the tragedies on earth, especially the desecration and destruction of the temple; (2) verses 10–11 compound this with the silence and apparent inactivity of God; (3) verses 12–17 lift the curtain and give a glimpse of that greater battle waged on the cosmic scale; (4) verses 18–23 speak of the continuing mystery and suffering.

An interesting parallel is found in the book of Daniel, with chapters 1 – 6 describing events on earth and chapters 7 – 12 showing the activities in the heavenly realms of which earthly events are a reflection. More relevant, for this study, are significant parallels with Job: Job's bewilderment, God's anger and the unfolding of the real solution in the smiting of the monster which is parallel with the act of creation itself. Kidner comments usefully: 'It forestalls our hasty conclusions in the same way as the closing chapters of Job, by looking beyond the immediate problem to the total scene which God co-ordinates in wisdom.'[14]

This psalm evokes the 'total scene' by a vivid reminder of God the Creator and God the Lord of history, who at the exodus rescued his people, brought them through the flood waters (see 'Song of the Sea', Exod. 15) and created a new community. Creation is not simply one of the acts of God 'in the beginning' but the continuing providence by which his living power is seen throughout the earth. The exile, like the flood (cp. the imagery in Jer. 4), appears to have undone not only the exodus but creation, and returned the world to primordial chaos. Thus, faced with the cruel realities of exile, the psalmist here calls on God the king who defeated the chaos monster, Leviathan, and drove back the waters of the Red Sea. The God of creation and history is one God and the use of the words 'day and night' and 'sun and moon' underlines this for they are natural phenomena but they are also

[14] Kidner 1975: 269.

markers of time and thus belong to both spheres. Again the imagery is borrowed from Canaanite myth and is used here to evoke the atmosphere of cosmic struggle.[15]

As in Job 26, details of creation are paralleled with the smiting of the monster. God's power is active in both the seen and unseen worlds. The earthly counterpart of Leviathan is the enemy who 'burned your sanctuary to the ground . . . and defiled the dwelling-place of your Name' (Ps. 74:7) and who still is responsible for 'haunts of violence' (74:20). The monster, already smitten, is still active, and this same idea occurs in Revelation 17:8: 'The beast . . . will come up out of the Abyss . . . because he once was, now is not and yet will come.'

Psalm 104:26

This is a majestic hymn of praise to the Creator for his manifold works and in it we find the phrase 'There is the sea . . . and the leviathan, which you formed to frolic there.' Many view this as inconsistent with the other monster passages because Leviathan appears to have lost his fearsome qualities. However, close attention to the structure and imagery of the psalm shows this to be a superficial view. The psalm's resemblance to Genesis 1 has often been noted and this gives us a clue to discerning the significance of Leviathan here.

Psalm 104, like Genesis 1, emphasizes the unapproachable transcendence of God in the heavens, on the earth, on the land and its creatures and the sea and its inhabitants. Before the awesomeness of this God the fearsome Leviathan is cut down to size and becomes merely a plaything. This reminds us of Job 40:29 (Eng. 41:5) where God ironically asks if Leviathan can be a pet on a leash; here he is just that.

This emphasis on the transcendence of God is picked up in the theophany language of verses 4–9. The 'deep' is a garment, and the flood waters flee at the 'rebuke' of God, recalling both the flood and the exodus. God is the thunderer (v. 7b) and the one who curbs the waves (v. 9a). It is this power of the Creator that tames the majestic procession of human, animal and natural life of verses 10–30.

In such a setting, Leviathan, so fearsome and awful when he confronts Job, is a mere plaything for Yahweh. This in no way lessens the impact of the other passages but places them in the widest

---

[15] There are parallels with *CML* 3D, ll. 35–44 where Anat boasts of her victory over a number of monsters, esp. l. 39: 'the tyrant with the seven heads'.

possible context of God's power in creation. This is the emphasis of
Job 42:2:

> 'I know that you can do all things;
> no plan of yours can be thwarted.'

This brings us to the final Old Testament passage to mention
Leviathan.

Isaiah 27:1

> In that day,
> the LORD will punish with his sword,
> his fierce, great and powerful sword,
> Leviathan the gliding serpent,
> Leviathan the coiling serpent;
> he will slay the monster of the sea.

In this passage, the smiting of Leviathan is eschatological and occurs
in the so-called 'Isaiah Apocalypse' (chs. 24 – 27).[16] There are also
unmistakeable allusions to Canaanite mythology.[17] What is different
here is that this verse looks to the new creation and the final destruction of the beast when the returned exiles 'will come and worship the
Lord in the holy mountain in Jerusalem' (v. 13).

It would be interesting to trace this motif throughout Isaiah. Space
permits only a brief reference to the smiting of the evil power: the
King of Babylon brought down to Sheol (14:12ff.); the destruction of
Sennacherib, an earthly manifestation of the evil power (ch. 37); the
historical and eschatological smiting of Rahab (51:9ff.). Leviathan
here sums up all that is evil and opposed to God, no matter if its
earthly manifestation is Assyria, Babylon, Edom or any other power.
Motyer comments: 'The picture of the power of the air, the coiling
serpent on the ground, and "the dragon which is in the sea" shows the
whole creation infested with alien powers which will be sought and
destroyed wherever they are.'[18]

---

[16] Oswalt (1986: 440) points out that 'the material is not truly apocalyptic, however
that may be defined, but more correctly eschatological'.

[17] As in Ps. 74 and Job 26, the allusion is to *CML* 3D, ll. 35–44:

> Was not the dragon captured and vanquished?
> I did destroy the wriggling serpent,
> the tyrant with seven heads.

[18] Motyer 1993: 222.

The eschatological nuances of 'that day' complement and complete the creation theology of Leviathan in Job and the Psalter. The final smiting of the monster leads to that new creation that is the final answer to Job's agonies.

General comments

There are few passages like Job 41 in the Bible (although comparison has been drawn with Ezek. 28, and similar extended descriptions of evil occur in Rev. 13 and 17). Plainly the poet is underlining the awesomeness and significance of the Leviathan figure and showing how it is vital for Job, and for us, to grasp this reality in order to come to terms with what has happened. A further reflection on three areas (literary techniques, exegetical implications and biblical theology) will help to draw together some of the threads of the last four chapters.

Literary techniques

Three matters call for comment here.

First, it is significant that in chapters 40 – 41 pictures are drawn from the whole range of imagery in the book: the worlds of nature, death, law courts, domestic and commercial life. This is another demonstration of the thematic unity of the book and the climactic nature of the speech. Chapter 40:25–31 (Eng. 41:1–7) builds up a picture of a world of fishing, domestic life, trading and hunting. Doubtless the main effect of this is ironical, as already noted, but the poet is also suggesting the influence of Leviathan pervading the whole of life.

Secondly, the main cascade of images relates to the appearance and haunts of Leviathan (i.e. 41:5ff.; Eng. 41:13ff.) and the nuances of these phrases are important in establishing not just who Leviathan is, but the atmosphere of menace and terror he creates. For example, the images of fire evoke associations both of the divine presence and of an elusive and untameable force. The balancing of those with images of armour suggesting weight and strength reinforces the idea of a creature which is both rooted in an actual place and time and yet untameable and virtually impossible to pin down. There is a further level of suggestion too. By using images from the natural world, the poet is reminding us of the tragic ambiguity that lies at its heart; fire is both life-sustaining and destructive. The poet describes Leviathan in terms drawn from the world of nature of which he is a part and to which he is a threat. In doing so, the poet, with the vividness and compression that are the hallmark of great poetry, has memorably undergirded this theology.

Thirdly, the language used is marked by a subtle weaving of natural and supernatural images, as illustrated in 41:22–23 (Eng. 41:30–31). Verse 22 is a vividly naturalistic image of a crocodile or some such animal leaving a trail in the mud. Then in verse 23 we move to the world of the sea. The $t^eh\hat{o}m$ is the familiar ocean we can sail on, yet it is also the haunt of primordial evil where Leviathan presides over the 'sons of pride'. The poet, in his choice of words, is conveying the complexity and ambivalence at the heart of the fallen creation.

Exegetical implications

Much of the preceding four chapters has been concerned with the exegesis of the second divine speech, and with demonstrating that Behemoth and Leviathan are not new figures introduced at this late stage, but the climax of a carefully orchestrated preparation. Two questions remain: why are they in that particular order, and why is the Leviathan passage so much longer and more overwhelming?

To take the question of order, it has already been argued that the concentration on the underworld (40:13), as well as the increasing emphasis on death at the end of chapter 39, prepares the way for the figure of death itself. But death, fearsome as he is, is ultimately a lesser power. Indeed, when death eventually comes for Job at the end of chapter 42, it is robbed of much of its terror for he passes away honoured and surrounded by family and friends. It is not so much death, as 'the dread of something after death' (*Hamlet*) which haunts the most terrifying passages (for example, ch. 18). More fearsome than death is the power that stands behind death and 'can destroy soul and body in hell' (Matt. 10:28 RSV) and that 'holds the power of death' (Heb. 2:14). Living before the cross and the resurrection, Job only glimpsed the realities of the principalities and powers to be given that death-blow by Christ, but part of his greater insight was to recognize the reality of those powers. Thus the exegesis of the Behemoth passage has important implications for the understanding of earlier parts of the book (not least Job's long meditation on death in chs. 13 – 15), as well as implications for the analysis of the Leviathan passage.

Leviathan plainly is introduced deliberately as the climax of the supernatural imagery of the poetic dialogue. First of all we have an inclusio: in 3:8 the rousing of Leviathan corresponds to the permission given to Satan, and now chapters 40 and 41 bring that to a stirring conclusion. At the beginning Leviathan was a rather shadowy figure who appeared in various disguises throughout the dialogue, but now he is being comprehensively unmasked. God knows all there is to know about him, and thus his words are not a series of abstract statements about the power of evil but a vivid and unforgettable insight into its nature and how this is bound up with the innermost workings of the universe.

Commentators have been led astray by interpreting the many details in a naturalistic way and ignoring the important nuances of the words. This reflects the rationalizing tendency of much of the work of scholars such as Driver, Gray and Dhorme whose primary concern was philology and who gave relatively little thought to the theological significance of Leviathan.

This lengthy passage clears the way for the very different atmosphere of chapter 42 (see ch. 9, p. 183). Leviathan/Satan has no place in the final outcome, but it is imperative that Job and the reader are not 'left in ignorance of his devices'.

Implications for biblical theology

More will be said in our final chapter about Job and biblical theology as a whole, but two points can be made here.

First, Leviathan, as already noted, is firmly linked with creation; however fearsome, he is simply a creature (a fact underlined in Ps. 104). Thus he cannot be seen in isolation from the poet's theology of creation, especially in chapters 28 and 38 – 39. Creation itself has violence as well as beauty and is shot through with pain and distress. This is the fallen creation and the agonies of Job have been an example of 'the bondage to decay' that runs through the whole of creation and waits for 'the glorious freedom of the children of God' (Rom. 8:21).

This first point is linked with another point. Unlike Psalm 74 and Isaiah 51, Job does not emphasize the smiting and final destruction of the monster. That is implied in the control of God over the whole created universe but it needs the eye of faith to discern this. The implications of God's control will be further explored in the next chapter. Standing at the other side of the cross and the resurrection we know that the evil one has been defeated, that Christ has the victory. The vindication of Job is part of the biblical witness pointing to Satan's defeat and yet it shows vividly the many agonies and stern challenges to faith which still remain. In this world the realities of God's providence and victory can be perceived only by faith, and that is the victory which overcomes the world.

Chapter Nine

The vision glorious

'Nothing of difficulty in this verse.' Thus, and wearily, Sebastian Schmidt writes on Job 42:17.[1] This sense of weariness appears to grip many commentators when they reach chapter 42. Few take seriously the immense importance of this chapter for a final assessment of the theology of the book.[2] To set the scene I want to make two introductory observations.

First, chapter 42 is crucial in demonstrating the unity of the book. I explored this theme in chapter 1 of my study and will be returning to it later in this chapter. Secondly, my interpretation of Job, especially the figures of Behemoth and Leviathan, must be consistent with, and indeed illuminate, chapter 42. I intend to examine three main areas: the structure of the chapter; the theological implications and the place of Job in the canon as a whole.

Structure

Most commentators discern a threefold structure: (1) verses 1–6 which end the poetic dialogue; (2) verses 7–9 which tie up loose ends in the narrative; and (3) verses 10–17 which look to the future. Each of these sections deals with unfinished business and that applies even to the third which points beyond itself.

When we examine verses 1–6 we realize that we are at the climax and moment of understanding in the poetic dialogue. Job had longed, indeed insisted, that God should appear in the court and give an answer (9:3, 32; 10:4; 16:19; 19:25–27; 24:1 etc.). This has now happened and Job (more fully than in 40:4) is responding. There is an urgency and passion here that is the result of the amazing confrontation of chapters

[1] Schmidt's 1670 commentary on Job; cited in Clines 1989: xxx.
[2] An exception is Janzen (1985) who wrestles seriously with ch. 42's links with the rest of the book. Although I have grave reservations about much of what he says (not least his conflation of Yahweh and Satan), at least he recognizes the immense importance of the chapter.

38 – 41. By quoting the challenge in God's words from the whirlwind, Job shows that both the first and second divine speeches are in view. His use of words like 'know' and 'understand' reflect the pattern of God's own words in chapters 38 and 39.

The second quotation (v. 4, quoting 38:3) focuses on Job's listening to the divine words. As we shall see, there is a fine balance of hearing and saying. Moreover, his 'repentance' in dust and ashes completes a movement that began in 2:8 with Job sitting among the ashes. Janzen rightly points out that so far in the speech-cycles all has been confrontation but now reconciliation is achieved.[3]

The 'debate' does not reach a 'resolution' in the sense that all the profound issues and huge problems explored are given detailed answers. Rather the words of God have produced first silence (40:4) and then words of restored relationship (42:1–6).[4] Thus the dialogue ends with Job in the same physical location as at the beginning but with a far deeper knowledge and experience of God.

The second section (vv. 7–9) resumes the prose narrative broken off in 2:13 and links it intimately with the poetic dialogue ('After the Lord had said these things to Job'). Again the early chapters of the book are echoed ironically. In 2:11–13 the three friends had come to visit Job in his distress and had sat silent for seven days and seven nights.[5] Thus they failed both in their silence and their speech. Job again appears as intercessor (cp. 1:5). Once again, four times in fact (vv. 7–8), Job is described by the Lord as 'my servant'. In this section the questions posed in chapters 1 and 2 are faced and resolved.

The third section (vv. 10–17), with a limpid and lucid grace, takes the story of Job to a happy and satisfying conclusion. I shall comment on the theology later, but a number of narrative and structural matters deserve mention. First, the movement begins with Job's prayers and this is neatly balanced with reference to the providence of God both in grace (v. 10) and trial (v. 11).

Secondly, there is a renewed emphasis on the physical blessings of family and possessions which had been at the heart of the terrible

---

[3] Janzen 1985: 248.

[4] This is a very different situation from that in the third speech cycle. Thus Eliphaz (ch. 22) urges Job to repent of evil; Bildad (ch. 25) ends in a sour tirade, and Zophar has sputtered out in angry denunciation (ch. 20).

[5] The significance of 2:11–13 is disputed. Some take the seven days' silence as empathy. It is also possible to take it as evidence that the friends already think of Job as a dead man, a man without a future; seven days is normal period of formal mourning for the dead (see e.g. Gen. 50:10).

reversal of Job's experience in chapters 1 and 2. The emphasis here is on generous and lavish blessing.

Thirdly, the narrative ends on a patriarchal note (cp. Abraham's death in Gen. 25:8). Death, which had been such a menacing presence, now comes at the end of a long and fulfilling life. This ending is a reminder that the Creator loves to bless (see Gen. 1:28). Job who had wished the day of his birth to be blotted out (3:2–6), now lives to praise and glorify God.

Thus the structure of this chapter contains important pointers to the unity of the whole book. The links between the narrative and dialogue are crucial to a true understanding of the ending of Job. The main characters (with the exception of Satan and Elihu) reappear. I shall comment later on the absence of Satan from the final scene. Moreover, the theological emphases of the book are given final treatment and it is to these we now turn.

Theological issues

There are nine issues of theological importance that will be useful to our discussion at this point.

What Job now knows

The first relates to what Job now 'knows' and 'understands' (vv. 2–3). These words, at the heart of so much wisdom literature, underlie the unfolding pattern of the first divine speech. God, who made the world by wisdom, continually asks Job whether he 'knows' such things as the place where light dwells (38:19–21) or when the mountain goats give birth (39:1). Job does not 'know' these things in the sense that he is not the creator and what he knows about them is partial and limited. Yet here Job is now claiming to 'know', and God does not contradict him.

What is it that Job now knows? First, he is convinced of God's sovereignty over the universe. He had already, of course, been convinced of this, most especially in chapter 9, but then he had seen this sovereignty as hostile. The huge difference in Job's understanding has come about since God spoke to him and revealed to him the intricacy and providential care evident in every part of the natural order.

Job further develops this in verse 2b: 'No plan of yours can be thwarted.' The word translated 'plan' is $m^e zimm\hat{a}$, used, for example, in Jeremiah 23:20 for the purposes of God's heart (there referring to the judgment of the exile). In the discussion of chapter 39, reference was made to the strong underlying idea of providence and thus Job is here addressing the God of creation who works out everything according to the purpose of his will.

This knowledge merges into confession in verse 3. It is important to understand clearly what is happening here. Job does not confess to sins he has not committed; neither to the overt sins of Eliphaz's allegations in 22:4–11, nor to the secret ones implied by Bildad in chapter 8. No-one, not even Satan, convicts Job of that. Rather Job is acknowledging that his idea of God had been limited. However, I suggest that this goes rather further than the revelation of chapters 38 and 39 to which Job had already responded with a resolve to be silent (40:4–5). This confirms the thrust of this study that the portraits of Behemoth and Leviathan are further revelation rather than simply an intensifying of chapters 38 and 39. I shall develop this further in the next comments but will point out here that Job's reaction is like that of others who receive such an awesome revelation (cp. Hab. 3:16–18).

What Job now sees

Not only does Job 'know', he now 'sees'; and two aspects of this change need to be considered. First, in what sense does he see, and what is it that he sees? The seeing is linked by many commentators to 19:26–27:

> '. . . yet in my flesh I will see God;
> I myself will see him
>   with my own eyes'.

Yet there are grounds for thinking that this is only partially true. The earlier passage, as already discussed, places emphasis on the physicality of the experience. Whatever we may make of the phrase 'in my flesh' (see earlier discussion on pp. 51–52), the expression 'with my own eyes' implies a bodily and post-resurrection experience. This 'seeing' is important here but, as we shall see, still leaves unanswered questions.[6]

Further light is thrown on the phrase 'with my own eyes' when we consider some of the other great theophanic passages in the Bible. In Exodus 34:18 Moses asks Yahweh to show him his glory, a request partially answered by Yahweh allowing Moses to see his back. Yet the

[6] See also Andersen 1976: 292.

true 'seeing' is the revelation which follows in chapter 34 and is embodied in the tablets of the covenant. Similarly, in Isaiah 6, when the prophet sees Yahweh, the revelation is embodied in the message he is given, and indeed the whole of the prophetic book. This is neatly encapsulated in Isaiah 1:1–2, detailing a vision that the prophet sees and yet the first words of that vision are 'hear' and 'listen'. Further, in Revelation 1, John on Patmos sees a vision of the risen Christ, a vision that controls the entire book. Yet the purpose of that vision is that it might be written (1:11), and the closing words of the vision urge a hearing of the words of the prophecy of that book (22:18). To see God is inextricably bound up with hearing God.

We must take care not to misunderstand the dynamics of verse 5, as if they were contrasting hearing and seeing *per se*. Rather, the difference lies in a comparison between, for example, chapters 9 and 28 and the divine speeches from the whirlwind. Chapter 9 makes profound comments on the mystery and majesty of the Creator and chapter 28 on the wonder and wisdom of the created order. But chapters 38 – 41 have one major difference. There it is God himself who outlines these mysteries and marvels and who exposes the powers of evil. Mystery remains, as in the other theophanies mentioned above, yet the appearance of God himself means that the words spoken are words of revelation.

Two observations follow from this. The first is that mere hearing in the sense of 'hearing of' is not sufficient. This is well illustrated in 4:12–17 in Eliphaz's 'vision', which I have already argued is a deception of the enemy (see pp. 145–147). There Eliphaz hears a 'word' and a form stands before his eyes. This uncanny experience leads to nothing but platitudes, nor does it give him increased sensitivity. Eliphaz and the other friends do not truly hear.

The second observation is that true hearing and vision belong together. Truly to hear God is to see God. It is because Job has listened to God that he now sees God.

What Job now does

According to the NIV of 42:6, Job says to God:

> 'Therefore I despise myself
> and repent in dust and ashes.'

Both the verbs call for comment. The verb translated 'despise' is *'em'as*, which may either be related to *mā'as* ('despise', 'loathe'; with

NOW MY EYES HAVE SEEN YOU

object 'myself' supplied from contexts) or to *māsas* ('to sink down', 'to melt away'). Habel argues that it suggests, dismisses or retracts his case against God (citing 31:13) as a parallel.[7] This argument fits well with the acknowledgment that he failed to understand the divine pattern of creation; an acknowledgment that is a further result of listening to and seeing God.

'Repent' does not mean he now confesses to sins he has not committed. Rather it is the reaction that would be expected after the theophany of chapters 38 – 41. Thus Isaiah cries 'I am ruined' (Is. 6:5) and John on Patmos falls before the risen Christ 'as though dead' (Rev. 1:17). Job, like Jacob, has wrestled with God and this will mark him for the rest of his life. However, he now recognizes that, while he has not committed sins which have led to his afflictions, he has been guilty of presumption and he wishes to turn from that.

'Dust and ashes' began the dialogue (2:8), and symbolize mourning and exile. But here the story has moved on and that brings us to our next comment.

Speaking what is right about God

The epilogue is tied very closely to the preceding dialogue by the Lord's condemnation of the friends for not speaking what is right and his commendation of Job for speaking what is true. This point must be related to God's own speaking in chapters 38 – 41 and the revelation of reality given there.

The friends had effectively misrepresented God although appearing to speak from within the mainstream Wisdom tradition. A few words on how they fail to say what is right would be useful at this point. Eliphaz is essentially a philosopher whose characteristic mode of discourse is: 'as I have observed' (4:8) or 'we have examined' (5:27).[8] At the start he appears reasonable, even kindly, but by chapter 15 he has become harsh and intolerant. Bildad is a traditionalist who counsels learning from former generations (8:8–10), but by chapter 18 he has become vicious and vindictive. Zophar is a dogmatist and theorist and is probably the least attractive of the friends. Right from his opening speech in chapter 11 he lacks compassion. He is blunt and uses his debating skill in a heartless way. Often all three use ideas which may be right in themselves but fail to see that they do not apply to Job's situation.

---

[7] Habel, 1985: 576.
[8] See Gibson 1975.

They are self-appointed spokesmen for God and what they say is exposed in all its shallowness by the devastating grandeur expressed in chapters 38 – 41. They have a mechanical view of creation and providence and fail utterly to glimpse the supernatural dimensions of Job's agony. Even when they blunder against it, as Eliphaz does in his vision in chapter 4 and Bildad in his evocation of the 'king of terrors' in chapter 18, they simply use these as sticks with which to beat Job.

Job, on the other hand, while confessing, as we have seen, to ignorance and presumption had nevertheless glimpsed the great realities unfolded in chapters 38 – 41. First, he had used the language of awe, mystery and wonder in chapters 9, 26 and 28, which anticipate the first divine speech. Second, he had often, as already noted, perceived the mystery of evil which lay at the heart of creation and which is embodied in Behemoth and Leviathan. This, in my view, strengthens the case for the supernatural interpretation of these figures. It is the extra element in the second divine speech which completes the revelation God gives to Job.

Job's intercession

Also in verses 7–9 Job intercedes for his friends in a manner which recalls Abraham's intercession for Sodom (Gen. 18:22–33) and Moses' intercession for the people after the golden calf incident (Exod. 32:30–31). Significantly, four times in these three verses God calls Job 'my servant', giving him a Moses-like status.[9] Two matters deserve comment.

First, this ties the beginning and ending of the story together. Not only is Job called 'servant', but his intercession here recalls his similar activity in relation to his family (1:5). Job has always been a man of prayer. Even his fiercest denunciations and angriest cries have been a determination not to let God go until he blesses him.

Secondly, there is the delicately nuanced relationship between Job's prayer and God's answer. The prayer is the initiative of God: 'My servant Job will pray for you' (v. 8). Yet this is not a knee-jerk reaction on Job's part but evidence of the restored and deepened relationship he has with the Lord. The fact that the Lord accepts the prayer shows that it is genuine. James, in his comment on the Job story, notes 'The Lord is full of compassion and mercy' (Jas. 5:11). This compassion is

[9] 'Servant' is a title used in the OT most frequently for Moses (37 times) and David (38 times). Its use for Job underlines his special status and, incidentally, supports the historicity of the story.

shown not only in the restoration of Job but in the way the friends are accepted back into his grace.

Prayer and Job's restoration

We come now to the 'happy ending' which many have found an anti-climax or have speculated that it is the work of a pious writer who was afraid the book was not sufficiently orthodox. However, a number of points can be made in defence of this ending.

First, it is important to note that God's restoration of Job was an act of grace shown by the fact that it was a twofold restoration (v. 10). It is not a bargain. Also Job's restored relationship with God and his intercession for the friends happen before the blessing comes. In this respect Job is like the sufferer in many of the lament psalms, who although his situation is as yet unchanged, praises God and declares his faith (e.g. Pss. 22:22; 31:14). Yet seen as part of the story of God's eternal purposes, Job must be vindicated. God's providence will always be mysterious, but because of his purpose to create a new heaven and new earth it is possible even now to live the life of faith.

Secondly, the expression 'made him prosperous again' is character-istically used for the nation restored from exile (e.g. Jer. 29:14 and Ps. 126:4). The basic text is Deuteronomy 30:3 which promises restora-tion from exile if there is a turning to God: 'then the LORD your God will restore your fortunes and have compassion on you and gather you again from all the nations where he scattered you'. It is probably unwise to press the link between Job and the exile too far, but it is valid to note here the connection between Job and the nation, for both are the objects of divine providence.

Thirdly, the specific linking of prayer and restoration shows that it is the *relationship with God* that is at the heart of all that happens. Prayer is thus not an incidental ingredient but the essential link between the mystery of God in creation and providence and the events in this story.

The Lord and Job

Two important expressions crystallize the events as they have unfolded and are yet to happen. Verse 11 speaks of 'all the trouble the LORD had brought upon him', and verse 12 says that 'The LORD blessed the latter part of Job's life more than the first.' *The Lord* is the sole cause of all that has happened and will happen. Verses 11–12 raise a number of questions that bear especially on the relationship of God and evil.

The first is that here, after the revelation of God in creation and providence, no secondary agents or causes are identified. This indeed was the perspective at the beginning: 'shall we accept good from God and not trouble?' (2:10). That perspective has now been demonstrated in a much fuller and deeper way.

Moreover this perspective explains the absence of Satan from the final scene. Some commentators have failed to see the significance of this absence. Andersen rightly comments that Job is not presenting dualism and that Satan is small compared to the Lord. But he also states, inaccurately I believe, that 'The contribution of the Satan to the action of the book is minor. His place in its theology is even less. In the subsequent discussions the misfortunes of men are never traced to a diabolical foe.'[10]

The problem of the 'subsequent discussions' is that it is just this presence of a diabolical foe that the friends have failed to perceive. Trapped in their mechanical universe, they rightly believe that God is supreme but fail to see the sheer power and personality of evil. That power which has masqueraded in many guises has been exposed in chapter 41. Here, however, God and his servant Job are face to face again, but now Job's faith and understanding are immeasurably deeper. Satan has been and is a terrible adversary, but he cannot thwart the final outcome. Even now – and this is part of the mystery of providence – he cannot act except with God's permission.

The Lord's blessing

Verses 12–16 speak of Job's new family and possessions. We must avoid being over-spiritual in our analysis of Job's renewed prosperity. We must never forget that God delights to bless humans. One of the key verbs in Genesis 1 is 'bless', which is particularly associated there with procreation (Gen. 1:28). Similarly 'descendants' are a vital part of the blessing to Abraham and we are told in Genesis 13:2 that he 'had become very wealthy in livestock and in silver and gold'.

Furthermore, such material blessings do not take away Job's or Abraham's need for faith. Job still has one hundred and forty years ahead of him, and there is no guarantee that his new family and possessions will be immune from trouble. Also, Job's consciousness that these blessings were gifts of grace is reflected in his own conduct. No law required Job to give an inheritance to his daughters, but the grace which had blessed him now flows out to others.

[10] Andersen 1976: 83.

Job's death

In my earlier analysis of the structure of this chapter (pp. 175–177), I suggested that each of the sections pointed beyond themselves and this includes verses 16–17 which speak of Job dying 'old and full of years'.

Again the patriarchal echoes sound, for similar words are used of Abraham in Genesis 25:8. This long life, as much as the new family and possessions, was a gracious gift of God. Death here, having also been exposed in chapter 41, comes gently at the end of a full and fruitful life.

And there is more. Plainly the life beyond the grave awaits the resurrection of Jesus before it can be revealed. Yet what has happened in this chapter is a partial unfolding of that. Job has indeed seen God, but the ultimate fulfilment of his leap of faith in 19:24–27 awaits a fuller experience beyond the grave. Mystery remains, but death is under the control of the Lord whom Job has already seen and heard.

Job and biblical theology

If the thrust of this study is correct, then the issues raised are central not only for the interpretation of Job but for biblical theology as a whole. I want now to outline three areas of major significance.

Job and Wisdom

In our opening chapter we looked briefly at the Wisdom tradition in ancient Israel (pp. 23–24). Here I want to comment particularly on the relationship between Job and Proverbs. It is often thought that Proverbs presents a simplistic and over-idealized picture of the 'good life', with little sense of the agonies and pains of mortal life, and puts forward a mechanical view of the righteous being rewarded and the evil punished in this life. It is held that the book of Job demonstrates the inadequacy of such a mechanical and naïve theology; the theology, in fact, of Job's friends. It would be more true to say, however, that Job *prevents* such a simplistic reading of Proverbs.

A careful reading of Proverbs illustrates this. In Proverbs 8:21 Wisdom speaks of 'bestowing wealth on those who love me and making their treasuries full'. However, the last verses of the chapter do not allow us to interpret that promise in a crassly literalistic way. There the issues are no less than life and death (vv. 35–36). Job indeed is so blessed that the restored and deepened relationship with God is seen as ultimately more important than material blessing.

This nuanced presentation of the issues of life and death that we find in Proverbs is also evident in Psalm 1. Clearly Job is a model of the blessed man in that psalm. The imagery is very important: the blessed are compared to the living world of nature, to fruit trees and running water. This comparison shows that they are people who live their lives the way the Creator intended. Moreover, there is no implication that the final destiny will be reached easily any more than trees escape storm and attack by other natural phenomena.

Thus the view that Job is a critique of the Wisdom tradition, as represented by Proverbs, cannot be sustained. The relationship is rather one of complementarity. Both explore the implications of the doctrine of creation rather than the issues of salvation history. Yet something needs to be said of Job's relationship, if any, to Old Testament history.

Job and salvation history

At first sight, the book of Job seems remote from issues such as history, covenant and law. Yet the issues of creation and providence that lie at the heart of Job also lie at the centre of the story of God's mighty acts, and this is demonstrated particularly clearly in the exodus narrative. There are at least two areas where the theology of Job relates to that of Exodus.

The first is the way in which Exodus 7 – 19 represents the plagues as a contest between Yahweh and the gods of Egypt.[11] This contest is made explicit in Exodus 12:12: 'I will pass through Egypt . . . and I will bring judgment on all the gods of Egypt. I am the LORD.' The world Job experienced, with his sense of hostile powers such as Yam and Mot, is also what the covenant people experienced in the most crucial event of Old Testament history.

The other area of particular significance is the Red Sea crossing and its imagery which is particularly associated with the chaos battle, in the ancient poem which is Exodus 15. This aspect of the exodus also occurs in the Psalter, for example in Psalm 77:16:

> The waters saw you, O God,
>   the waters saw you and writhed;
>   the very depths were convulsed.

---

[11] The plague narratives can be seen as an attack on various members of the Egyptian pantheon; e.g. the darkness is a blotting out of Amon-Re, the sun god. For a useful recent study see Currid 1997: 83–121.

Yet there is a strong emphasis on the incomparability of Yahweh (Exod. 15:11) that is similar to Job's understanding after seeing Yahweh's power in the stunning panoramic vision of chapters 38 – 41.

A related issue is the way the writers of the historical books explore the influence of supernatural evil in the course of events. Some such incidents are: Dagon's idol smashed before the Ark of the Covenant (1 Sam. 5); the evil spirit that tormented Saul (1 Sam. 16:14ff.); the witch of Endor (1 Sam. 28); Satan's incitement of David to number Israel (1 Chr. 21); the lying spirit in the vision of Micaiah ben Imlah (2 Kgs. 22:19ff.); and, perhaps, Manasseh's pagan worship (2 Kgs. 21). Ultimately these are evidences of the great struggle adumbrated in Genesis 3:15. Once again, Job, with its picture of the fundamental reality of the heavenly court, belongs in the same area as these and many other passages. Just as Job's story did not fit into the neat parameters of the mechanical theology of the friends, so the history of God's people is not to be seen purely in terms of the power politics of the Ancient Near East.

Another area of great importance is the legal framework of the book (discussed in ch. 2 of this study) which has many connections with other parts of the Old Testament. Job's character, in chapter 1 and in his final summing up of his case in chapters 29 – 31, is set in a legal framework. Chapter 29 is a fine evocation of Job as a leading figure in an old Israelite community, looking forward to a ripe old age and then dying like Moses with vigour unabated. In this community Job experienced all the blessings promised to the covenant people. In 29:6 he speaks of the time

'when my path was drenched with cream
and the rock poured out for me streams of olive oil'.

This plentiful existence was to be the experience of Israel in the promised land with springs, wine, olive oil and honey (Deut. 8:6ff.). Job has also practised the active virtues of social justice, compassion to the poor, widows, orphans and foreigners, as prescribed in Deuteronomy 22ff. Yet in Job 30 we have a picture of Job in the present: mocked and derided and certain that he is the object of God's hostility. The curses for breaking the covenant have come on him (30:16ff.): wasting disease (Deut. 28:21–22) and painful boils (Deut. 28:35). These are part of his affliction (2:7); he is ridiculed and scorned (cp. Deut. 28:37 with 30:9–10).

This use of covenant language in Job is important both for the theology of that book and more widely for the theology of covenant itself. It places Job within a recognizable Old Testament context and forces us to consider fundamental questions about that context. It prevents us understanding covenant in a mechanical way and underlines that covenant is a gift of grace. It shows that while punishment is an inevitable consequence of disobedience, blessing is an act of grace and that suffering will be an inextricable part of the road to that blessing.

It is worth mentioning here that the legal metaphor, while not totally comprehensive as a description of the relationship between Yahweh and the community or an individual, is an essential component of that relationship.

Job and the canon

In spite of the apparent unorthodoxy of some parts of Job, its canonicity was never questioned (unlike the book of Ecclesiastes). Its profundity and spiritual power were recognized from the beginning and interest in it continues unabated. In this final section I shall comment on how some of its major concerns are addressed in a unique way and yet form an important part of the biblical canon as a whole.

First, we have the picture of God which illustrates well how the book of Job is both Jewish and universal. The God of the dialogue is usually called 'Eloah' or 'Shaddai' or some such name, but it is clear not only from the framing story but from the divine speeches (38 – 31) that this God is Yahweh the Covenant Lord. He is the God who both reveals and hides himself. He is the God who, as in John's Gospel, reveals himself fully in the Word made flesh (John 1:1–14) and also hides himself (John 12:20–36).

This paradoxical aspect of God is displayed in the depiction of the heavenly court whose doings are concealed from Job and form no part of the revelation in 38 – 41. A parallel might be drawn with Daniel 10 – 12, although there the angel who comes from the heavenly court draws aside the veil for both Daniel and the reader.

God is both the judge and disposer of destinies and the God of Israel. To put that another way, he is the God of Genesis 1 – 11 as well as the God of Genesis 12 and the story of Abraham and his descendants. Canonically, Job's portrait of God is linked to both these great themes of creation and providence. Moreover, the book of Job shows a God whose ways are beyond our ways (Is. 55:9ff.) and yet whose Word comes down from heaven and causes transformation. God who appears so distant is also the God who speaks at length to his servant and brings him to new depths of understanding.

The importance of both aspects of the picture of God cannot be overstated. Ultimately, the wonder and mystery of God are the surest protection against idolatry. This God cannot be confined in temples, intellectual systems or our limited experience, much less can he be represented by material artefacts. Yet the fact that this God also speaks and reveals himself prevents mystery becoming a vague and spurious mysticism detached from ethics, thought and true worship. Thus, in coming to a truly biblical understanding of God, the book of Job is of enormous importance. For a proper understanding of the book it is vital that we discern the very heart of its message: we need to know and hear God. Other themes and ideas flow from this.

There is, secondly, a profound concern with creation. The canonical shape of the Bible, with creation in Genesis 1 and 2 and new creation in Revelation 21 and 22, reflects the fundamental importance of the doctrine in the biblical revelation. This was our concern in chapter 3 of this study and only a few further comments are needed here.

In microcosm, the flow of the book reflects that of the canon itself. The 'blessedness' of the first few verses and the greater blessedness of the last few verses frame a profound struggle with the mysteries of creation, during which Job longs for the created order to be dissolved (ch. 3), expresses both awe and dismay at its mysteries (ch. 9), uses profound language of worship (ch. 26) and wrestles with great theological issues of wisdom and creation (ch. 28).

There is also a profound concern with providence, especially God's just government of the created order. Among other things, chapters 38 and 39 insist that no part of creation is beyond God's control. The book of Job powerfully combines the most searching and organized questions about the justice at the heart of creation with the most deep-rooted conviction that God is good. Such concerns surface in many other places in the Bible and Job shows both the anguish of creation as it groans in the pains of childbirth and the hope of liberation from its bondage to decay (Rom. 8:19–22).

Thirdly (and this has, of course, been central to this study), is the concern with evil in the created order. I have argued in detail for the supernatural character of Behemoth and Leviathan and again only a few comments on the canonical appropriateness of this are needed.

This interpretation places the book of Job firmly in the overall thrust of the Bible's plot-line. Evil comes into the good creation from a creature. In Genesis 3:1 the serpent is a creature, as are Behemoth and Leviathan. In that sense Yahweh creates evil (Is. 45:7); not in the sense that he made evil creatures, but that he made free creatures with the capacity to disobey. Thus evil springs from within the created order. On a cosmic scale, in Revelation 12 and 13 the dragon summons two beasts from sea and earth. The evil which attacks Job is no abstraction; it is expressed first in shadowy figures which haunt him and then in solid physical reality in the giant powers of chapter 41.

The story of Job is an outcropping of that great struggle begun in Genesis 3:15 where God himself takes the initiative: 'I will put enmity', and predicts the result: 'he will crush your head'. This culminates in the revelation that the death and resurrection of Jesus Christ will destroy the works of the devil.

The picture of evil powers in the created order never becomes dualism. God is Creator and Satan is a creature. As C. S. Lewis points out in the *Screwtape Letters*, the opposite of Satan is not God but Michael.[12] Satan is a terrifying adversary, and at times Job may well feel he is in a dualistic universe, but in the end, as in the end of the book of Revelation, Satan is banished for ever.

Fourthly, there is the problem of suffering which can be truly seen only when these other issues have been faced. Suffering is part of that world which emerges from the fall and is inextricably bound up with sinfulness. Job, however, like John 9, is concerned with that kind of suffering which bears no relationship to the specific sins of individuals. The friends, however, are bound to a rigorously deterministic view in which virtue is always rewarded by prosperity and sin is always punished by adversity.

Canonically, Job takes its place alongside Jeremiah, 2 Corinthians and some of the lament psalms (e.g. Ps. 73). The calm at the end of Job is one that was reached by intense suffering, whose final explanation will come only when God wipes away every tear from our eyes.

Two closing observations can be made. First, it is important to avoid making the book of Job into something it is not. It does say profound and illuminating things about suffering, but those who turn to it hoping to find 'answers' to their particular situation often find it fails to provide the kind of solutions they hope for. Similarly, preachers turning to Job hoping it will help people through a time of crisis will have to be careful not to spend so much time refuting the friends' arguments that they draw out little of positive value. The answer to

[12] In C. S. Lewis, 1942: 11.

this, I suggest, is to see that the book is not so much about suffering *per se* as about creation, providence and knowing God, and how, in the crucible of suffering, these are to be understood.

Secondly, we must see Job's suffering in a wider biblical context. Job takes his place with Joseph in prison, with Moses in the desert, with Jeremiah in the dungeon, with the Paul of 2 Corinthians 11. Suffering, in all these cases and in many others, such as the nameless faithful of Hebrews 11, is both transformed in their own lives and part of what God has to teach us in our Christian pilgrimage. This is emphasized in James 5:11: 'You have seen what the Lord finally brought about.'

Reading and studying Job can be an alarming and unpredictable experience. Many apparent certainties disappear and familiar landmarks seem few and far between. Yet to glimpse even a little of the book's awesome picture of God's providence, expressed in glorious and richly resonant language, is to undergo both a chastening and healing experience. To listen to this book is to listen to the Master's voice.

Appendix

Job and Canaanite myth

Frequent reference has been made to the Ugaritic texts and more broadly to Canaanite myth, and the purpose of this appendix is to draw some of these threads together and provide background information. Four issues will be outlined: (1) the significance of Ugarit; (2) the relevance of the Baal sagas; (3) some illustrative examples; and (4) some comments on theological significance.

The significance of Ugarit for Old Testament studies

The discovery of Ugarit is like a story-book episode. In the spring of 1928 an Arab peasant, while working his land, struck a large flagstone. He cleared the earth and found a subterranean passage. Subsequent excavation uncovered an ancient tomb. This was the mound of Ras Shamra near the north Syrian coast. Within months a team was sent out under Claude F. A. Schaeffer of the Archaeological Museum in Strasbourg. They uncovered the lost city of Ugarit, mentioned in Babylonian, Hittite and Egyptian texts, whose site hitherto had been unknown.

The archaeologists found thousands of clay tablets written in alphabetic cuneiform. This previously unknown language was deciphered with remarkable speed. In addition to these tablets in the Ugaritic language, many other texts in Akkadian, Sumerian, Hittite and Egyptian were discovered. The tablets are extremely varied and include administrative and economic texts. But those most significant for biblical study are poetic texts, especially those dealing with the god Baal and other members of the Ugaritic pantheon. Many of these were written down some time between 1400 and 1350 BC and were compiled or edited by a scribe called Elimelek. They give us a fascinating glimpse into the thought-world of Canaanite culture just before the conquest.

Their significance for Old Testament studies is threefold. First, especially in the poetic books of the Old Testament such as Job, many difficult words can be understood in the light of Ugaritic. Secondly, many themes and motifs, such as the divine council and the battle with the sea god, appear to be echoed in Scripture. Thirdly, there appear to be important connections with the thought-world of the texts and the Old Testament.[1]

The relevance of the Baal sagas

A number of the tablets found in the temple library of Ugarit contain sagas of the exploits of the god Baal. Baal and his sister (or consort) Anat appear to have been the main focus of worship among the pantheon. Two sagas in particular are relevant.

The first is Baal's battle with Yam (or Yammu) the sea god. This is one of a number of such stories in the Ancient Near East and in it Yam represents the primeval forces of chaos, while Baal represents order and life. My argument is that the Job author has found in this story a powerful metaphor for the triumph of God over the evil in creation. This saga culminates with a long poem of the building of Baal's palace which is a symbol of his victory. We may compare this with Psalm 93 which speaks of Yahweh's power over the raging waters and then, with apparent irrelevance, speaks of holiness becoming his house (v. 6). The house is, however, not only the temple but the orderly universe, secure and dedicated to God because of his victory.

The second saga tells of Baal's struggle with Mot whose name means 'Death'. Baal is worsted but restored, and, helped by Anat, resumes the conflict. Mot is an earth monster, and in this study I have argued that Behemoth is the figure of Death.

Both these sagas speak of the great discords in creation and of people's fear of the powers of chaos and death. The Job poet uses these well-known materials in a way consistent with his own worldview.

Some examples

At various points specific reference has been made to the Ugaritic texts and here I shall mention only two examples.

---

[1] Craigie 1983 is a judicious account of the discovery of the city, and in ch. 5 makes some shrewd and sane comments on Ugarit and the Old Testament. For details of the edition of the texts I have used see *CML* in the abbreviations list. For a fuller edition see Wyatt 1998.

First, Job 19:25. This text was discussed in chapter 2 as part of the material on the heavenly court. Here I want to look at it in connection with a passage in the Baal/Mot saga:

> that I may know that mightiest Baal is alive,
> that the prince lord of the earth exist.
>
> (*CML* 6, col. iii, ll. 8–9)

Many commentators mention these lines but fail to demonstrate a link with the Job passage. However, it is possible to find some connections. Baal, in his battles with Yam and Mot, is not only fighting in an individual capacity but as champion of the gods. Thus he rebukes the other gods for their cowardly behaviour at the presence of Yam's envoys (*CML* 2, col. i, ll. 24ff.). Similarly, the consternation and sense of helplessness in the divine assembly at the death of Baal is evident in the words 'Baal is dead! What will [become of] the people of Dagon's son?' (*CML* 6, col. i, l. 6).

From these passages it appears that Baal acts, in a way, as a *gô'ēl* for the fine court and that without him there is an air of vulnerability and desolation.

Secondly, Job 41:4 (Eng. 41:12). This is one of the more difficult verses in the extended description of Leviathan, and Pope had discerned in it a further allusion to the battle of Baal and Yam.[2] He renders the verse:

> Did I not silence his boasting
> By the powerful word Hayyin prepared?

He argues that *baddāyw* does not mean 'limbs' (as in 18:13) but 'boasting' (e.g., as in Is. 44:25 of false prophets). There the nuance of incantation is present. In Ugaritic the root means 'sing' or 'song'. That in itself is unexceptional and is the meaning I have used in my own translation.

However, less convincing is Pope's highly original treatment of the puzzling *ḥyn*, which he understands as an epithet of the god Koshar or Kothar mentioned in the Ugaritic texts as an artisan and enchanter. It was Koshar who supplied Baal with the weapons to fell Yam. Not surprisingly, perhaps, this undoubtedly ingenious suggestion has not been accepted widely.

---

[2] Pope 1973: 338–339.

Theological significance

I have already commented on the Job poet's use of Canaanite material (see ch. 1) and here I simply make some observations on the significance of the material.

There was undoubtedly a tendency, which peaked in the work of Mitchell Dahood, to find Ugaritic explanations for everything in the Old Testament. More than twenty years after his death, the value of Dahood's contribution is still vigorously debated, and some, in their reaction against it, have gone too far in their dismissal of the value of some of the evidence.

The real value is in demonstrating the antiquity of many ideas and motifs. Although the Ugaritic texts were probably written about 1400 BC, they embody material from a much remoter antiquity. Much of the evidence calls into question the late dating beloved of earlier generations of scholars.

The use of these Ugaritic motifs shows the writer interacting with the culture and thought-world of his time. Thus Job can be seen genuinely to have an apologetic purpose which speaks well beyond the bounds of Israel. This engagement with surrounding culture is one of the many glories of the book and we may be grateful for whatever light Ugaritic sheds on our understanding of the background.

Bibliography

Commentaries and major works

These are referred to constantly and are cited by author and date or by abbreviation.

Andersen, F. I. (1976), *Job: An Introduction and Commentary*, TOTC, Leicester: IVP.

Brown, F., Driver, S. R. and Briggs, C. A. (1906), *A Hebrew and English Lexicon of the Old Testament*, Oxford: Clarendon.

Clines, D. J. A. (1989), *Job (1 – 20)*, WBC, Dallas, Texas: Word Books.

Dhorme, E. (1967), *A Commentary on the Book of Job* (trans. H. Knight), London, Nelson.

Driver, S. R. and Gray, G. B. (1977), *A Critical and Exegetical Commentary on the Book of Job*, ICC, Edinburgh: T. & T. Clark.

Day, J. (1985), *God's Conflict with the Dragon and the Sea: Echoes of a Canaanite myth in the Old Testament,* Cambridge: Cambridge University Press.

Gibson, J. C. L. (ed.) (1956 and 1978), *Canaanite Myths and Legends*, Edinburgh; T. & T. Clark.

Gibson, J. C. L. (1985), *Job*, DSB, Edinburgh: St Andrews Press.

Habel, N. C. (1985), *The Book of Job: A Commentary*, OTL, London: SCM Press.

Hartley, J. E. (1988), *The Book of Job*, NICOT, Grand Rapids, Eerdmans.

Michel, W. L. (1987), *Job in the light of Northwest Semitic*, vol. 1, Rome: Biblical Institute Press.

Pope, M. H. (1973), *Job: Introduction, Translation and Notes*, AB, Garden City, NY: Doubleday.

Tromp, N. J. (1969), *Primitive Conceptions of Death and the Nether World in the Old Testament, BibOr* 21, Rome: Pontifical Biblical Institute.

Wakeman, M. K. (1973), *God's Battle with the Monster: A Study in Biblical Imagery*, Leiden: Brill.

Other books and articles

Alter, R. (1981), *The Art of Biblical Poetry*, London: Allan and Unwin.

Alter, R. and F. Kermode (eds.) (1987), *The Literary Guide to the Bible*, London: Collins.

Anderson, B. W. (1984), *Creation in the Old Testament*, Issues in Religion and Theology 6, Philadelphia: Fortress.

Baker, J. (1978), 'The Book of Job: Unity and Meaning', JSOT Sup 11, 17–26.

Beuken, W. A. M. (ed.) (1994), *The Book of Job*, Leuven: Leuven University Press. A collection of papers given at the Colloquium Biblieum Lovaniease, 1993.

Blommerde, A. (1969), *North West Semitic Grammar and Job*, BibOr 22, Rome: Pontifical Biblical Institute.

Brenner, A. (1981), 'God's Answer to Job', *VT* 31, 129–137.

—— (1989), 'Job the Pious? The Characterization of Job in the Narrative Framework of the Book', *JSOT* 43, 37–52.

Burns, J. B. (1987), 'The Identity of Death's First-Born in Job xviii:13', *VT* 37, 362–364.

Carson, D. A. (1990), *How Long, O Lord? Reflections on suffering and Evil*, Leicester: IVP.

Ceresko, R. J. (1980), *Job 29 – 31 in the light of Northwest Semitic*, Or 36, Rome: Biblical Institute Press.

Clifford, R. J. (1972), *The Cosmic Mountain in Canaan and the Old Testament*, Cambridge, MA: Harvard University Press.

Clines, D. J. A. (1986), 'Job', in F. F. Bruce (ed.), *The International Bible Commentary*, Basingstoke, Hants.: Marshall Pickering, 520–551.

—— (1990), 'Deconstructing the book of Job' in *What does Eve do to help? And Other Readerly Questions to the Old Testament*, Sheffield: Sheffield Academic Press, 106–123.

—— (1994), 'Why is there a book of Job and what does it do to you if you read it?' in W. A. M. Beuken (ed.) (1994), *The Book of Job*, Leuven: Leuven University Press.

Cooper, A. (1990), 'Reading and Misreading the Prologue to Job', *JSOT* 46, 67–79.

Craigie, P. C. (1969), 'The Conquest and Early Hebrew Poetry', *TynB* 20, 76–94.

—— (1971), 'The Poetry of Ugarit and Israel', *TynB* 22, 3–31.

—— (1973), 'Helel, Aththar and Phaeton (Jes. 14:12–15)', *ZAW* 85.

—— (1976), *The Book of Deuteronomy*, NICOT, Grand Rapids: Eerdmans.

—— (1982), *The Book of Psalms* (1–50), WBC 19, Dallas TX: Word.

—— (1983), *Ugarit and the Old Testament*, Grand Rapids: Eerdmans.

—— (1985), 'Job and Ugaritic Studies', in W. E. Aufrecht (ed.), *Studies in the book of Job*, Waterloo, Ontario: S.R. Supplements, Wilfred Laurier University Press, 28–35.

Cranfield, C. E. B. (1959), *A Commentary on Saint Mark*, Cambridge: Cambridge University Press.

Crenshaw, J. L. (1984), *A Whirlpool of Torment: Israelite Traditions of God as an oppressive presence,* Philadelphia: Fortress Press.

—— (1994), *Trembling at the Threshold of a Biblical Text*, Grand Rapids: Eerdmans, 223–225.

Cross, F. M. (1973), *Canaanite Myth and Hebrew Epic*, Cambridge, MA: Harvard University Press.

Currid, J. D. (1997), 'An Exegetical and Historical Consideration of the Ten Plagues of Egypt', in *Ancient Egypt and the Old Testament*, Grand Rapids: Baker.

Curtis, J. B. (1983), 'On Job's Witness in Heaven', *JBL* 102, 549–562.

Dahood, M. (1957), 'Some Northwest Semitic Words in Job', *Bib* 38, 306–320.

—— (1961), '*Mišmar*: Muzzle in Job 12', *JBL* 80, 270–271.

—— (1965), *Ugaritic–Hebrew Philology*, Rome: Pontifical Biblical Institute.

—— (1966, 1968, 1970), *Psalms* (3 vols.), AB, Garden City, NY: Doubleday.

Dalley, S. (trans.) (1989), 'The Epic of Creation', *Myths from Mesopotamia* 4, Oxford: Oxford University Press.

Davidson, A. B. (1984), *A Commentary: Grammatical and Exegetical on the Book of Job*, Cambridge: Cambridge University Press.

Davidson, R. (1983), *The Courage to Doubt: Exploring an Old Testament Theme*, London: SCM.

Day, P. L. (1988), *An Adversary in Heaven: Satan in the Hebrew*, Harvard Semitic Monographs 43, Cambridge, MA: Harvard University Press.

Dell, K. J. (1991), *The Book of Job as Sceptical Literature*, BZAW 197, Berlin: Walter de Grutyer.

—— (2000), 'Wisdom in Israel', in A. D. M. Mayes (ed.), *Text in Context – Essays by Members of the Society for Old Testament Study*, Oxford: Oxford University Press.

Dick, M. (1979), 'Job XXVII: 4: a new translation', *VT* 29.

Driver, G. R. (1953), 'Two Astronomical Passages in the Old Testament', *JTS* 4, 208–212.

Eaton, J. M. (1985), *Job*, Old Testament Guide 5, Sheffield: Sheffield Academic Press.

Fishbane, M. (1971), 'Jeremiah 4:23–26 and Job 3:3–13a: a recovered use of the creation pattern', *VT* 1.21, 151–167.

Fisher, L. R. (ed.) (1972, 1975 & 1981), *Ras Shamra Parallels: The Texts from Ugarit and the Hebrew Bible* (3 vols.), Rome: Pontifical Biblical Institute.

Fohrer, G. (1968), *Introduction to the Old Testament*, trans. D. Green, Nashville: Abingdon Press.

Freedman, D. N. (1968), 'The Structure of Job 3', *Bib* 49, 503–508.

Frye, N. (1982), *The Great Code: The Bible and Literature*, London; Ark Paperbacks.

Fulco, W. J. (1976), *The Canaanite God Rešep*, New Haven, Connecticut: AOS.

Gaster, F. H. (1966), *Thespis: Ritual Myth and Drama in the Ancient Near East*, New York: Harper Torchbooks.

Gehman, H. S. (1944), ' "Sepher" – an inscription in the book of Job', *JBL* 58, 304–307

Gesenius, W. (1910), *Hebrew Grammar*, ed. E. Kautzsch, rev. by A. E. Cowley, Oxford: Oxford University Press.

Gibson, J. C. L. (1975), 'Eliphaz the Temanite: Portrait of a Hebrew Philosopher', *SJT* 28, 259–272.

—— (1984), 'The Theology of the Ugaritic Baal Cycle', *Or* 53, 202–219.

—— (1988), 'On Evil in the Book of Job', in L. Eslinger and G. Taylor (eds.), *Ascribe to the Lord: Biblical and other Studies in Memory of Peter C. Craigie*, Sheffield: Sheffield Academic Press.

—— (1990), 'The Book of Job and the Cure of Souls', *SJT* 42, 303–317.

Ginzberg, L. (1909), *The Legends of the Jews* (7 vols.), trans. H. Szold, Philadelphia: Jewish Publication Society.

Gordis, R. (1965), *The Book of God and Man: A Study of Job*, Chicago: University of Chicago Press.

Gordon, C. H. (1965), *Ugaritic Manual*, *AnOr* 35, Rome: Pontifical Biblical Institute.

Grabbe, L. L. (1977), *Comparative Philology and the Text of Job: A Study in Methodology*, *SBLDS*, Chico, CA: Scholars Press.

Gray, J. (1952), '*Dtn* and *Rpum* in Ancient Israel', *PEQ* 84.

—— (1965), *The Legacy of Canaan: The Ras Shamra Texts and their relevance to the Old Testament*, 2nd edn., *VTS* 5, Leiden: Brill.

—— (1970), 'The Book of Job in the context of Near Eastern Literature', *ZAW* 82, 251–269.

Greenback, J. H. (1985), 'Baal's Battle with Yam – A Canaanite Creation Fight', *JSOT* 33, 251–269.

Habel, N. C. (1972), 'He who stretches out the Heavens', *CBQ* 34, 417–432.

—— (1975), *The Book of Job*, Cambridge: Cambridge University Press.

—— (1983), 'The Narrative Art of Job: Applying the principles of Robert Alter', *JSOT* 27, 101–111.

Harris, S. L. (1983), 'Wisdom or Creation? A New Interpretation of Job 28:27', *VT* 33, 419–427.

Healey, J. F. (1986), 'The Ugaritic Dead: Some Live Issues', *UF* 18, 27–32.

Irwin, W. A. (1962), 'Job's Redeemer', *JBL* 81, 217–228.

Janzen, J. G. (1985), *Job*, Atlanta: John Knox Press.

Kapelrud, A. S. (1963), *The Ras Shamra Discoveries and the Old Testament*, Oklahoma: University of Oklahoma Press.

Keel, O. (1984), *Die Welt der altorientalischer Bild symbolic und das Alte Testament*, 4th edn., Zurich: Neukirchener.

Kidner, T. D. (1973, 1975), *An Introduction and Commentary on the Psalms* (2 vols.), TOTC Leicester: IVP.

—— (1985), *Wisdom to Live By: An Introduction to the Old Testament's Wisdom Books – Proverbs, Job and Ecclesiastes*, Leicester: IVP.

Kloos, C. (1986), *Yhwh's Combat with the Sea: A Canaanite Tradition in the Religion of Ancient Israel*, Leiden: Brill.

Lang, B. (1980), 'Job XL:18 and the "Bones of Seth"', *VT* 30, 360–361.

L'Heureux, C. E. (1979), *Rank among the Canaanite Gods: El, Ba'al and the Repha'im*, Harvard Semitic Monographs 21, Montana: Scholars' Press.

Lewis, C. S. (1942), *The Screwtape Letters*, London: Geoffrey Bles.

—— (1979), *God in the Dock*, ed. W. Hooper, Glasgow: Collins.

Lowenstamm, S. E. (1959), 'The Muzzling of the Tannin in Ugaritic Myth', *IEJ* 9, 260–261.

McFague, S. (1983), *Metaphorical Theology: Models of God in Religious Language*, London: SCM.

McKay, J. W. (1970), 'Helel and the Dawn-Goddess', *VT* 20, 451–461.
McKenzie, R. A. F. (1959), 'The purpose of the Yahweh speeches in the book of Job', *Bib* 40, 435–445.
Meek, T. J. (1956), 'Job 19:25ff.', *VT* 6, 99–103.
de Moor, J. C. (1987), *An Anthology of Religious Texts from Ugarit*, Leiden: Brill,
Motyer, J. A. (1993), *The Book of Isaiah*, Leicester: IVP.
—— (1996), *Look to the Rock: An Old Testament Background to our Understanding of Christ*, Leicester: IVP.
Mowinckel, S. (1963), 'Shahal', in W. Thomas and W. D. McHardy (eds.), *Hebrew and Semitic Studies Presented to G. R. Driver*, Oxford: Oxford University Press.
Mullen, E. T. (1980), *The Assembly of the Gods: The Divine Council in Canaanite and Hebrew Literature*, Harvard Semitic Monographs, Chico, CA: Scholar's Press.
Nielsen, K. (1989), *There is hope for a tree: The tree as metaphor in Isaiah*, *JSOT*, Sheffield: Sheffield Academic Press.
Oswalt, J. N. (1986, 1998), *The Book of Isaiah* (2 vols), NICOT, Grand Rapids: Eerdmans.
Parker, S. B. (1972), 'The Ugaritic Deity Rapiu', *UF* 4, 87–104.
Patrick, D. and A. Scult (eds.) (1990), 'Finding the Best Job', in *Rhetoric and Biblical Interpretation*, JSOT Sup 82, Sheffield: Almond Press, 81–102.
Perdue, L. G. (1991), *Wisdom in Revolt*, Sheffield: Almond Press.
—— (1994), *Wisdom and Creation*, Nashville: Abingdon Press.
Pfeiffer, C. F. (1962), *Ras, Shamra and the Bible*, Grand Rapids: Eerdmans.
Pope, M. H. (1955), *El in the Ugaritic Texts*, *VT* Sup 2, Leiden: Brill.
Pritchard, J. B. (ed.) (1950), *Ancient Near Eastern Texts relating to the Old Testament*, Princeton: Princeton University Press.
Propp, W. H. (1987), 'On Hebrew SADE (H), "Highland"', *VT* 37, No. 2.
Rabin, C. (1946), 'Bariah', *JTS* 47, 38–41.
Roberts, J. J. M. (1975), 'Sapon in Job 26:7', *Bib* 56, 554–557.
Sarna, N. M. (1957), 'Epic Substratum in the Book of Job', *JBL* 76, 13–25
—— (1963), 'The Mythological Background of Job 18', *JBL* 82, 315–318.
Schiaparelli, G. (1905), *Astronomy in the Old Testament*, Oxford: Clarendon.
Smick, E. B. (1988), 'Job', *EBC* 4, Grand Rapids: Zondervan.

Smith, M. S. (1986), 'Interpreting the Baal Cycle', *UF* 18, 313–339.

Snaith, N. (1968), *The Book of Job: Its Origin and Purpose*, London: SCM.

Tsevat, M. (1954), 'The Canaanite God Šalah', *VT* 4.

Tsmura, D. S. (1989), *The Earth and the Waters in Gensis 1 and 2: A Linguistic Investigation*, JSOT Sup 83, Sheffield: Sheffield Academic Press.

Vanhoozer, K. J. (1998), *Is there a meaning in this text?*, Leicester: Apollos.

Van Selms, A. (1970), 'Yammu's dethronement by Ba'al', *UF* 2, 251–268.

Van Zizl, P. J. (1972), *Baal, A Study of Texts in connection with Baal in the Ugaritc Epics*, Neukirchen-Vluyn: Kevelaar.

Vaughan, P. H. (1974), *The Meaning of 'bama' in the Old Testament: A Study of Etymological, Textual and Archaeological Evidence*, SOTS Monograph 3, Cambridge: Cambridge University Press.

Von Rad, G. (1972), *Wisdom in Israel*, London: SCM.

Westermann, C. (1981), *The Structure of the Book of Job*, Philadelphia: Fortress.

Wharton, J. A. (1999), *Job*, Westminster Bible Commentary, Kentucky: John Knox Press.

Whedbee, J. W. (1977), 'The Comedy of Job', in R. Polzin and D. Robertson (eds.), *Semeia* 7 (Studies in the book of Job), 1–39.

Whybray, R. N. (1998), *Job – Readings: A New Biblical Commentary*, Sheffield: Sheffield Academic Press.

Wilson, J. V. K. (1975), 'A Return to the problems of Behemoth and Leviathan', *VT* 25, 1–14.

Wolfers, D. (1995), *Deep Things Out of Darkness: The Book of Job, Essays and a New English Translation*, Grand Rapids: Eerdmans.

Wyatt, N. (1987), 'Sea and Desert: Symbolic Geography in West Semitic Religious Thought', *UF* 19, 375–389.

—— (1990), 'The expression *Bekôr Mawet* in Job XVIII:13 and its mythological background', *VT* 40 (2), 207–216.

—— (ed.) (1998), *Religious Texts from Ugarit*, Sheffield: Sheffield Academic Press.

Zink, Z. K. (1965), 'Impatient Job: An Interpretation of Job 19:25–27', *JBL* 84, 147–152.

Zuckerman, B. (1991), *Job the Silent: A Study of Historical Counterpoint*, Oxford: Oxford University Press.

Index of modern authors

Index of Scripture references